african BIOGRAPHY

Volume 1
A-K^{im}

Virginia Curtin Knight, Editor

U·X·L®

AN IMPRINT OF GALE

DETROIT · NEW YORK · LONDON

African Biography

Virginia Curtin Knight, Editor

Staff

Sonia Benson, *U•X•L Senior Editor*
Carol DeKane Nagel, *U•X•L Managing Editor*
Thomas L. Romig, *U•X•L Publisher*

Mary Beth Trimper, *Production Director*
Evi Seoud, *Assistant Production Manager*
Deborah Milliken, *Production Assistant*

Cynthia Baldwin, *Product Design Manager*
Barbara Yarrow, *Graphic Services Director*
Pamela A. E. Galbreath, *Senior Art Director*
Shalice Shah-Caldwell, *Permissions Associate*
LM Design, *Typesetter*

Library of Congress Cataloging-in-Publication Data

African Biography / Virginia Curtin Knight, editor

p. cm.
Includes bibliographic references and index.

Summary: Presents biographical entries on seventy-five noteworthy Africans, historical and contemporary, in a variety of fields, from a wide range of sub-Saharan countries.

ISBN 0-7876-2823-9   ISBN 0-7876-2824-7 (volume 1)
   (set : alk. paper)   ISBN 0-7876-2825-5 (volume 2)
                               ISBN 0-7876-2826-3 (volume 3)

1. Africa, Sub-Saharan—Biography—Juvenile literature. [1. Africa, Sub-Saharan—Biography. 2. Blacks—Africa, Sub-Saharan—Biography.]. I. Knight, Virginia Curtin.

CT1920.A39 1998
920.067—dc21   98-14069
                                                   CIP

african BIOGRAPHY

Contents

Nelson Mandela

Volume 2

Volume 3

Entries by Nationality

Bold numerals indicate volume numbers.

Moshoeshoe

Entries by Field of Endeavor

Bold numerals indicate volume numbers.

Fela Kuti

Heads of Government: prime ministers, presidents, dictators

Heads of International Organization

Labor Leaders

Medicine

Military Leaders

Musicians

Nobel Prize Winners (peace)

Nobel Prize Winners (literature)

Political Activists

Publishers (book)

Publishers (newspaper)

Religious Leaders

Rulers: kings, queens, chiefs, and emperors

Slave Traders

Translators

Writers

Reader's Guide

Miriam Makeba

For students and interested browsers who want to learn more about the world, *African Biography* presents biographical entries on some of its most remarkable people. Spanning most of the recorded history of Africa, this three-volume reference resource includes people living from the year 1182 to modern times from areas that now comprise 23 nations of sub-Saharan Africa. Through reading about the lives of its noteworthy people, the reader will confront many of Africa's important historical and social issues, such as the ancient kingdoms, the early Muslim and Christian influences, Europeans and the devastating slave trade, the colonial governments, African nationalism, and the triumphs and struggles of the newly formed independent nations. The people profiled are the kings, presidents, and dictators, religious and military leaders, musicians, activists, traders, environmentalists, and writers who have helped to shape the continent's history.

In *African Biography* readers will find:

- 75 alphabetically arranged biographical entries, each focusing on the childhood and formative experiences of the subject as well as his or her career; the background and traditions held by the subject; and the overall historical or political situation in the nation or area upon which the subject made an impact.

- Sidebars that provide information on people, events, historical background, and other fascinating facts related to the entry.

- Sources for further reading and a full bibliography that inform students where to delve even deeper.

- More than 150 portraits, illustrations, and maps.

- Locator maps in most entries that identify the nations within the continent.

Each volume of *African Biography* begins with a listing of biographical entries by nationality and by field of endeavor; an introduction to, and timeline of, important events in African history; and a glossary of terms used in the text. Volumes conclude with a subject index so students can easily find the people, places, movements, and events discussed throughout the set.

Acknowledgments

The editor would like to thank the U•X•L staff, particularly the photo research department, for all their hard work behind the scenes. Special thanks to U•X•L senior editor Sonia Benson for her enthusiastic support for this project. Thanks are due also to Remer Tyson who worked on the biographies and enjoyed the research as much as I did.

Special thanks are due for the valuable comments and suggestions of U•X•L adviser Ann Marie Laprise, Detroit Public Library, Elmwood Park Branch, Detroit, Michigan.

Comments and Suggestions

We welcome your comments on *African Biography* as well as your suggestions for topics to be featured in future editions. Please write: Editors, *African Biography,* U•X•L, 27500 Drake Rd., Farmington Hills, Michigan 48331-3535; call toll-free: 1-800-877-4253; or fax (248) 699-8066.

Preface: An Overview of Africa's History

Félix Houphouët-Boigny

The inscription welcoming researchers to the building housing Zimbabwe's historical records says: "There is a history in all men's lives." Just as each person's life holds a history, each life also reveals part of the history of a specific time and place. In these biographies of 75 African men and women, the history of the continent emerges.

The Africans included in these volumes are people living south of the Sahara Desert. For centuries the desert has divided the peoples of the continent. Those living along the Mediterranean and north Atlantic Ocean coasts have a history different from those living to the south. The people in the North were part of the history of Egypt and the early Roman empire while the South remained largely untouched by the experiences of the North.

Historians such as Herodotus (c. 425-484 B.C.) made occasional isolated tours into Africa as early as the fifth century B.C. But historians began to collect comprehensive knowledge of Africans living in the vast regions south of the Sahara with the beginning of Portuguese exploration in the 1400s. From the records and diaries kept by the sailors, priests, and representatives of the kings, the lives of prominent African men and women come alive. Their history and those of future generations reveal a pattern of resistance, perhaps because of the nature of their relationship with the Europeans. In the earlier period, Africans clashed with outsiders who were seeking to exploit the continent's mineral wealth and later to expand the horrendous trade in slaves. Later, resistance took the form of nationalism and demands for independence from European rule. Today, Africans are demanding an end to the corrupt and tyrannical African governments that have cheated them of their share of their countries' resources.

Majesty and wealth

For the early historical period of the great empires in West Africa the documented history is scant. Along the reaches of the Niger and Senegal rivers in West Africa, Africans developed large powerful kingdoms based on trade and warfare. These early empires of the 400s to 1500s—Ghana, Mali, and Songhai—stretched from the Atlantic Ocean as far as the northwest of modern Nigeria. So fabulously wealthy were these kingdoms that Arab traders from the north crossed the Sahara Desert with their huge camel caravans to trading centers like Timbuktu and Gao along the Niger River. There they traded their salt and textiles for the gold of the western African kingdoms. In southern Africa, from the Zambezi River to the Indian Ocean, the rulers of Great Zimbabwe (1000-1400s) controlled the trade in gold and ivory. African traders brought their goods to the Indian Ocean Coast where they traded with Arab merchants from Kilwa and Mombasa along the Kenyan coast.

Along the Red Sea, the Christian kingdom of Aksum reached its height in the 1100s. **Lalibela** (1182-1255), the Emperor of Aksum (Ethiopia), is the first person about whom we have enough information to form a biography. Lalibela was responsible for the construction of 11 Christian churches, still standing today, built into the sides of stone cliffs in northern Ethiopia. In this earlier period **Mansa Musa** (1312-1337), the enormously wealthy ruler of the kingdom of Mali, gained a place in history when he made a pilgrimage, or *haj,* from his capital at Timbuktu to the Muslim holy city of Mecca, in today's Saudi Arabia. The trip took him two years. On his return, he established in Timbuktu one of the leading Islamic intellectual centers in the world.

European interests

In the 1400s the Portuguese sailed around the West African Coast and in their wake European slave traders followed. This trade distorted the normal development of African communities for nearly 500 years. Faced with expanding penetration by Portuguese traders in the East and Arab traders along the Indian Ocean coasts, African communities reacted in several different ways. Some adapted themselves to the trade and grew wealthy from the capture of slaves and the trade in guns. Others resisted.

Sent out by Portuguese Prince Henry the Navigator to make their way around the continent, the Portuguese set up trading posts along the coast. Stimulating the early explorers was the myth of the fabulously wealthy realm of an African Christian king named Prester John. Islam, the faith founded by the prophet Muhammad, had rapidly spread from Saudi Arabia into Africa and Asia from the 600s onward. The Christian church in Europe wanted to believe that Christian kingdoms existed beyond the reach of Islam, and the myth of Prester John suited their purpose. To avoid the Muslim-controlled Sahara Desert, Prince Henry planned to sail along the Atlantic Coast, and then follow the large rivers inland until he found Prester John.

As they explored along the coast, the Portuguese established settlements. Following their discovery of Brazil in the 1500s and the development of plantations there, they began taking slaves from Africa to work these plantations. They sailed around the Cape of Good Hope and along the Indian Ocean Coast. There they explored the inland river systems and wrote descriptions of **Mwene Mutapa Negomo Mupunzagutu,** the ruler of the Mutapa dynasty along the Zambezi River in the 1550s. As in other earlier African kingdoms, the Portuguese were welcomed and provided with accommodation. Often, their Christian priests converted the African rulers and their courts to Christianity. In many instances this caused dissent within the ruler's court between the traditional authorities and priests and those who adopted the new ways. Struggles for power within the kingdom were fueled by the outsiders who supported one side against the another.

Later, other European explorers kept diaries of their contact with African rulers and their societies: among these were the Dutch in the 1600s and the French, British, and Germans in the 1700s and 1800s. On the heels of the explorers came the missionaries, adventurers, and traders. Confronted by European expansion, African societies were forced to turn outward to respond to the pressures. There were some fascinating exceptions, like **Afonso I** of the Kongo in the 1480s, but most ultimately resisted the European presence. Sometimes resistance followed accommodation. The West African kings of Dahomey, for instance, initially profited from the slave trade with the Europeans and strengthened their kingdom. Later, however, French colonial forces defeated the Dahomeans and exiled their king. From the East Coast of Africa, the Arabs and later the Portuguese followed the rivers inland to open up the continent to Europeans from the Indian Ocean Coast.

Anna Nzinga, the queen of the Ndongo in the 1600s in present-day Angola, was a good strategist and formed alliances with the Dutch to try to keep the Portuguese from destroying her kingdom. Ultimately, however, the wealth derived from the trade in slaves won the day. The slavers destroyed African societies, corrupted their leaders, and sent thousands of people into slavery in the Americas. Some men, such as **Olaudah Equiano** and **Samuel Ajayi Crowther,** who were taken as slaves, gained their freedom and wrote descriptions of their experiences. Crowther returned to his native Nigeria and became the first black bishop in the Anglican Church of England. Others became wealthy from trading in slaves. **Tippu Tib** from Zanzibar was one of the greatest African slavers in the interior.

In southern Africa resistance took other forms. Internal conflicts in the region had much more impact on the societies than slavery did. In the early 1800s, **Shaka,** the Zulu king, displaced tens of thousands of people as he sought to increase his powerful kingdom. Later, as the whites from the Cape Colony began moving northward, the conflicts centered on white encroachment and African resistance. The intensity of resistance escalated toward the end of the 1800s as the governments of Europe vied with one another for control of Africa. The British faced armed resistance in southern Africa from the Afrikaners under **Paul Kruger,** from the Zulus under **Cetshwayo**, and from the Matabele under **Lobengula.** In South West Africa (Namibia), **Samuel Maherero,** leader of the Herero, put up stiff resistance to German occupation. Elsewhere in Africa, in the Belgian Congo **Simon Kimbangu** began a religious movement that opposed the repressive, cruel treatment meted out to Africans by the agents of Belgian King Leopold II. In Madagascar, Queen **Ranavalona I** used her authority to keep all

Christian missionaries out of her country for nearly 40 years, thus allowing the traditional culture to flourish unimpeded by European culture. In Ethiopia, **Menelik II** took up arms to defend his country against the Italian invasion. His troops defeated the Italians at the battle of Adowa in 1896, one of the greatest defeats of a European power in Africa.

Demands for independence

During the Second World War, Africans fought in the armies of the colonial powers. When they returned home from the war, they began demanding the same rights for themselves that they had fought for in Europe and Asia. They formed political parties and nationalist movements to rid their countries of European rule. Over a period of 30 years, some by arms and others through negotiation, the African leaders achieved independence for their countries. **Kwame Nkrumah** was the first president of Ghana, the first sub-Saharan African country to win its independence. Nkrumah was a formidable intellectual presence who promoted the idea of Pan-Africanism, a united Africa. During the 1960s, the flood gates opened and in 10 years' time nearly 30 African countries won their independence from their colonial rulers. Some countries under leaders such as **Félix Houphouët-Boigny** in Côte d'Ivoire and **Léopold Sédar Senghor** in Senegal experienced a smooth transition to independence and kept close ties with the French, their former colonial power. Other countries under nationalist leaders like **Patrice Lumumba** in the former Belgian Congo (Zaire and now the Democratic Republic of the Congo) experienced turmoil and bloodshed at independence.

Nationalists and independence leaders

Once African countries had become independent, many leaders experienced difficulties administering their nations and reconciling the conflicting interests of regional and cultural groups. Some leaders like Nigeria's **Abubakar Tafawa Balewa** fell under the gun of military rule. Other rulers ignored constitutional limits and declared themselves presidents for life. Men such as **Hastings Banda** of Malawi, **Kenneth Kaunda** of Zambia, and **Julius Nyerere** of Tanzania all ruled over governments that recognized only one political party—theirs.

In the aftermath of World War II, rivalry grew up between China, the Soviet Union and the Communist bloc countries, and the West. The period of Great Power rivalry is known as the Cold War. It lasted until 1989 when the Communist governments of Eastern Europe fell. During this time, the East and West provided their supporters with arms and ammunition. Africans fought major wars in Angola, Mozambique, Somalia, Ethiopia, and Eritrea. To prevent the East from influencing other governments, the West supported friendly dictators such as **Mobutu Sese Seko** of Zaire to keep them in power. The West wanted to prevent Communist countries from coming in and exploiting the continent's mineral resources and from gaining strategic bases in Africa.

African writers used their powers to criticize and interpret the changes taking place in their societies. Among the most prominent of the writers in the post-World War II period were Nigerians, **Chinua Achebe** and **Wole Soyinka. Alan Paton** used the power of his novel *Cry the Beloved Country* to personalize the plight of Africans in his home country of South Africa. Resistance to the racist policies of the South African government of **Hendrik Verwoerd** continued under such people as Chief **Albert Lutuli, Miriam Makeba, Steve Biko, Winnie Madikizela-Mandela, Nelson Mandela**, and former Archbishop **Desmond Tutu.**

With the collapse of Communism in eastern European and the Soviet Union, the African nations were left alone and some were able to bring stability to their countries. The major benefactors of the end of the Cold War were black South Africans and South Africa's neighbors, Namibia, Mozambique, and Angola. In the absence of the Communist threat, South African National Party leader **Frederick Willem de Klerk** could justify to his followers the advantages of releasing **Nelson Mandela** from nearly 30 years in prison. Mandela's release opened the way to a multiparty system in South Africa and the normalizing of relations with African countries in the southern region.

Today, the leaders of African countries are being evaluated for their competence rather than their loyalties. In many cases they do not stand the test of providing a leadership for the benefit of their people. Many have performed miserably; some have stayed in power for many years and enriched themselves and their families while impoverishing their countries. With the broader vision of democracy and sound economic policies, African societies are beginning to demand a fairer deal from their leaders. In Uganda,

Yoweri Museveni has ended the terrible ethnic fighting and brought stability to his country, although he too refuses to allow competing political parties. In South Africa, **Nelson Mandela** turned over the presidency of his political party to a younger generation, and he has promised to leave office by 1999—setting a precedent that an African leader can serve his or her people by leaving office at the peak of power.

A note about this collection

In these volumes the numbers of prominent political South African activists are greater than in any other single country. Various circumstances account for this. The struggle for freedom and majority rule lasted longer in South Africa than in other countries, and the struggle gave rise to activists, black and white. Of the sub-Saharan African countries, South Africa also has the most developed economy and infrastructure, giving greater opportunities and outlets for activism.

African women are noticeably underrepresented in these biographies. Many African cultures are dominated by men, and they have assigned women to inferior positions. That some women have emerged as powerful leaders is all the more tribute to their strengths and perseverance. In modern Africa, women such as Kenyan environmentalist **Wangari Maathai** are in the forefront of women who have succeeded despite the prejudices of their families, husbands, peers, and governments. Women in many contemporary cultures are challenging the traditional ways that have kept them in subservient positions.

Finally, one of the most difficult aspects of compiling this collection of biographies was to limit the number of entries to 75. Many interesting and noteworthy people were necessarily omitted in an effort to achieve a wide representation of people by region, race, sex, and field of endeavor.

Virginia Curtin Knight
Harare, Zimbabwe
January 1998

Desmond Tutu

Words to Know

A

Abolitionist: someone who is in favor of, or works for, the elimination of slavery.

Advocate: to support or speak in favor of; or someone who speaks in favor of.

African nationalism: a strong loyalty to the traditions and political and economic interests of Africa and its people. The term generally refers to Africans who tried to free Africa from colonial governments and worked for self-rule.

Afrikaans: a language derived from the Dutch language of the seventeenth century, spoken by the Afrikaners or Boers and one of the official languages of the Republic of South Africa.

Afrikaner: an Afrikaans-speaking South African native of European descent, usually Dutch, German, or French. Afrikaners started arriving in South Africa in the middle of the seventeenth century, where the majority became farmers.

African National Congress (ANC): the oldest black political organization in South Africa, founded in 1912 by a group of black lawyers for the purpose of promoting the interests of blacks in the newly created Union of South Africa. After 1948 the organization led the opposition to apartheid, and it was outlawed in the 1960s. In the 1990s the ban on the ANC ended; in 1994 the party won in the first elections open to all races in South Africa.

Afro-Beat: a modern musical style that fuses jazz with the sounds of traditional African music with lyrics in both a native African language and in pidgin English.

Agnostic: someone who believes that human beings cannot know if God or any supreme being exists, or understand what the nature of the supreme being is.

Amnesty: the granting of pardon—forgiveness without punishment—to a group of people by the authorities involved (as a government).

Anarchy: lawlessness or disorder due to the absence of government or authority.

Ancestral lands: lands passed down within a group or family from one generation to the next.

Anthropology: the study of the way humans have lived and developed over the ages.

Apartheid: the policy of segregating and practicing economic and political discrimination against non-European groups; *apartheid* policies were in effect in South Africa from 1948 until the early 1990s.

Archaeology: the study of past human life by digging up and examining the material remains, such as fossils and artifacts.

Asceticism: the practice of strict self-denial for the purpose of gaining spiritual discipline.

Assimilation: the absorbing of an individual or a group into the cultural mainstream.

Atrocities: appalling and brutal acts.

Authoritarianism: placing a nation's power in a leader or group of leaders who are not accountable to the people for their actions.

Autocracy: a government in which one ruler has unlimited power.

Autonomy: self-governing.

Axiom: an established principle or rule.

B

Banning order: legal restrictions imposed by the National party government of South Africa upon an individual that prohibited travel from a set area, speaking in public, appearing in certain public places, and restricted who, or how many people, could visit at one's home, and placed other limitations on the individual's freedoms of movement and speech.

Baptism: a Christian ritual in which a person is purified by means of water and then accepted into the Christian community.

Boer: a South African of the Afrikaans-speaking community.

Boycott: a united effort of refusing to deal with an organization, such as a company, or its products, in order to express disapproval.

Bureaucracy: a system of administration, generally known for its inefficiency, in which decisions and tasks must be filtered through many different specialized officials and conform to many rules in order for an action to be taken.

C

Cabinet: a body of advisers to a ruler.

Caliph: a ruler in an Islamic state who is considered a successor of Muhammad and rules politically as well as spiritually.

Calvinism: a Christian sect developed by John Calvin (1509-1564) that emphasizes the idea of predestination, the belief that some people are fated for salvation and are guided by God.

Capitalism: an economic system in which property and businesses are owned by individuals and corporations (rather than being owned by the government or by the society as a whole). Profits in a capitalistic system are based on competition and enrich the individual owner or the investors in a corporation.

Caravan: a group of people who travel together through deserts or hostile territories.

Censorship: the system of examining public statements or the arts, written or spoken, for ideas or material that is objectionable to the interests of a governing body, and not allowing these statements to be expressed in a public forum.

Centralization: the placement of the majority of power in one concentrated office, as in a strong central government as opposed to a federation of individually governed states.

Civil rights: the nonpolitical rights of a citizen, as in the rights of personal liberty guaranteed to U.S. citizens: equal treatment and equal access to housing, free speech, employment, and education.

Civil disobedience: the refusal to go along with government orders, as in purposely disobeying a discriminatory law or ordinance. Usually *civil disobedience* is carried out by a group in order to protest something or to get concessions from the government.

Civilian government: a government that is not led by the military or police forces.

Coalition government: a temporary joining together of two parties or interest groups within the government for a common goal.

Cold War: a term used to describe the tensions between the West and the Communist bloc countries of Eastern Europe and the former Soviet Union that arose after World War II (1939-45) and ended when the Berlin Wall fell and the Soviet Union dissolved at the end of the 1980s.

Collaboration: cooperation between two individuals or groups that are not normally connected.

Collective farm: a farm formed from many small farms, run jointly by the group of owners and usually supervised by the government.

Colony: a territory in which settlers from another country come to live while maintaining their ties to their home country, often setting up a government that may rule over the original inhabitants of the territory as well.

Colonialism: control by one nation or state over a dependent territory and its people and resources.

Communism: an economic theory in which there is no private property—all goods are owned in common; also the doctrine of the former Soviet Union, in which a single authoritarian governing body controls all means of production.

Confederation: to be united in a league or alliance for mutual support or common goals, as in the union of the 11 states that seceded from the United States in 1860 as the Confederate States of America.

Consensus: an agreement by most or all concerned with an issue.

Conservation: protection and preservation of something (often the environment); a carefully planned management system to prevent exploitation, destruction, or overuse.

Conservative: wishing to preserve what is already established, such as traditions or political or economic structures.

Consolidate: to join different elements or groups together to form one solid unit.

Constitution: a written document that sets forth the basic principles and laws of a nation, establishing the powers and duties of a government and the basic rights of its citizens.

Consul: an official appointed by one nation to live in a foreign country and to represent the business interests of his or her home nation in the foreign country.

Convoy: a protective escort.

Coptic church: a Christian sect that differed from the Western church in the belief that Jesus had only one nature, a divine one; orthodox creed holds that Jesus had both a divine and a human nature.

Corruption: the state of being outside of moral, legal, and proper behavior; acting in ways that benefit oneself or one's connections but hurt the society, such as offering or accepting bribery.

Coup: (from the French *coup d'etat,* "stroke of state") the violent overthrow of a government by a small group.

Cultural integration: to bring many cultures together into a whole as equals within a society, but not necessarily as distinct entities with separate beliefs and traditions.

Culture: the set of beliefs, social habits, and ways of surviving in the environment that are held by a particular social group. *Culture* is also a word for a group that shares these traits.

D

Delegation: a group of people chosen to represent a larger group, such as an organization, a political party, or a nation.

Democracy: a government in which the people hold the power and exercise it either directly or through elected representatives.

Denounce: to publicly criticize, accuse, or pronounce someone or something evil.

Depose: to remove a monarch from the throne or a leader from power.

Dictator: a ruler who has absolute authority and is often oppressive in his use of it.

Diplomacy: the art of handling affairs and conducting negotiations, especially between nations or states, without creating tensions.

Disfranchise: to deprive of the right to vote.

Diviner: someone who practices the arts involved in foreseeing the future or finding hidden knowledge.

Dominate: to exert mastery and control over another.

Dynasty: a powerful family that stays in power over many generations.

E

Elite: a group considered to be socially superior; or a powerful minority group.

Emirate: a state under the control of an *emir,* a ruler in an Islamic country.

Entourage: a group of attendants; the people who surround an important or famous person.

Environmentalist: someone who supports the preservation and improvement of the natural environment.

Ethnic group: a group of people that shares customs, language, beliefs, and a common history and origins.

Evacuate: to leave, or be removed from, a place in an organized way, often for protection from danger.

Évolué: a Western-educated African.

Evolution: in the struggle for survival, the process by which successive generations of a species pass on to their offspring the characteristics that enable the species to survive.

Excavation: to dig up or uncover in order to expose to view, as in digging up ancient fossils.

Exile: removal from one's native country, often forced but sometimes voluntary.

Expatriate: someone who lives in a foreign country.

Expedition: a journey taken for a specific reason.

Expropriate: to take property and put it in one's own name; to take away someone's property rights.

F

Famine: an extreme shortage of food causing starvation within a certain area.

Fascism: a political system headed by a dictator in which the nation is exalted above its individual citizens, all opposition to the government is prohibited, and powerful police and military forces use strong-arm tactics to ensure obedience and conformity to strict government regulation.

Fetish: an object that is believed to have magical powers that will protect its owner.

G

Garrison: a military station.

Genocide: the deliberate killing of everyone belonging to a particular ethnic group.

Grass roots: at the local community level, often referring to rural society away from the political centers.

Guerrilla: someone who fights, generally with a small group of rebels, using nonmilitary methods, such as sabotage and harassment.

H

Harlem Renaissance: a highly creative period among artists and writers in the community of Harlem in New York City that started in the early 1920s and lasted until the Great Depression in 1929.

Hereditary rulers: leaders who inherit the right to rule by reason of being born into a particular station within the ruling family.

Heretic: someone who will not conform to the established beliefs or doctrines of the prevailing religion.

I

Impeach: to accuse a public official or ruler of a crime against his or her office.

Indentured servant: someone who enters into a binding contract to work for someone else for a set period of time and in return usually receives travel and living expenses.

Indigenous: being native to a particular place or having one's origins there.

Inflation: a growing rise in the prices of goods due to an economy in which more money and credit are available than goods.

Infrastructure: the basic structure underlying a system; in a nation, the *infrastructure* includes government and public works, roads and other transportation systems, and communication networks.

Insurrection: rebellion against a government or other authority.

Integration: incorporation of different groups of people into a society as equals.

Isolationism: the chosen condition within a nation or territory of keeping apart from other nations, abstaining from alliances, trade, or intermingling of populations.

J

Judicial system: the system within a state or nation that administers justice, generally through a network of courts and judges.

K

Koran: the holy book of Muslim people, containing sacred writings that are revelations given to the prophet Muhammad by the Muslim god Allah.

L

Labor union: a group of workers organized to bargain together as a strong unit with employers for better wages, benefits, and working conditions.

Legislative body: the group within a government that is in charge of making laws and collecting taxes.

Liberal: broad-minded and open to the reform of established rules, authorities, traditions, and social structures.

Lobby: to attempt to persuade public officials to take action or vote a particular way on an issue.

M

Martial law: the law administered by a country's military forces during a declared emergency situation, when the normal security forces are not sufficient to maintain public safety and order. *Martial law* often involves a temporary suspension of certain individual civil and legal rights.

Mercenary: a soldier who is hired to fight with an army for pay, often coming from a foreign land and serving for profit, without any patriotic motivations.

Migrant worker: a person who moves from place to place to find temporary work.

Migration: the movement of a group of people from a home territory to another region.

Military rule: a government run by the armed forces, as opposed to a civilian government.

Missionary: a person belonging to an organized effort by a religious group to spread its beliefs in other parts of the world.

Monopoly: the exclusive control, ownership, or rights to something, like a product or a particular business.

Mosque: a building where Muslims practice public worship.

Multiparty politics: a political system in which parties representing different interests run against each other in elections, giving individual voters a variety of options and allowing for opposition to be expressed.

Muslim: a follower of the Islam religion, who worships the god Allah as revealed to the prophet Muhammad through the Koran, the holy book of Islam.

Mutiny: resistance to authority; particularly, revolt against a superior officer, as in the crew of a ship against the commander.

Mysticism: the belief that one can obtain a direct knowledge of God or spiritual truth through inner, or subjective, experience.

N

Nationalism: pride and loyalty toward one's nation, usually to the extent of exalting that nation above all others.

Nationalization: investing control and ownership, usually of a business or property, to the national government.

Nation-state: a political unit in which a particular group sharing the same beliefs, customs, history, and political interests comprises its own state and is self-ruled.

Negritude: the state of being pridefully aware of the culture and history of the African people.

Nomad: a member of a group of people who do not live in one set place, but move around as necessary, usually in pursuit of a food supply.

O

Opposition: the position of believing and expressing something contrary to another; in politics, the *opposition* party is one that disagrees with and is ready to replace the party in power.

Organization of African Unity (OAU): An organization founded in 1963, currently with more than 50 member nations, to promote unity among African states, to eliminate colonialism, to develop sound health and economic policies, and to maintain defense of the African nations.

Overlord: a supreme ruler, who rules over other less powerful rulers within his or her realm.

P

Pagan: a word used by Christians and westerners to identify people who believe either in many gods or in no gods.

Pan-Africanism: a movement for greater cooperation and unity among the different regions or nations of the African continent.

Parliament: the highest legislative body of a nation, which meets regularly and is the forum for gathering and discussion among different assemblies.

Pass laws: laws under which blacks in South Africa had to carry documents that identified them and certified that they had authorized jobs in white areas.

Passive resistance: nonviolent defiance of a government or power usually exerted through noncooperation (as in not following commands).

Patronage system: a method of distributing jobs, often used in appointing government jobs, in which jobs are granted as a reward for increasing the political or financial standing of the person or group making the appointments.

Peasant farmers: members of a social class of either small landowners or laborers who work the land, who are generally quite poor and often uneducated and lacking in political influence.

Philanthropist: one who works to promote the welfare of others or the society.

Pidgin English: a simple form of English-based speech used for communication between someone who speaks English and someone who speaks a different language; or, a mixture of English and another language.

Pilgrimage: a journey to a sacred place.

Plantation: a large farming establishment in which the labor is usually provided by workers who live on the premises.

Plateau: a region of high, flat land that is raised sharply above land next to it on at least one side.

Police state: a nation or other political unit under the power of a repressive government that uses a powerful and often secret police force to administer the areas of government usually left to civilians, such as judicial and social matters.

Political prisoner: someone who is jailed because of beliefs or actions that are perceived to be contrary or in opposition to the government.

Polygamy: the practice of having more than one spouse at a time, applicable to either sex.

Polygyny: the practice of a male having more than one wife at a time.

Premier: the prime minister, or the leader who is first in rank as head of the cabinet or ministry of a nation or state.

Prime minister: the leader who heads the cabinet or ministry of a nation or state.

Protectorate: the relationship that occurs when a state assumes the authority position over another state.

Province: a regional division of a nation, like a state, with a regional government of its own, but ruled in federal matters by the national government.

Puppet government: a political body that is controlled by an outside authority, usually referring to a leader who appears to rule but is in fact carrying out the demands of a more powerful and less apparent entity.

Purge: literally, to rid (the nation) of something that is undesirable; *purges* have taken place in many areas in which one ethnic group attempts to destroy another.

R

Recession: a time of decreased economic activity.

Refugee: someone who flees from his or her own country, often to another country, to escape persecution.

Regent: someone who governs a kingdom standing in for the sovereign ruler, generally because the sovereign is under the legal age, absent, or disabled.

Regime: a government in power.

Reparations: payments made after a war by the defeated nation for damages another nation or group of people suffered as a result of the war.

Resistance: the act of opposing the dominant authority; *resistance* can also refer to a political organization that fights an occupying power within its nation, using underground methods such as guerrilla warfare and sabotage.

S

Sabotage: a deliberate act of destruction or obstruction, designed to damage an enemy's ability to carry out its functions.

Sanctuary: a place of protection from persecutors or immunity from the law.

Secession: a formal withdrawal from an organization or a political unit.

Secretary-general: the main administrative officer of an organization.

Socialism: an economic and political system in which the government owns businesses and distributes goods to the people.

Solitary confinement: a punishment used in prisons that involves being placed in a cell by oneself and not allowed to see or speak with others for a set amount of time.

Sovereignty: freedom from controls from outside; self-government.

Statesman: someone who is wise in the arts of leadership and can govern fairly, without becoming involved in factions and partisanship.

Strategic: necessary in the conduct of war and not available in the warring nation's own country; of great importance.

Strike: a stoppage of work by an organized group of workers in order to make an employer respond to demands about wages, job security, or work conditions.

Sub-Saharan Africa: part of Africa south of the Sahara desert (see map, inside front or back cover).

Subsidize: to grant money to a business or another nation in order to provide assistance or to obtain favors.

Subsistence farming: a system of farming in which a family farms a small amount of land to grow just the things they need to live, without significant extra harvest to be sold.

T

Terrorism: using threats and violent acts to inspire extreme fear in an enemy in order to force the enemy to agree to demands.

Textiles: cloth.

Totalitarian: describing a dictatorial state in which one powerful person or group rules with near total control and the state is exalted above the individual.

Tradition: a custom or institution from among the beliefs, social habits, methods, systems, arts, etc., of a people that is handed down from generation to generation, such as a ritual, a story, or a courtship practice.

Treason: the offense of trying to overthrow a government or kill its ruler.

Tribute: a payment made from one nation or group to another, usually when the paying group has been conquerred by the group they are paying. *Tribute* is either payable to the dominant party as a kind of tax, or it is paid in exchange for protection.

Tyranny: excessive and repressive power exerted by the government.

U

Unify: to bring together different elements and make them into a coherent whole.

Unitary state: an undivided state or nation: one with only one political party and a strong central government.

United Nations: an international organization established after World War II for the purpose of maintaining international peace, developing good relations among nations, and finding solutions to economic, social, and humanitarian problems throughout the world.

V

Vanguard: those who lead a movement or action, or the forefront of a movement.

W

West: a term referring to the countries of western Europe and the United States, usually those countries that have not been under Communist regimes in the twentieth century and have some similarities in customs, political and economic philosophy, and ethnicity.

Westernization: the adoption of, or conversion to, traditions and qualities of the West.

White supremacy: a belief in the superiority of the white race over the black race and the consequent need to maintain whites in powerful positions over blacks.

White-minority government: a government led and administered by white people in a population that is comprised of a majority of non-whites who are excluded from the political process.

World Bank: The International Bank for Reconstruction and Development, an agency of the United Nations that loans money to member nations for the purpose of developing economic growth.

Picture Credits

Nadine Gordimer

The photographs and illustrations appearing in *African Biography* were received from the following sources:

On the cover: Haile Selassie I, Miriam Makeba, and Nelson Mandela: **AP/Wide World Photos. Reproduced by permission.**

Photograph by J. P. Laffont. United Nations: xlix; **Photograph by Jerry Bauer. Reproduced by permission:** p. 1; **AP/Wide World Photos. Reproduced by permission:** v, xv, xxiii, lv, lviii, lix, 18, 23, 39, 44, 50, 55, 59, 64, 93, 138,143, 147, 157, 162, 166, 173,175, 177, 181, 183, 229, 232, 235, 261, 269, 283, 306, 309, 315, 328, 346, 359, 379, 396, 400, 418, 433, 437, 441, 448, 454, 466, 471, 498, 502, 504, 510, 525, 530, 534, 543, 554, 562; **Photograph by Reuters/Jeff Christensen. Archive Photos. Reproduced by permission:** p. 28; **Photograph by Rick Wilking. Archive Photos. Reproduced by permission:** 32; **Library of Congress:** 34, 119, 292, 350; **Archive Photos. Reproduced by permission:** lvii, 47, 187, 192, 238, 241, 254, 263, 341, 362, 364, 365, 427, 521, 571, 587, 589, 596; **United Nations:** 62, 578; **Corbis-Bettmann. Reproduced by permission:** lii (top and bottom), 73, 201, 285; **The Granger Collection, New York.**

Reproduced by permission: 79, 220, 388; **Photograph by Howard Burditt. Archive Photos. Reproduced by permission: 86, 385; Photograph by Van Lierop. United Nations:** 90; **Illustration by Donna V. Benson, Gale Research:** 95, 195, 294, 459, 478; **Reuters Corbis-Bettman. Reproduced by permission:** lxi, 112, 116, 319; **Photograph by Wyatt Counts. AP/Wide World Photos. Reproduced by permission:** 125; **Photograph by Juda Ngwenya. Archive Photos. Reproduced by permission:** 130, 282; **Reproduced with the kind permission of the Estate of Bessie Head:** 149; **Zimbabwe National Archives. Reproduced by permission:** 246, 248, 249, 515; **Tony Stone Images. Reproduced by permission:** 206; **Photograph by Tom Costello. AP/Wide World Photos. Reproduced by permission:** 212; **Photograph by Robert Caputo. Time Magazine. Reproduced by permission:** 216; **Corbis Images. Reproduced by permission:** 223; **Adrian Arbib/Corbis Images. Reproduced by permission:** 271; **Photograph by Hos Maina. Archive Photos. Reproduced by permission:** 275; **Photograph by Peter Andrews. Archive Photos. Reproduced by permission:** lx, 277; **Photograph by Chester Higgins Jr. Photo Researchers, Inc. Reproduced by permission:** xxi, 304; **Kenya Information Services.** 321; **Corbis Corporation. Reproduced by permission:** 330; **Express Newspapers/L932/Archive Photos. Reproduced by permission:** 353; **Photograph by Reinhard W. Sander. Reproduced by permission:** 443; **The Kobal Collection. Reproduced by permission:** 476; **Mansell Collection/Time Inc/The New York Times Magazine. Reproduced by permission:** li (bottom), 485, 489; **Photograph by Caton Woodville. Mansell Collection/Time Inc/New York Times Magazine. Reproduced by permission:** li (top), 518; **Archive Photos/Trappe. Reproduced by permission:** 536; **Photograph by Y. Nagata. United Nations:** 561; **Photograph by Peter Van Niekerk. Reproduced by permission:** xxxi, 580.

A Timeline of Important Events in African History

Angolan children celebrate their nation's independence.

300 Aksum, the first recorded kingdom of Ethiopia (founded by Arab traders in the first century A.D.), adopts Coptic Christianity.

700 Mombasa (Kenya) develops as a center for Arab trade in slaves and ivory.

1000-1400 Great Zimbabwe, the largest and strongest city of its time in central and southern Africa, controls the gold trade in southern Africa. Lying in the high plateau area of present-day Zimbabwe, the population of Great Zimbabwe reached about 18,000 and its rulers controlled an area of about 60,000 square miles.

1182 Lalibela becomes emperor of Ethiopia.

c. 400
Beginning of Middle Ages in Europe

c. 610
Muhammad founds Islam religion

800
Charlemagne crowned emperor of Romans

1096
European Christians begin Crusades against Muslims

300   500   700   900   1100

1324- 27 Ruler of Mali Kingdom **Mansa Musa** makes pilgrimage to Mecca, the holy city of Islam, and returns to rebuild the capital city of Timbuktu into an urban center of commerce and learning.

1400-96 Sunni Ali, the great leader of the Songhai Empire in Mali, takes Timbuktu; his empire becomes the largest in ancient Western Africa.

1482 Afonso I of the Kongo welcomes Portuguese explorers into his kingdom and establishes relations with Portugal; in addition to bringing Christianity and Western education, the Europeans establish an enormous slave trade in the Kongo kingdom.

1482 The Portuguese establish a trading post at Elmina, Gold Coast.

1505 Portuguese burn Kilwa (in Kenya) and continue penetration along the Indian Ocean Coast and inland.

1550 Mwene Mutapa Negomo Mupunzagutu rules the Mutapa Dynasty in current-day Zimbabwe.

1591 Moroccans invade Songhai, defeat its army, and occupy Timbuktu (in Mali).

1591 The Portuguese invade Angolan kingdoms and increase the slave trade to Brazil.

c. 1600 African trading states develop along the Atlantic Coast as partners of Europeans in slave trade.

1622 Anna Nzinga represents the Ndongo (Angola) in negotiations with the Portuguese.

1652 Dutch East India Company establishes a settlement at the Cape of Good Hope in southern Africa.

1673 Dahomey (Benin) becomes a powerful slave trading kingdom.

1789 Former Nigerian slave **Olaudah Equiano** publishes his memoirs.

Slavers moving captives.

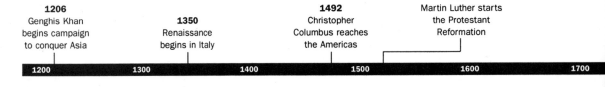

1206
Genghis Khan
begins campaign
to conquer Asia

1350
Renaissance
begins in Italy

1492
Christopher
Columbus reaches
the Americas

1517
Martin Luther starts
the Protestant
Reformation

| 1200 | 1300 | 1400 | 1500 | 1600 | 1700 |

1804 Usuman dan Fodio declares a holy war in northern Nigeria and founds the Islamic Sokoto Empire.

1807 British parliament passes the Slave Trade Abolition Act outlawing maritime (at sea) slave trade.

1815 The British take Cape Colony in southern Africa from the Dutch.

1818 Zulu chief **Shaka** begins 10 years of expansion in southern Africa. His warriors raid villages, causing chaos and forcing millions of people to flee. People displaced by Shaka in turn displace or absorb other peoples, changing forever the mixture of people, language, and culture throughout southern Africa and parts of central Africa. This period in African history is referred to as the *mfecane* or the "crushing."

Shaka meets Lieutenant Farewell.

1818-58 King **Guezo** of a newly strong and independent Dahomey directs his army to move eastward in a relentless pursuit of slaves.

1833 Slavery is outlawed in the British Empire.

1835-43 Afrikaners begin Great Trek northward from Cape Colony in southern Africa to get beyond the influence of the British colonial government.

1835 Queen **Ranavalona I** of Madagascar forbids all religious teaching in the country in an attempt to eliminate foreign influence and preserve the traditional culture of her people.

Ranavalona I.

1843 Gambia and Natal (in southern Africa) become British colonies.

1847 Liberia becomes a republic. American blacks had begun settling there in 1821, and by 1867 approximately 20,000 people had settled in Liberia, mostly on land that had been purchased from local tribes.

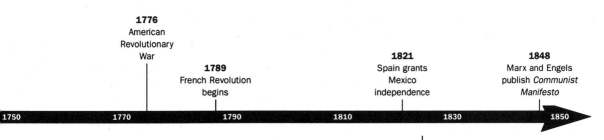

1776
American
Revolutionary
War

1789
French Revolution
begins

1821
Spain grants
Mexico
independence

1848
Marx and Engels
publish *Communist
Manifesto*

1750   1770   1790   1810   1830   1850

Slaves leaving ship.

1860 M'Siri becomes leader of the Katanga Kingdom in Congo. M'Siri expands his territory methodically, taking captives and trading them for more guns and powder, which he uses to take more slaves. At the height of his reign M'Siri controls a territory larger than the state of California.

1861 British establish colonial presence in modern-day Nigeria.

1862 Mutesa I is the first Bugandan king to receive Europeans in his kingdom.

1867 Tippu Tib establishes himself as one of the greatest traders in ivory and slaves in eastern and central Africa. He amasses such a great fortune that he is recognized as the overlord of a vast area.

1868 Moshoeshoe, the chief of a small Sotho clan, arranges for Basutoland to become a British protectorate after Afrikaners move North and settle on land claimed by Moshoeshoe. His diplomacy laid the foundation for the current-day nation-state of Lesotho.

1871 Gold is discovered in the Transvaal (southern Africa).

1873-74 Kumasi (Ghana) is burned in the Ashanti-British War.

1874 The Gold Coast becomes a British colony.

1879 Zulu leader **Cetshwayo**'s army, with weaponry consisting mostly of *assegais* (short stabbing spears) and some firearms, defeats the British army at Isandhlwana (South Africa).

1883 Paul Kruger is elected the first president of the Transvaal Republic (South Africa) after successfully leading his people against the British army in 1880 to restore independence to the Transvaal.

1884-85 At a conference in Berlin, European nations carve out their spheres of influence in Africa.

Cetshwayo.

1865
U.S. Civil War ends; slavery abolished in United States

1870
15th Amendment grants all male U.S. citizens the right to vote

1875
Alexander Graham Bell invents telephone

1881
Booker T. Washington founds Tuskegee Institute

| 1855 | 1860 | 1865 | 1870 | 1875 | 1880 |

1885 The Mahdi, a Muslim visionary who declared himself the successor to the prophet Muhammad, defeats British general Charles Gordon at Khartoum (Sudan) in an uprising against the territory's Egyptian overlords and their British administrators.

1885 King Leopold II of Belgium creates the Belgian Congo as his personal kingdom.

1889 Menelik II becomes emperor of Ethiopia. He is the only African leader to keep control of his country as European powers carve up the continent into colonies.

1889 Great Britain grants the British South Africa Company a royal charter for Rhodesia (Zimbabwe). A large, permanent white settlement is established at Fort Salisbury the next year.

1893-94 Matabele chief **Lobengula** is defeated by British South Africa Company in Rhodesia. With Lobengula's death in 1894, the line of inherited leadership of the Ndebele ends.

1894 Samuel Crowther is consecrated bishop of Nigeria and becomes the first black bishop in the Anglican Church.

1895-96 Ethiopians defeat Italian invaders at the battle of Adowa.

1896 Ashanti king **Prempeh I** negotiates with the British in order to save his 200-year-old kingdom.

1896-97 Ndebele and Shona revolt against the British (in Zimbabwe).

1899-1902 The Boer War is fought between Afrikaners in the Transvaal and Orange Free State against the British. Although the Boers win early victories, the British win the war and the Afrikaners accept British rule.

1900 The first Pan African Congress is held in London. Early Pan-Africanism advocates the merging of smaller African states into one huge African nation.

The Mahdi.

Samuel Crowther.

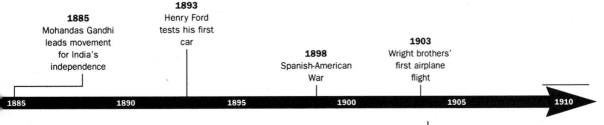

1885
Mohandas Gandhi leads movement for India's independence

1893
Henry Ford tests his first car

1898
Spanish-American War

1903
Wright brothers' first airplane flight

1885　　1890　　1895　　1900　　1905　　1910

Boer soldiers.

Adelaide Smith Casely Hayford and pupils.

1900 Queen mother of the Ashanti **Yaa Asantewa** leads Ashanti army in war against the British in a heroic but futile battle against the colonizers.

1908 German troops defeat the Herero army at Waterberg (Namibia). **Samuel Maherero,** supreme chief of the Herero nation, makes a brave but ultimately hopeless attempt to get the land back from the Germans. When the Herero revolt begins, the population stands at about 80,000, but within one year more than 65,000 Herero are dead.

1915 Malawi nationalist **John Chilembwe** leads uprising against British colonists. Chilembwe, an African Christian leader in Nyasaland (present-day Malawi) whose "Rising" failed miserably, became a folk hero to the people of Nyasaland, a symbol of resistance to white rule.

1919 Adelaide Smith Casely Hayford establishes her Girls' Vocational and Industrial School in Freetown, Sierra Leone.

1921 Congolese religious leader **Simon Kimbangu** establishes a following after starting one of the most important independent Christian religious movements in central Africa.

1921 Sobhuza II is installed as "Lion" or king of the Swazi. Sobhuza will become the world's longest-reigning monarch, ruling for 60 years.

1930 Haile Selassie I becomes emperor of Ethiopia. During his rule, he abolishes slavery, institutes tax reform, promotes education, creates a constitution, and plays a dominant role in the formation of the Organization of African Unity (OAU).

1935 Italy invades Ethiopia under the orders of Italian dictator Benito Mussolini. **Haile Selassie** appeals to the League of

1914
World War I
begins

1917
Russian
Revolution

1918
World War I
ends

1927
Joseph Stalin
becomes
dictator of the
Soviet Union

1929
Great
Depression
begins

1912   1916   1920   1924   1928   1932

Nations for help to stop the Italian invaders, but England and France refused to cooperate. The next year, Italy occupies Ethiopia and Haile Selassie goes into exile.

1941 Italy is evicted from Ethopia; **Haile Selassie** is restored to the throne.

1944 William V. S. Tubman is named president of Liberia.

1946 General rise of African nationalism throughout colonial Africa at end of World War II.

1948 Kenyan anthropologist **Mary Leakey** discovers fossilized bones of *Proconsul africanus,* an apelike creature between 25 and 40 million years old. This is the first significant find to suggest that humans may have originated in East Africa

1948 Olufunmilayo Ransome-Kuti organizes Nigerian market women. The Abeokuta women's campaign protest abuses of British rule.

1948 The National party, comprised mainly of conservative Afrikaners, wins elections in South Africa and establishes a society based on racial separateness and discrimination, or apartheid.

1948 South African writer **Alan Paton**'s novel *Cry, the Beloved Country* is published, bringing South Africa's racial policies worldwide attention.

1952 The Mau Mau uprising in Kenya begins, a violent rebellion by Kikuyu terrorists who fight against the seizing of Kikuyu land by the British. In the next few years, nearly 3,000 Kikuyu die, many at the hands of the Mau Mau rebels, who terrorize blacks suspected of supporting the white regime. By the end of 1955 the revolt is put down.

Haile Selassie I.

Louis S. B. Leakey.

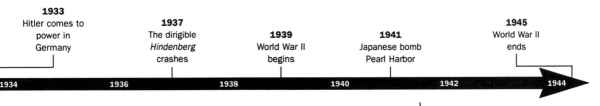

1933 Hitler comes to power in Germany

1937 The dirigible *Hindenberg* crashes

1939 World War II begins

1941 Japanese bomb Pearl Harbor

1945 World War II ends

1934   1936   1938   1940   1942   1944

1953 Federation of Northern and Southern Rhodesia and Nyasaland is formed. Following pressure from the white settler groups in Southern Rhodesia, Northern Rhodesia (now Zambia), and Nyasaland (now Malawi), Great Britain allows the three territories to unite as the self-governing Federation of Rhodesia and Nyasaland. Black Africans strongly oppose the formation of the white-run federation, which lasts until 1963.

1955 Alice Lenshina forms the Lumpa Church, which will become the largest and most powerful peasant movement in Zambian history. The expanding Lumpa Church challenges the state, the established churches, and the traditional leaders.

1957 Kwame Nkrumah becomes prime minister of independent Ghana, the first British colony in Africa to achieve independence after World War II.

1958 Sékou Touré becomes president of Guinea as it achieves independence from France.

1958 Hendrik Verwoerd takes over as prime minister of South Africa and reinforces Bantustan policies that were initiated in South Africa in 1951. Under these policies, citizenship and voting rights for blacks is restricted to nine districts or Bantus. The land reserved for blacks is of poor quality and equals about 14 percent of South Africa's total land, whereas blacks make up about 85 percent of the population.

1958 Nigerian writer **Chinua Achebe**'s *Things Fall Apart* is published.

1960 Joshua Nkomo is elected president of the National Democratic Party, the forerunner to the Zimbabwe African People's Union, one of the main groups that successfully fought for the independence of Rhodesia.

Sékou Touré, Kwame Nkrumah,
and William V. S. Tubman

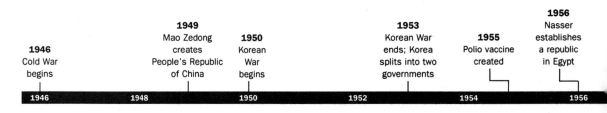

1946
Cold War
begins

1949
Mao Zedong
creates
People's Republic
of China

1950
Korean
War
begins

1953
Korean War
ends; Korea
splits into two
governments

1955
Polio vaccine
created

1956
Nasser
establishes
a republic
in Egypt

1946   1948   1950   1952   1954   1956

1960 South African singer and political activist **Miriam Makeba** begins exile from South Africa that will last 30 years. Singing throughout the world, she uses music as her forum in the fight against apartheid and racial discrimination.

1960 At a mass demonstration pushing for an end to pass laws for blacks in Sharpeville, South Africa, policemen fire into a crowd of 5,000 unarmed demonstrators, killing 69 and wounding 300.

1960 **Patrice Lumumba** of the Congo Republic, **Félix Houphouet-Boigny** of Côte d'Ivoire, **Léopold Sédar Senghor** of Senegal, and **Julius Nyerere** of Kenya are sworn in as heads of their newly independent nations.

1960 South African chief and African National Congress (ANC) president **Albert John Lutuli** wins the Nobel Peace Prize.

1960 **Moïse Tshombe** declares Katanga independent from Congo and becomes the president of the secessionist state.

1961 Tanganyika, Rwanda, and Sierra Leone become independent.

1962 Uganda and Burundi achieve independence.

1963 Organization of African Unity is founded to promote unity among African states.

1963 **Nnamdi Azikiwe** becomes president of the Republic of Nigeria.

1964 **Kenneth Kaunda** becomes president of Zambia.

1964 **Jomo Kenyatta** is inaugurated president of Kenya.

1965 Prime Minister **Ian Douglas Smith** declares Rhodesia's independence from Great Britain to avoid an independence granted by the British that would be based on majority rule.

Julius Nyerere

Jomo Kenyatta and Tom Mboya

1959	**1961**	**1964**	**1965**
Castro creates Communist government in Cuba	Berlin Wall divides East and West Germany	First wave of racial riots in large U.S. cities	U.S. troops become involved in Vietnam War

1958 1960 1962 1964 1966 1968

1966 Nigerian writer **Flora Nwapa** publishes her first novel, *Efuru.*

1966 In a military coup in Nigeria, Prime Minister **Abubakar Tafawa Balewa** is assassinated. Another military coup occurs this year in Ghana.

1966 Hastings Banda becomes president of Malawi.

1966 Sir Seretse Khama becomes president of independent Botswana.

1966 Basutoland becomes independent Lesotho.

1967-70 Civil war erupts in Nigeria. In the second military coup since independence, military officers from the Muslim North overthrow the existing government. A Muslim-dominated government takes over, and tens of thousands of Ibos who live in the North are killed. The federal government announces plans to split the Eastern Region, the home of the Ibo, into three separate states. In response, the Eastern Region secedes and proclaims itself the independent Republic of Biafra. Nigerian troops go into Biafra to put down the rebellion. A two-and-a-half year bloody conflict follows before Biafra falls to federal forces. An estimated one million Biafrans die of starvation because of the food shortages caused by the war.

1967-97 Mobutu Sese Seko establishes himself as president of Congo (Zaire).

1968 Swaziland and Mauritius become independent.

1969 Mozambique nationalist **Eduardo Mondlane** is assassinated.

1969 Kenyan trade unionist **Tom Mboya** is assassinated.

1969 Exiled South African writer **Bessie Head** publishes *When Rain Clouds Gather.*

1971 Idi Amin takes power in Uganda.

Mobutu Sese Seko and troops.

Idi Amin being sworn in.

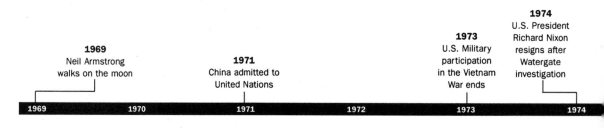

1969
Neil Armstrong walks on the moon

1971
China admitted to United Nations

1973
U.S. Military participation in the Vietnam War ends

1974
U.S. President Richard Nixon resigns after Watergate investigation

| 1969 | 1970 | 1971 | 1972 | 1973 | 1974 |

1974 A military coup in Portugal ends the fight in Mozambique for independence from Portugal. The Portuguese army—tired of the endless wars they were sent to fight in Africa and desiring a democratic system at home—overthrow the government of Marcello Caetano. The new government in Portugal hold a series of meetings with Mozambique's nationalist leaders and works out a plan for independence.

1974 Ethiopian emperor **Haile Selaisse I** is assassinated.

1975 Mozambique becomes independent.

1976 Soweto, South Africa, erupts in violence as school children demonstrate against the school authorities' decision to use Afrikaans as the language for teaching.

1977 South African authorities banish activist **Winnie Madikizela-Mandela** to Orange Free State for eight years.

1977 South African activist **Steve Biko** dies in police custody.

1977 Kenyan environmentalist **Wangari Maathai** establishes the Green Belt Movement; in years to follow 50,000 people involved in the effort will plant an estimated 10,000,000 trees.

1978 Daniel arap Moi becomes president of Kenya after **Jomo Kenyatta**'s death.

1980 Robert Mugabe becomes prime minister of Zimbabwe, the last of the British colonies in Africa to become independent.

1981 Jerry Rawlings overthrows the elected Ghanaian government in his second coup as Ghana's economy nears collapse.

1984 South African Anglican archbishop **Desmond Tutu** wins Nobel Peace Prize.

1986 Nigerian writer **Wole Soyinka** wins Nobel Prize for literature.

Winnie Madikizela-Mandela.

1975
Bill Gates
cofounds
MicroSoft

1978
Egypt and Israel
negotiate peace
in Camp David
Accords

1979
Ruhollah
Khomeini
creates Islamic
state in Iran

1983
The Internet
is born

1975   1976   1978   1980   1982   1984

1986 Joaquim Chissano is named president of Mozambique.

1986 Yoweri Museveni takes over as the head of government in Uganda.

1990 Nelson Mandela is released from prison after 27 years.

1990 The first president of Namibia, **Sam Nujoma,** is sworn in.

1991 Nigerian writer **Ben Okri** wins the Booker Prize.

1991 South African fiction writer **Nadine Gordimer** wins the Nobel Prize for literature.

1992 President **Joaquim Chissano** helps to end the 16-year-long civil war in Mozambique and brings the rebel group headed by Afonso Dhlakama into the government through the country's first multiparty elections.

1993 South Africans **Nelson Mandela** and **Frederick Willem de Klerk** are jointly awarded the Nobel Peace Prize for their efforts to form a democratic, representative government in South Africa.

1994 Nelson Mandela is inaugurated as the first black president of South Africa. His political party, the African National Congress, is elected as the majority in South Africa's parliament.

1996 Ghanaian diplomat **Kofi Annan** is named Secretary General of the United Nations.

1997 Nigerian Afro-Beat singer **Fela Kuti** dies of AIDS.

1998 U.S. embassies in Nairobi, Kenya, and Dar es Salaam, Tanzania, are bombed.

Nelson Mandela and Frederick Willem de Klerk.

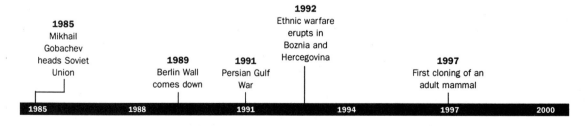

1985
Mikhail Gobachev heads Soviet Union

1989
Berlin Wall comes down

1991
Persian Gulf War

1992
Ethnic warfare erupts in Boznia and Hercegovina

1997
First cloning of an adult mammal

| 1985 | 1988 | 1991 | 1994 | 1997 | 2000 |

african BIOGRAPHY

Chinua Achebe

Born November 16, 1930
Ogidi, Nigeria

Nigerian writer

hinua Achebe (*CHIN-yoo-uh ah-CHAY-bee*) is one of Nigeria's best-known and most respected authors. He has written a number of novels, short stories, poems, essays, and articles earning worldwide critical acclaim and popular success. In addition to his numerous awards for his written works, including the 1972 Commonwealth Poetry Prize, Achebe has received more than 20 honorary doctorates from universities around the world. In an interview published in the scholarly journal *Callaloo,* literary critic Charles H. Rowell told Achebe that "here in the United States, those of us who read 20th century world literature think of you as one of the most important writers in this era."

Achebe's role as a socially committed storyteller stems from his ethnic Ibo traditions. As he explained his literary goals to *Callaloo,* the author described an Ibo festival of art that celebrates

"Art cannot be in the service of destruction, cannot be in the service of oppression, cannot be in the service of evil."

—Achebe, commenting on his belief that all literature should have a higher purpose humanity in all of its good and evil aspects. In this ceremony, called the *mbari,* art is made with the involvement of the community and in the service of the community. The festival itself is called into being by an Ibo goddess named Ala or Ani. She is both earth goddess and goddess of creativity and as such is responsible for creativity and morality in the world. In this way, commented Achebe, "a statement is being made about the meaning of art. . . . Art cannot be in the service of destruction, cannot be in the service of oppression, cannot be in the service of evil." The author's writings reflect his belief in the need for all stories to have a purpose and to teach a lesson.

Writes to preserve tradition

Achebe was born on November 16, 1930, in Ogidi, Nigeria, to Janet N. Iloegbunam Achebe and Isiah Okafo Achebe. He was raised in what was then the colony of Nigeria under British rule. Achebe's father was one of his village's earliest converts to Christianity and a teacher at the Church Missionary Society. As a result, young Chinua was taught to reject the traditional religion of his Ibo people and to embrace Christian teachings. Still, he felt drawn to the ways of his non-Christian neighbors and—against his parents' wishes—attended traditional village festivals.

At the colonial government secondary school, Achebe studied the works of English writers Charles Dickens (1812-1870), Jonathan Swift (1667-1745), and William Shakespeare (1564-1616), as well as a number of "African" books such as *Heart of Darkness* by Polish-born English novelist Joseph Conrad (1857-1924). While he enjoyed these works early in high school, by the time he graduated in 1947 Achebe realized he was forsaking his African roots by identifying with the white man—not the African, who was often portrayed in such literature as a savage. Achebe was thus inspired to counter such stereotypes of Africa and Africans.

Achebe entered the University College in Ibadan, Nigeria, to study medicine. He quickly transferred to liberal arts, however, an area of far greater interest to him. Through his studies he came across the 1939 novel *Mister Johnson* by Anglo-Irish novelist Joyce Cary. This book disturbed Achebe with its superficial and grossly inaccurate depiction of Nigeria. His exasperation at the novel convinced him to try his own hand at writing.

As an undergraduate Achebe wrote short stories about Nigeria and published a number of them in the campus newspaper, the *University Herald.* He began work as a journalist for the Nigerian Broadcasting Corporation in 1954, one year after graduating with a bachelor's degree in literature. Around this time, Achebe first imagined the character of Okonkwo, who would become the tragic hero of his first novel, *Things Fall Apart,* published in 1958.

Nigeria

Nationalist response to colonial rule

Things Fall Apart firmly established Achebe's reputation as a writer. The book has been translated into 45 languages, has sold over 8 million copies, and has been adapted for film, stage, and the small screen. Through *Things Fall Apart,* the author rejects the negative view of Africa and Africans that he had unconsciously accepted during his upbringing in the British colonial era. In its rediscovery of the beauty and uniqueness of African culture, the novel forms a part of what Achebe terms a "mental revolution"—a revolution occurring within the consciousness of the African people that accompanied the independence movement in British West Africa.

Independence leads to frustration and disenchantment

In his 1966 novel *A Man of the People,* published only six years after Nigeria's independence from British rule, Achebe addresses the failures of Nigerian democratic politics. The author's autobiographical note in *Contemporary Novelists* describes the quick passing from one era in Nigerian history to the next and the corresponding shift of emphasis in Nigerian novels:

> Europe conceded independence to us and we promptly began to misuse it, or rather those leaders to whom we entrusted the wielding of our new power and opportunity [misused it]. So we got mad at them and came out brandishing novels of disenchantment.

A Man of the People was one such novel of disenchantment. *World Press Review* reprinted Chuks Iloegbunam's summary of the novel: "In *A Man of the People,* Achebe focuses on the mess that African politicians made of nationhood once [they were given] political authority. . . . Abuse of power, corruption, politi-

Background to Biafran War

Nigeria gained its independence from Great Britain in October 1960. Sir Abubakar Balewa (see entry) became the nation's first head of state. But Balewa's nonmilitary government would not last long in Nigeria, where ethnic tensions run deep.

Nigeria has the largest population of any country in Africa, estimated in the late 1990s to be about 100 million. The country is dominated by three distinctive ethnic and religious groups. The Muslim Fulani-Hausa live in the northern part of the country. The South, however, is generally Christian, with the Ibo people living in the eastern region and the Yoruba people living in the western region.

In January 1966 Ibo army officers overthrew Balewa's government, killing him and two regional prime ministers and ending civilian rule in Nigeria. Six months later, another group of military officers from the Muslim North overthrew the existing government. At that time, many Ibo traders were living in the North. When the Muslim-dominated government took over, tens of thousands of Ibos were killed; others fled to the East. In 1967 the federal government announced plans to split the Eastern Region, the home of the Ibo, into three separate states. This move would have cut the Ibo off from access to the Atlantic Coast and the oil-rich areas of the delta. In response, the Eastern Region seceded (separated) from Nigeria and proclaimed itself the independent Republic of Biafra.

The Nigerian government sent its troops into Biafra to put down the rebellion. A long and bloody conflict followed. Two and a half years later, in January 1970, Biafra fell to federal forces. An estimated one million Biafrans died of starvation because of the food shortages caused by the war.

cal thuggery, and electoral malpractices walked the streets in broad daylight." Achebe's vision proved all too accurate. He had predicted the fall of civilian government and the rise of military coups (overthrowing an existing government) and political chaos. Days after *A Man of the People* was published in 1966, a coup ended Nigeria's first republic (nonmilitary government). In the following chaos, nearly 30,000 Ibo people were massacred. (See box titled "Background to Biafran War.")

Civil war in Nigeria

By the time civil war had erupted in Nigeria, Achebe was ranked among the nation's leading novelists. But the outbreak of the war drove him away from writing long fiction for over two decades. He felt that the horrors of his nation's struggle could not be expressed through fiction.

The author could not avoid involvement with the chaotic events of the time and chose to throw himself into the cause of his Ibo people. In the spring of 1967 the Ibos declared the Eastern Region of Nigeria an independent state. The region, which they called the Republic of Biafra, had seceded, or separated itself, from the federal government. Achebe was in the new capital, Enugu, at the time, starting up the Citadel Press with fellow Nigerian poet Christopher Okigbo (who was later killed in the war). After Enugu fell to federal troops in October 1967, Achebe traveled to foreign capitals to publicize the plight of Biafran peoples, which included mass starvation as well as widespread casualties from the war. He worked through the duration of the war as Biafran Minister of Information.

Although Achebe's preoccupation with the painful realities of the Nigerian civil war made it difficult for him to write long fiction in the late 1960s, he did write poetry, short stories, children's fiction, essays, and articles. In the volume *Christmas in Biafra,* which won the Commonwealth Poetry Prize in 1972, Achebe expresses his fierce anger, despair, and sorrow at the forces that were tearing his nation apart.

Peace brings cautious hope

Biafra fell to the Nigerian federal government in January 1970. The secessionist state was then reincorporated into Nigeria. Achebe continued his efforts in publishing by assuming the position of director of both Nwamife Publishers Ltd., based in Enugu, Nigeria, and Heinemann Educational Books (Nigeria) Ltd., based in Ibadan. He had begun his work in publishing in 1962 as general editor of the Heinemann African Writers' Series, and he viewed his new directorial positions in publishing as vehicles to combat racism in literature and to foster the efforts of African writers. He also founded *Okike: A Nigerian Journal of New Writing* in 1971. During the 1970s Achebe began teaching at the University of Nigeria at Nsukka and overseas at the universities of Massachusetts and Connecticut. He delivered numerous addresses and wrote critical essays on racism in Africa, the aftereffects of colonialism on his people, and the need for more young voices in African literature.

Selected writings of Chinua Achebe

- *Things Fall Apart* (1958), novel
- *No Longer at Ease* (1960), novel
- *The Sacrifical Egg and Other Stories* (1962), short stories
- *Arrow of God* (1964), novel
- *Chike and the River* (1966), children's book
- *A Man of the People* (1966), novel
- *Beware, Soul Brother and Other Poems* (1971), poetry
- *How the Leopard Got His Claws* (1972; with John Iroaganachi), children's book
- *Christmas in Biafra and Other Poems* (1973), poetry
- *Girls at War and Other Stories* (1973), short stories
- *Morning Yet on Creation Day* (1975), essays
- *Don't Let Him Die: An Anthology of Memorial Poems for Christopher Okigbo* (1978; coeditor with Dubem Okafor), poetry collection
- *The Drum* (1978), children's book
- *The Flute* (1978), children's book
- *The Trouble with Nigeria* (1983), essays
- *African Short Stories* (1984; coeditor with C. L. Innes), short stories collection
- *Anthills of the Savannah* (1988), novel
- *Hopes and Impediments: Selected Essays* (1988), essays
- *Another Africa* (1997; with Robert Lyons, photographer), nonfiction

During the 1980s and early 1990s, Achebe continued to teach and lecture while he wrote general essays, literary criticism, and a fifth novel, *Anthills of the Savannah*. Many critics at the time found this his most powerful novel. *Anthills of the Savannah* differs from his other works of long fiction. In this novel women take the most significant role by inventing a new kind of storytelling—and thereby offering the glimmer of hope in the work's ambiguous ending. This marks a tremendous change in tone from Achebe's earlier writings, especially *Things Fall Apart*.

Throughout his remarkable career, Chinua Achebe has

worked variously as a journalist, publisher, teacher, and writer, focusing at different times on different literary styles. In all of his works, though, his commitment to his ideals has remained clear and uncompromised. In 1961 he married Christiana Chinwe Okoli. They have four children: two daughters (Chinelo and Nwando) and two sons (Ikechukwu and Chidi).

Further Reading

Black Literature Criticism. Detroit: Gale, 1992.

Black Writers. Detroit: Gale, 1989.

Callaloo, winter 1990, pp. 87-101.

Contemporary Black Biography. Volume 6. Detroit: Gale, 1994.

Contemporary Novelists. Detroit: St. James Press, 1991.

Duerden, Dennis, and Cosmo Pieterse, eds. *African Writers Talking: A Collection of Radio Interviews.* Africana Publishing, 1972.

Killam, G. D. *The Novels of Chinua Achebe.* Africana Publishing, 1969.

King, Bruce. *Introduction to Nigerian Literature.* Africana Publishing, 1972.

Larson, Charles R. *The Emergence of African Fiction.* Bloomington: Indiana University Press, 1972.

Petersen, Kirsten Holst, and Anna Rutherford, eds. *Chinua Achebe: A Celebration.* North Pomfret, VT: Heinemann, 1991.

World Press Review, June 1986.

Afonso I

Born c. 1461
Kingdom of Kongo (called Zaire, 1971-97;
renamed Democratic Republic of the Congo,
May 17, 1997)
Died c. 1543
Kingdom of Kongo

King of the Kongo people

"We need from your Kingdoms no other than priests and people to teach in schools, and no other goods but wine and flour for the holy sacrament. . . . It is our will that in these kingdoms there should not be any trade in slaves nor market for slaves."

—Afonso, in a letter to the Portuguese king

fonso I (*AH-fon-so*) was a Christian king of western-central Africa's Kongo empire from 1506 to 1543. He welcomed the early Portuguese explorers who journeyed to the kingdom in the 1480s and 1490s, and he established a partnership of equals with kings of Portugal. At his request, Catholic priests and artisans (crafters) visited his kingdom and taught the royal family and nobles of the court reading, writing, grammar, and the humanities. In 1518, after studying in Lisbon, Portugal, and in Rome, Italy, Afonso's son Henrique became a bishop in the Roman Catholic church. Afonso corresponded frequently with the kings of Portugal. His letters and those of various Portuguese observers document the development and eventual destruction of the Kongo kingdom.

As explorations in the New World and the route to India became the main preoccupation of sixteenth-century Portuguese explorers, the profitability of a quickly growing slave trade refocused attention on the Kongo. Eventually, Afonso lost control of his subjects and the kingdom disintegrated into warring and slaving factions (or groups). The promise of wealth in the increasing slave trade was so great that even some Portuguese educators and missionaries participated.

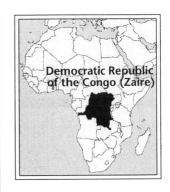

Democratic Republic of the Congo (Zaire)

Kongo empire expands

About 150 years before the Portuguese made their way down the coast to the land of the Kongo, Kongo-speaking settlers from north of the Congo River had conquered smaller, weaker groups and consolidated (or united) them into the Kongo kingdom. During the conquest of the smaller chiefdoms, the leaders of Kongo took many captives or slaves. Some historians speculate that as the kingdom expanded, the number of slaves may have actually outnumbered the free population. The kingdom ran roughly from the Congo River in the north to the Kango River in the east and from the Dande River in the south and the Atlantic Ocean to the west. It consisted of six divisions—the *manikongo* (king of the Kongo people) appointed a leader for each one—and its capital was located at Mbanza. At the time of the Portuguese's arrival, the kingdom of the Kongo was probably the most advanced civilization on the western coast of Africa.

In 1483 Diogo Cão discovered the place where the Congo River empties into the Atlantic Ocean. The Portuguese explorers made contact with the king of the territory, the manikongo known as Nzinga a Nkuwu. Afonso was the son of the manikongo and the heir apparent to the throne.

Diogo Cão left four Portuguese behind when he returned to Lisbon from his first trip and took four young Kongo men home with him. Portuguese king John II (reigned 1477-95) received them warmly and assumed responsibility for their education. Likewise, the manikongo welcomed the Portuguese and treated them as royal visitors. When the Portuguese returned home two years later, the two kings sought to establish a policy of peace and friendship between their kingdoms. In a gesture of good faith and respect—and with the hope that the Kongo would benefit from the Europeans' wealth and power—the manikongo sent gifts and representatives back to King John II. Afonso would profit greatly from this relationship. In the future, however, European powers

Portuguese explorers

The recurring myth of an African Christian king named Prester John stimulated Portuguese exploration of the West Coast of Africa. Christian rulers in Europe believed the fabulously wealthy kingdom of Prester John could be found in Ethiopia, so they sent explorers along Africa's Atlantic Coast to find a river route across the continent to his kingdom. The hunt for the imaginary king contributed to the discovery of the Americas, the exploration of the Congo River, and the establishment of a sea route around southern Africa to India. Portuguese prince Henrique de Aviz (Henry the Navigator; 1394–1460) set up a school of navigation in 1420 and financed the early expeditions himself. The initial explorers set sail from Lisbon, inching their way along the coast of Africa until, at the time of Prince Henry's death in 1460, they had reached the western coastal region of Sierra Leone. Year after year they ventured farther south.

Meanwhile, other expeditions set sail from Lisbon in search of a sea route from the European Coast to India. In 1487 Bartholomeu Dias sailed along the entire length of the Atlantic Coast and rounded the Cape of Good Hope at the tip of the African continent.

would not establish a relationship of equality with any other African ruler.

In 1490 King John dispatched a representative to establish diplomatic relations with Kongo's king. He sent three ships, a dozen priests, soldiers, masons, carpenters, printers, farmers, and various other artisans, as well as women skilled in domestic arts such as bread baking and sewing. The Catholic priests quickly succeeded in converting the manikongo, his wife, and their son Afonso to Catholicism. For the occasion of their baptism into the Christian faith in 1491, the king employed 1,000 Kongo people in the construction of a church of stone. Portuguese masons and carpenters also worked on the project. Despite the frenzied work, the church was not completed in time. In its place, the carpenters built a wooden hut for the ceremony. According to some reports, 100,000 people gathered to participate in the historic event. On his baptism, the African king took the name of his benefactor, King John, and his wife took the name Eleanor, after the queen of Portugal. The manikongo's son and heir to the throne was also baptized. He took the name Afonso, after Portugal's royal heir.

Not all the nobles in the king's court approved of this swift embrace of a foreign religion. Some refused to be baptized. One such dissenter (or opponent) was the king's son by another wife, Mpanzu a Nzinga, chief of the Mpemba.

In time, the Kongo Christians became increasingly resistant to the teachings of the church. They refused to give up some of their traditional beliefs and practices. While professing a belief in the existence of a supreme being, the Kongo people did not believe that this being—an all-knowing and all-powerful God to Christians—exerted an influence over their everyday lives. Instead, they placed their faith in their ancestors, communicating with them through various intermediaries. Traditional healers and diviners (people thought to possess supernatural powers) were believed to correspond with the spirit world. The Catholic priests realized that if the Kongo people continued to cling to their rituals and fetishes (carved idols) for guidance, they would never truly embrace Christianity. The Africans held fast to their beliefs, and in their frustration the priests resorted to violence, destroying ritual centers and even whipping the Kongo people in a misguided attempt to instill Christian beliefs in a non-Christian land.

When the missionaries attacked the traditional practice of polygyny (having more than one wife), they went too far. Many African societies allow their male members to practice polygyny; in such cases, a man may take as many wives as he is able to support. For a king, polygyny provides an opportunity to consolidate (enlarge by merging and therefore strengthen) his kingdom by marrying the daughters of powerful subjects and chiefs. The Catholic priests' disregard for traditional African practices helped the anti-Portuguese faction to gain increasing support. As a result, many of the Kongo's Christian converts turned away from the church. Eventually, Afonso's father, the manikongo, renounced Christianity and the Catholic faith.

Afonso, however, did not. As a punishment, the king banished Afonso and the remaining Portuguese in Mbanza to Afonso's inherited district of Nsundi in 1495. Afonso remained in exile (forced absence from one's homeland) for about 11 years, during which time he held fast to his Christian beliefs. He reportedly attended mass daily and continued his study of the Christian faith. He also destroyed and outlawed the fetishes in the district and expelled those who used them.

With such strong anti-Christian sentiments in the Kongo kingdom, Portuguese relations cooled. Nevertheless, King John II and his successor, Manuel (who reigned from 1495 to 1521), sent a few expeditions out to Kongo. By that time, however, the Portuguese were absorbed in the new paths and lands that their explorers had discovered: the sea route to India in 1497 and the discovery of Brazil in 1500.

The manikongo died in 1505, and although Afonso was the heir apparent, his half-brother Mpanzu threatened his ascent to the throne. Queen Eleanor, who had secretly held on to her Christian beliefs, arranged a three-day delay in the announcement of her husband's death, thereby allowing enough time for Afonso to get to the capital and prepare for battle with his brother. Although Afonso and his troops were outnumbered 20 to 1 by Mpanzu's army, Afonso defeated him because he had the support of the well-armed Portuguese. The people interpreted Afonso's victory over such incredible odds as the miracle of Christianity, and it won the new manikongo, King Afonso, many supporters.

Takes the helm

When Afonso rose to power, he was probably less than 30 years old. During the 11 years he spent in exile, he had studied with European priests and had learned as much as he could about Christian Europe. He had also learned something about court politics. One of his first acts as king was to rid the court of his non-Christian enemies. He ordered many to be hanged or sent into exile. Freed of active opposition, Afonso then took steps to heal the split in the court. For example, he appointed the chief earth priest, one of the highest ranking traditional priests, as supervisor for the maintenance and construction of the churches. Afonso also agreed to respect and practice certain traditional rituals and, having learned from the Christian priests' mistakes, maintained the practice of polygyny in the kingdom.

Afonso asked the Portuguese king to send more skilled Europeans to the kingdom. As an indication of his good intentions, he sent the Portuguese some of the kingdom's most valued riches: ivory, copper, parrots, and slaves. He also sent his own son, Henrique, and other sons of court nobles to be educated in Lisbon. Portugal's king welcomed the Kongo youth and enrolled them in the college of Santo Eloi in Lisbon. He also shipped a fresh group of 15 priests—along with various artisans, craftsmen, soldiers, and teachers—to Afonso.

Modernizes the kingdom

With this fresh supply of crafters, educators, and priests, Afonso oversaw the construction of a series of schools to fulfill his dream of creating a literate elite in the kingdom. As early as 1509, 400 students had enrolled in mission schools. Within seven years, about a thousand students were attending schools in the capital.

Afonso also put the artisans to work redesigning the capital city. Mbanza was a walled city; within the walls, artisans laid out straight, tree-lined streets and constructed houses made of ironstone. They built a special walled section of the city for Afonso and his nobles and set aside another walled-off section for the Portuguese. The capital, renamed São Salvador, had a population of 100,000 in its 20 square miles. Using the knowledge he had gained from his exposure to Europeans, Afonso helped advance the living conditions in his kingdom. He imported fruit-bearing trees such as guava, lemon, and orange to improve the diet of the people; he also brought in maize (corn), manioc (a tropical plant), and sugar cane for planting from Brazil and Asia. In addition, Afonso taught his people how to use contemporary weapons such as mortars, muskets, swords, and sabers.

Afonso personally assumed the dress and manners of the Portuguese. Duarte Lopes, Portuguese representative at the court, described the court style of dressing, as "cloaks, capes, scarlet tabards, and silk robes. . . . They also wear hoods and capes, velvet and leather slippers, [with] rapiers [swords] at their sides. . . . The women have adopted the Portuguese fashions, wearing veils over their heads, and above them black velvet caps, ornamented with jewels, and chains of gold around their neck." The nobles in the kingdom took the titles of Portuguese nobles: princes, dukes, marquises, counts, and barons. Afonso even had a royal coat of arms drawn up.

The glory fades

In their travels along the African coast in the late 1480s, the Portuguese established sugar plantations on an uninhabited island they called São Tomé. The island is situated on the equator, about 200 miles west of Gabon. Because sugar growing and processing are labor intensive, the Portuguese brought slaves with them from West Africa to do the work. São Tomé quickly became the leading

Slavers moving captives.

slave trade depot for the Lower Guinea coast and the Kongo territory. A company licensed by the Portuguese crown ran the island. Its leader did not want the king to interfere in his business. By 1512 São Tomé completely controlled the trade between Kongo and Europe. Rather than deal with African middlemen on the coast, the São Tomé traders went inland to buy their own slaves from the interior markets. They encouraged various groups to make war on one another so they might take captives to sell as slaves.

Afonso wrote a letter to the Portuguese king detailing the horrifying conditions the kingdom was experiencing. He asked the king to send a representative with the power to stop the whites. The king responded to Afonso's request for assistance for his own reasons—he realized just how lucrative the slave trade was and wanted to keep the São Tomé company out of it. Consequently, he made the Kongo a trade monopoly of the Portuguese crown and sent Simão da Silva, a nobleman, to represent the crown. He also sent the largest contingent yet of five ships loaded with missionaries, teachers, books, tools, and furniture. Most important, he prepared an official document, a *regimento,* for Afonso to sign. This document detailed Portuguese responsibilities to the kingdom of the Kongo and, in turn, the Kongo's responsibilities toward the crown. In exchange for teachers, missionaries, and soldiers, each year the Kongo had to fill the Portuguese ships with ivory, copper, and slaves. The agents from São Tomé learned of the Portuguese proposal to cut them out of the trade and went into the Kongo in advance. They ravaged the countryside for slaves, bribing or threatening local chiefs to turn away from the king.

In Mbanza, two factions developed in the kingdom—those who favored the alliance with the Portuguese and those who saw an opportunity to make a fortune and side with the São Tomé agents. For most people, greed won over religious principles: masons, carpenters, teachers—even some of the priests—joined in the trade and took their payment in slaves. So many slaves were traded to the São Tomé agents that a corral had to be built to hold them until they could be taken to the coast. Ironically, the corral was located next to the church.

Between 1505 and 1575, nearly 345,000 slaves were exported from the Kongo kingdom. In 1515 a Portuguese trader described the situation in Mbanza:

> Of all those who go there, few fail to sicken and of those who sicken few fail to die, and those who survive are obliged to withstand the intense heat of the torrid zone, suffering hunger, thirst, and many other miseries, for which there is no relief save patience. [Patience] is needed . . . not only to tolerate the discomforts of such a wretched place but . . . to fight the barbarity, ignorance, idolatry, and vices which seem scarcely human but rather those of irrational animals.

Afonso wrote several letters to the king requesting ships so that the Kongo might bypass São Tomé and deal directly with Portugal. His requests went unanswered. Portugal chose not to honor its agreement with Afonso because its interests lay in the slave trade, not in a modern Christian nation in Africa. In 1522 Portugal managed to take control of São Tomé, and the new king, John III (reigned 1521-27), declared it a colony of the crown.

In 1526, recognizing the terrible conditions the kingdom had fallen into, Afonso wrote another letter to the Portuguese king:

> We cannot reckon how great the damage is, since the above-mentioned merchants daily seize our subject, sons of the land and sons of our noblemen and vassals and relatives. . . . Thieves and men of evil conscience take them because they wish to possess the things and wares of the Kingdom. . . . They grab them and cause them to be sold. . . . So great, Sir, is their corruption and licentiousness that our country

is being utterly depopulated. . . . To avoid, this, we need from your Kingdoms no other than priests and people to teach in schools, and no other goods but wine and flour for the holy sacrament; that is why we beg your highness to help and assist us in this matter, commanding the factors that they should send her neither merchants nor wares, because it is our will that in these kingdoms there should not be any trade in slaves nor market for slaves.

Receiving no response to his letter, Afonso banned involvement in the slave trade. So great was the resistance, however, that he was forced to rescind (or cancel) the ban. Slave trading continued unimpeded. By the 1530s traders were shipping at least 5,000 slaves a year out of Kongo. One historian quoted by Peter Forbath in *The River Congo* stated that the "grand experiment of Europeanizing the African kingdom ground to a halt and, because of the ravages of the slavers, the Kongo fell into a state far more chaotic and primitive than it had ever been before the Portuguese arrived."

Afonso's nightmare

By this time only four missionaries remained in the entire kingdom. Afonso's son, Henrique, who had been ordained as the first African bishop in the Roman Catholic Church, received poor treatment at the hands of the Portuguese. After 13 years of religious study he returned to the Kongo as a bishop. The white clergy treated him so poorly that he became seriously ill.

Despite the terrible conditions in the kingdom caused by unleashed greed and disrespect for the king, Afonso did not lose faith in Portugal. He again entrusted young noblemen into the care of the Portuguese for their education. His trust was misplaced, however, for on their way to Lisbon half of the 20 were taken captive and enslaved on São Tomé. From there they were sent to Brazil as slaves for the plantations.

The kingdom had deteriorated into lawlessness and disrespect even for the king. Under the orders of a Catholic priest named Friar Alvaro, eight Portuguese traders tried to kill Afonso as he sat in church on Easter Sunday of 1539. They fired a cannonball into the church but it missed him, wounding other church goers instead. After that, Afonso became more remote and withdrawn. His dream of a civilized, modern African kingdom turned into a nightmare of disorder and decay.

Afonso died around 1543. The wars over his succession tore the kingdom apart. With the support of the Portuguese powers in São Tomé, Pedro I rose to power briefly, but the Kongo people rebelled after several years and installed Afonso's grandson, Diogo I (reigned 1545-61), as king. Diogo had been educated in Lisbon. He faced the same divisive issues that his grandfather had faced. Under his rule, the southern kingdom of Ndongo declared its independence from Kongo and began dealing directly with the traders on São Tomé. Later, the Portuguese invaded Ndongo and took the port of Luanda, located in present-day Angola.

The reign of Afonso was a brief but remarkable experiment in cooperative relations between a European power and a weak African state. Unfortunately for the history of Africa, it was an exception.

Further Reading

Curtin, Philip, and others, eds. *African History: From Earliest Times to Independence*. 2nd ed. New York: Longman, 1995.

Davidson, Basil. *Africa in History*. New York: Macmillan, 1974.

Dictionary of African Biography. Algonac, MI: Reference Publications, 1979.

Forbath, Peter. *The River Congo*. New York: Harper & Row, 1977.

Murphy, E. Jefferson. *The Bantu Civilization of Southern Africa*. New York: Thomas Crowell, 1974.

Wilson, Derek. *A History of South and Central Africa*. New York/UK: Cambridge University Press, 1975.

Idi Amin

Born 1925
Koboko, British East Africa (now Uganda)

Leader of Uganda

aking power in a military coup d'etat (the overthrow of an existing government) in 1971, Idi Amin Dada (*EE-dee ah-MEEN*) ruled Uganda for seven years. He headed a corrupt and ruthless regime (government). Amin could barely read or write, but he was cunning. He played opposing ethnic and religious interests in Uganda against each other in order to keep his opponents subdued and, when that failed, used brute force. An estimated 250,000 Ugandans were put to death during his rule of terror.

Childhood in a military barracks

Amin was born in northwest Uganda, near the border with the new Democratic Republic of the Congo (known as Zaire from 1971 to 1997) and Somalia. He was a Kakwa, a member of one of the smallest ethnic groups in the country. Amin's father, Dada—a

Kakwa and a Muslim—was a poor farmer trying to grow crops in an arid rocky region of the country. (Amin took his father's name in 1968.) His mother, a member of the Lugbara, another ethnic group, practiced witchcraft. When Amin was still a baby, she left her husband and took the child away with her to live with her family. Later, she went to live near the camp of the King's African Rifles (KAR) near Buikwe. (The KAR was a British regiment made up of local Africans.) She began a relationship with Yafesi Yasin, a corporal in the army, and moved into the barracks with him. For a time, Amin's mother had a reputation as a powerful woman because of her gift of healing. When she failed to cure an old woman, however, people lost respect for her, and her boyfriend sent her out of the barracks.

In 1946, when he was just 18 years old, Amin joined the King's African Rifles as a cook. The young man rose through the military ranks not so much because of his merit but because of the times. In the late 1890s Great Britain had declared the area occupied by the Buganda—the largest ethnic group in the region that is now Uganda—as a protectorate (a dependent political unit). Around the time that the British began having influence in the Lake Victoria region of eastern-central Africa (Uganda shares the lake with neighboring Kenya and Tanzania), the Buganda kingdom was a powerful, centralized monarchy. Britain gave the Buganda preferential treatment, building schools, hospitals, roads, and the railway in the region. Kampala, the capital, and Entebbe, the main commercial center, were within Buganda.

Uganda's problems profit the young Amin

Although the people of Buganda are the largest ethnic group in Uganda, they comprise only 17 percent of the population. Uganda has approximately 40 different ethnic and language groups, and about 10 of these have major populations. The country, therefore, lacks a single national identity—no ethnic group serves as the core for a stable and cohesive society.

The British administered Uganda for nearly 70 years, from 1890 until 1962, when African nationalists (people who sought strong, self-governed African nations) demanded independence. In preparing for independence, which came quite suddenly, the British administration speeded up its training and promotion of African military officers. Amin benefited from this policy. After

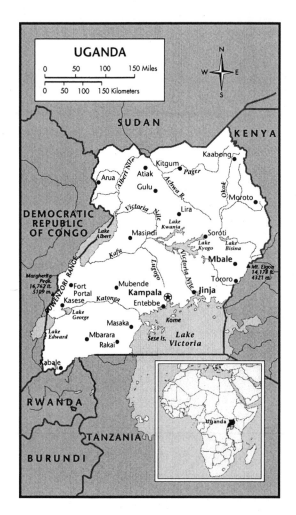

joining the KAR in 1946 as a cook, he was promoted to corporal within two years because of a policy that determined how many African soldiers would be promoted in each British colony in Africa. This began his rise to commander in chief of the entire army.

It did not take Amin long to get out of the kitchen. He had an imposing stature: he stood 6 feet 4 inches tall, was well-groomed, striking in appearance, and willing to obey orders. He was even the heavy-weight boxing champion of the army for 1951; he retired undefeated nine years later. After World War II (1939-45), as Africa's nationalist movements gained momentum, the British army sought out experienced African men to promote to officers. Amin was promoted quickly, achieving warrant officer rank in 1959. In the pre-independence Ugandan army, this was the highest rank an African could ever achieve. In the infantry during the 1950s, Amin saw action in Kenya and later served in the Karamojong District in northeast Uganda. In both cases, charges of brutality and excessive force nearly ended his career. He earned his paratroop wings in Israel. (Paratroops are troops trained to parachute from airplanes.)

Independence government makes enemies

On October 9, 1963, Uganda became fully independent. As a compromise, the British established a federal system whereby the king (or *kabaka*) of Buganda was made the symbolic head of the country—the president. However, the newly elected prime minister, Milton Obote, held the real power. On taking office, Obote set out on a course to restructure many of the British-dominated institutions in Uganda. He sent the British officers home and relied instead on Israeli troops for training. He alienated the British further with his "Move to the Left," nationalizing (taking over as a government) 85 mostly foreign-owned companies. The government also assumed 60 percent ownership of the major Ugandan businesses, like banking and the coffee and tea industries—the country's major exports. When the king of Buganda began to exercise more power than Obote thought he should have, the prime minister suspended the constitution and declared himself president, formally abolishing the kingships. The king went into exile (forced absence from one's country) in the United Kingdom in 1966. Obote promoted Amin to brigadier and then to general. Amin took the opportunity to strengthen his own personal base of support, enlisting and promoting his own people, the Kakwa, and the Nubians, also from his region of the country.

By 1969 many people in Uganda were dissatisfied with Obote's changes. He had made enemies of the Buganda people and of the capitalists (supporters of competition in a free market system), and he had not looked after his military supporters. After a failed assassination attempt in December 1969, Obote's relations with Amin began to cool. When Amin heard the news of the attempt on Obote's life, he fled from his home. This move sparked speculations that Amin himself had been involved in the death plot. His cowardice led to loud protests from fellow officers. The officer most critical of Amin's behavior was Brigadier General Pierino Okoya. On January 25, 1970, the day before he and Amin were scheduled to attend a follow-up investigative meeting on the assassination attempt, Okoya and his wife were found murdered.

Conditions set for a coup

Obote and Amin's relationship deteriorated further over foreign policy issues, especially the activities of a rebel group operating along the Uganda-Sudan border. (Amin was born in that part of the country and favored the rebels' presence there. The rebels were fighting against Muslim encroachment from the North.) Obote eventually decided to reduce Amin's authority and possibly arrest him, and Amin soon learned that Obote was out to get him. Obote planned to appoint several new army officers to undermine Amin's authority. In addition, Obote was pressing forward with the murder investigation of Brigadier Okoya and his wife, which implicated Amin. To put even more pressure on Amin, Obote demanded a full report as to the whereabouts of 2.1 million British pounds that had disappeared from army funds. Threatened by Obote on several fronts, Amin sprang into action. On January 25,

1971, he took control of the government while Obote was attending a conference in Singapore. Obote learned of the coup as he was returning to Uganda and went instead to Kenya.

Amin takes power

Although the army took power, Idi Amin did not establish a military dictatorship—he established a personal dictatorship. Despite his early appearance of heading a government ruled by a Council of Ministers, he personally took over the running of the government. In all, six men, directed by Amin, controlled the system; three security units—the military police, the Public Safety Unit, and the State Research Center—enforced their decisions. Amin ruled on impulse and whim. He gave the armed forces extensive powers to arrest citizens and to search and seize properties. Later, they were given the right to detain (or hold) citizens indefinitely.

On assuming power, Amin's first concern was the military. His takeover had been popular among certain elements in the military, but not all. Almost immediately, Amin ordered the execution of nearly all the original officer corps and half the enlisted personnel of the armed forces. He formed extermination squads that went from garrison to garrison and purged or cleaned out entire ethnic groups. They especially targeted Langi and Acholi officers (supporters of Obote) and massacred 600 soldiers who had served under Obote. Attacks on individuals and ethnic groups grew into campaigns against whole categories of people: judges, teachers, students, professors, and religious leaders among them. Their bodies were often dropped into the Nile River to be eaten by crocodiles.

The military police extended their reach beyond military matters into day-to-day life in Uganda. The Public Safety Unit (PSU) took over the role of the civilian (or nonmilitary) police, which had been denied funding in order to make it ineffective. PSU members carried submachine guns and terrorized the general population. The unit's headquarters were located on a main road. From the high-rise buildings surrounding the headquarters, people could see public executions taking place and actually hear the screams of the prisoners. The State Research Center conducted public executions in its headquarters in the center of Kampala. A tunnel linked it to one of Amin's houses. And, to bolster security

provisions, the State Security Center enlisted thousands of new recruits—mostly young men from the northern provinces who were barely able to read and write. These recruits soon became intoxicated with the power of force, arresting anybody they thought might have money or something they wanted. Through these three groups, Amin established the practice of using murder, brutalization, and intimidation to overcome opponents and to solve problems.

The attorney general under Amin, Godfrey Lule, quoted by Henry Kyemba in *State of Blood,* describes Amin:

> It is vital that the world understands clearly the true nature of the man who rules Uganda. For too long, Amin has been considered a clown. Indeed, he is a clown when he chooses. Face to face, he is relaxed, simple and charming. He seems incapable of wrong-doing or of sanctioning any crime. But this is no more than a facade. He is at heart a manipulator. Charm and generosity are his two greatest weapons. He will say anything to win the affection of the person he is with, but thinks nothing of saying exactly the opposite to his next visitor. He kills rationally and coolly.

Major General Idi Amin (left) speaks to the Ugandan people in Kampala after overthrowing President Milton Obote, 1971.

Expulsions destroy the economy

In the first year of his rule, Amin made several decisions that were popular with the native Ugandan population. For instance, he appeased the Buganda people when he arranged for the kabaka's (king's) body to be flown back to Uganda for burial. (The kabaka had died in exile in England in 1971.) Amin also expelled all the Indian traders in Uganda who were carrying British passports. This move was favored by the Africans because the Indians had gained a nearly complete monopoly in the trading sector.

The Indians (referred to as Asians) had first arrived in Uganda as indentured servants (people who sign up to work for someone for a set amount of time in return for travel expenses or food and shelter, generally when immigrating to a new country). They were sent to work on the 600-mile rail line being built from Mombasa, Kenya, through Nairobi to Kampala, Uganda, in the late 1890s. Indian traders followed to service the workers. The Asian community gradually took over the trading sector of the economy; they were the traders, the wholesalers, and the merchants. They owned splendid houses and drove fancy cars. When the Asians fled Uganda after Amin took power, they left behind nearly 4,000 shops and houses, which Amin promptly distributed to his military comrades—none of whom knew anything about the business of trading. The 50,000 or so employees of the Asians lost their jobs, and thousands more in the commerce and industry were dismissed. In a domino effect, Uganda's businesses collapsed.

Amin continued with Obote's nationalization policies. In 1973 the government took over more than 100 British-owned companies. Amin took delight in belittling and embarrassing others. In a much publicized event, he had himself carried on a platform by British expatriates (British people who had left their native country) into a meeting with the British foreign minister. Amin also spent excessive amounts of money on the military. In his first year in power he increased the military's share of the Ugandan budget from 20 percent to 60 percent. With the economy collapsing because of the Asians' expulsion and the trade chaos that followed, Amin found himself in an unenviable position: he could not repay his debts or finance new purchases. Suppliers of military goods were reluctant to give him credit. Furthermore, the British government sought to end its dealings in military equipment with Amin because of his extremism and apparent irrationality.

Foreign policy decisions prove disastrous

Whether or not Amin knew of his decreasing support, he made an unexpected deal with the northern African Arab nation of Libya. He denounced the Israelis in Uganda and ordered them out. This was an odd and inconsistent move, considering his earlier support of anti-Muslim rebels who had received backing from the Israelis.

In February 1972 Amin announced plans to make Uganda a Muslim nation. When he embraced the anti-Israeli Palestine Liberation Organization (PLO), the Libyans began sending money and military support to Amin's government. Libya also sent funds to support Muslim mosques and the spread of Islam (the religious faith of Muslims, including the belief in Allah as the sole God).

Later in 1972, Obote tried to overthrow Amin from his base in the eastern African nation of Tanzania. The attempt might have succeeded had it been better planned, since nearly all the communities in Uganda, except the Nubian and Sudanese, had withdrawn support from Amin's government. But the military alliance with the PLO proved useful to Amin. By the end of 1974 the PLO had 400 trainers in the country who served as military advisers, pilots, and Amin's bodyguards. When the PLO highjacked an Air France jet over Greece in 1976, it brought 91 hostages to Entebbe, the location of Uganda's major airport. Whether Amin knew of the organization's plan is not known, but Ugandan troops guarded the hostages when the PLO terrorists rested. The Israelis made a lightening-swift strike and freed the hostages with only a few deaths resulting. (The Ugandan troops and officers were reportedly drunk the night of the rescue.) When Amin learned of the Israeli raid the next morning, he was embarrassed and furious. He ordered the execution of 200 senior army officers and government officials, then had them buried in mass graves at a prison.

An end to a reign of terror

In eight years, Amin had devastated Uganda. The economy was in ruins, foreign trade had dried up, and the country had fallen into a state of lawlessness and brutality. Most educated and skilled workers had either been killed or had fled the country. The Libyans wanted the government to account for the millions of dollars they had contributed to the Muslim fund. Nothing worked and there were no goods to buy. Troops across the country began to rebel, demanding their pay.

At Christmastime in 1976, following an assassination attempt and another round of executions, a group of church officials went to Amin to ask him to end the suffering and lawlessness in Uganda. At the same time, a military delegation requested that Amin restore order in the nation. Under pressure from many groups, Amin responded with force. He ordered his troops to go throughout the country and launch massacres on a massive scale, concentrating on the Acholi and Langi peoples. One person especially targeted by Amin was Archbishop Janani Luwum, an Acholi. Amin's people falsified charges and arrested the archbishop for conspiracy. He died in detention. The official report stated that he had died in an automobile accident.

Other African nations respond

The death of the archbishop brought pressure from the outside world. Kenneth Kaunda (see entry), the president of Zambia, and Julius Nyerere (see entry), the president of Tanzania, had been criticizing the regime for years. But it wasn't until the 1977 Commonwealth Heads of State meeting in London that Britain began to apply pressure. The outside pressure began to increase, and it surfaced in internal fighting. Amin and his brother-in-law and close adviser, minister of defense General Mustafa Adrisi, had a falling out over a family matter. Over the years Adrisi had built up his own base of support in the military. Adrisi tried to soothe Amin's anger but a few days later was involved in an automobile accident. He was badly injured and went to Cairo for medical treatment. Amin then began to strip Adrisi's followers of power.

As various troop divisions began to rebel, Amin announced on Radio Kampala that Tanzania had invaded Uganda. The story was untrue, but it didn't matter. Amin wanted to divert attention away from the problems at home and focus on an outside enemy. The Ugandan air force bombed Bukoba in Tanzania, and five days later 3,000 Ugandan troops with tanks, armor, and air support invaded Kagera, Tanzania's western province.

The Ugandan troops met with no resistance and devastated the area, robbing and pillaging, burning and looting. Several hundred civilians were killed. The Tanzanians finally got their troops moved up to the northern area and pushed the Ugandans back across the border. Nyerere ordered 40,000 Tanzanian troops to pursue the Ugandans into Ugandan territory. On April 10, 1979, Kampala fell to Tanzanian troops. Idi Amin had already boarded a plane to Tripoli, Libya, with his several wives, girlfriends, and 20 of his children. He eventually went to Saudi Arabia where he was given sanctuary (protection from arrest by another nation). Twenty years after fleeing the devastated nation of Uganda, Amin was still living in Saudi Arabia, with many of his children. He is reported to be grossly overweight and, as a devout Muslim, to attend mosque services regularly.

Further Reading

Decalo, Samuel. *Psychoses of Power: African Personal Dictatorships.* Boulder, CO: Westview Press.

Omara-Otunnu, Amii. *Politics and the Military in Uganda: 1890-1985.* New York: St. Martin's, 1987.

Smith, George Ivan. *Ghosts of Kampala: The Rise and Fall of Idi Amin.* New York: St. Martin's, 1980.

Kofi Annan

Born April 8, 1938
Kumasi, Gold Coast (Ghana)

Secretary-general of the United Nations

"You never walk into a situation and believe that you know better than the natives. You have to listen and look around. Otherwise you can make some very serious mistakes."

—Annan, in a *New York Times* interview

n December 17, 1996, the General Assembly of the United Nations (UN) elected Kofi Annan (*COF-fee AH-nan*) to serve as its seventh secretary-general, or principal administrative officer. He is the first black African to lead the UN, an international organization formed after World War II to promote world peace. Annan brings to his post a wealth of knowledge and experience. Born on Africa's Gold Coast (now the west African republic of Ghana), he grew up in a developing country before being exposed to life in the industrialized Western world. Annan, who speaks English, French, and several African languages, has worked for the United Nations since the 1960s. Prior to his election, no other secretary-general had risen up to that post through the ranks of the International Civil Service.

From Africa to the States

Annan comes from a prominent Fante family from the Ashanti region of Ghana. Historically, the Fanti people occupied the southwestern areas along the Atlantic Ocean coast of the Gold Coast. Annan was born in 1938 in Kumasi and completed his high school education there. He then studied briefly at the University of Science and Technology at Kumasi before winning a scholarship from the Foreign Students' Leadership Project of the Ford Foundation in 1959. The project brought him to the United States, where he finished his undergraduate degree in economics at Macalester College in St. Paul, Minnesota, in 1961. Annan spent the next year taking graduate courses in economics at the Institut Universitaire des Hautes Études Internationales in Geneva, Switzerland.

Ghana

In an interview with the *New York Times* two days after his election to the UN's top post, he reminisced about his early years in the United States. "I entered the U.S. at Boston . . . and . . . did a summer program at Harvard," he said. "I then moved on to Macalester College in Minnesota. It was my first winter ever, and that was quite an experience." He said he dressed as warmly as he could but he could not bring himself to wear earmuffs:

> I resisted as long as I could, until one day, going to get something to eat, my ears nearly froze. So I went and bought the biggest pair I could find. . . . But even in that I learnt a very important lesson. You never walk into a situation and believe that you know better than the natives. You have to listen and look around. Otherwise you can make some very serious mistakes.

Annan arrived in the United States during the turbulent years of the civil rights movement. In the summer of 1960 he traveled around the nation as part of the "ambassadors of friendship" program. He stayed with families and even with poor, small-scale farmers, really getting to know a cross section of American society. "I had come from Ghana, and we had just gone through our own struggle for independence. People of my generation, having seen the change that took place in Ghana, grew up thinking all was possible. When I came to the United States, the social upheaval reminded me of some of the things that had gone on there."

Begins his career at the UN

In 1962 Annan joined the United Nations as an administrative employee and budget officer at the World Health Organization

(WHO). Then, in 1971, he won a Sloan fellowship to study at the Massachusetts Institute of Technology (MIT), where he received a master's of science degree in management. Taking another break from the United Nations beginning in 1974, he returned home on a two-year leave to work as managing director of the Ghana Tourist Development Company.

Over the years Annan held various low-profile positions in the UN and became familiar with many different aspects of UN operations. Apart from his service in the areas of management, administration, and finance, he worked on key issues affecting peacekeeping efforts and refugees (people forced to flee to a foreign country to escape danger and persecution). Annan is a successful negotiator because, as one colleague puts it, "he is respectful, he listens carefully . . . and he never loses sight of what is practical." He negotiated the release of Western hostages in Iraq following Iraq's invasion of Kuwait in 1990, which triggered the Gulf War. He also initiated the discussions on the Oil-for-Food Formula to ease the suffering of civilians in Iraq following the war. And in Bosnia (in the former Yugoslavia)—a war-torn region of southeastern Europe ravaged by brutal fighting between ethnic groups—he oversaw the enforcement of terms of the 1995 Dayton Peace Agreement, in which the UN peacekeeping forces stationed there were replaced by North Atlantic Treaty Organization (NATO)-led forces.

Annan stated in an address to the UN General Assembly that "a new understanding of peace and security must emerge" around the globe. The world is beginning to recognize, he said, that conflict has many roots, that peace rests on economic and social stability, and that "intolerance, injustice and oppression" can destroy nations. "We now know more than ever that sustainable economic development is not merely a matter of projects and statistics. It is, above all, a matter of people—real people with basic needs: food, clothing, shelter and medical care."

At Christmastime in 1996 Annan visited his homeland of Ghana and addressed his nation's parliament, pledging to work hard to solve the problems of the continent. For any assistance to be effective, though, he sees the need for the governments of various African nations to "get their own house[s] in order. They should open their political systems. They should take steps to reduce if not eliminate corruption."

Standoff with Saddam

Annan's greatest test to date as UN secretary-general came in February 1998, when Iraqi dictator Saddam Hussein defied the orders of UNSCOM, the UN's weapons-inspection team. Early in 1998 rumors circulated that Saddam was preparing to attack U.S. targets with biological and chemical weapons, which use deadly germs or chemicals to poison the enemy's environment.

Annan met Saddam Hussein in Baghdad, the Iraqi capital, and after hours of negotiations, Annan had successfully hammered out the terms of a deal that would give UNSCOM "unlimited access to palaces and other so-called 'sensitive' areas."

Ironically, Annan's most bitter criticism has come from an African country, Rwanda. During the 1994 massacres of between 500,000 and one million Rwandans, Annan had headed the UN peace-keeping department. Those killed in the massacres were mostly Tutsis, but some were Hutus who opposed the Hutu-dominated government in 1994. Hutus outnumber Tutsis by about eight to two in Rwanda. After the massacres, a Tutsi-dominated army that had attacked from neighboring Uganda took control of the government. The new Tutsi-dominated government accused Annan of ignoring advance warnings that the old Hutu-dominated government was preparing a genocide plan against the Tutsis and of failing to take action to prevent the massacres.

When Annan visited Rwanda in May 1998, top officials of the Tutsi-dominated government—including Rwanda strongman Paul Kagame—boycotted official UN events for the secretary-general to show their contempt for Annan. When Annan visited sites where mass killings had taken place in 1994, angry suvivors questioned him on why he had failed to send UN assistance to stop the slaughter of their families. During his visit to Rwanda, Annan acknowledged the UN had failed to stop the massacres because leading nations of the world lacked "political will" to do so. He said Rwanda and the UN must now look to the future.

Facing other challenges

Annan faces the difficult task of reducing UN expenditures and streamlining its administrative system. He must also persuade the United States to pay at least $1.4 billion it owes the UN in back dues. Annan generally has the support of the United States admin-

istration, and this is especially so after leaving Baghdad with the weapons-inspection deal the States wanted. The previous secretary-general, Boutros Boutros-Ghali from Egypt, who did not have U.S. support, served only one term. Under normal circumstances a secretary-general serves two terms, but U.S. opposition to Boutros-Ghali's reelection was so strong that it actually kept him out of office. He had infuriated the U.S. administration with his handling of the UN operation in Bosnia.

Annan's long career with the United Nations raises the question of whether he can objectively lead the organization's restructuring program. Many critics feel that the UN also needs to redefine its goals and objectives in the face of the world's changing political order.

A huge responsibility

Annan has cultivated good relations with the international press over the years, which should translate to more positive press on UN operations. He is on a first-name basis with many media correspondents and takes advantage of opportunities to meet with members of the press. Annan is a soft-spoken man, with the distinctive Ghanaian lilt to his words. His Swedish wife, Nane Annan, is a lawyer who is currently working as an artist. They have three children. Now under the constant watch of guards and unable to take his customary walks, Annan likens his high-profile position at the UN to the life of "a hamster in a cage."

Further Reading

Froehlich, Manuel. "The Old and the New UN Secretary-General." In *Aussen Politik,* 48:3, 1997, pp. 301-9.

Goshko, John M. "Soft-spoken Man Who Gets Things Done." In *Mail and Guardian*, December 20-23, 1996.

Newsweek, March 2, 1998, pp. 30-34; March 9, 1998, pp. 28-32.

The Star (Johannesburg, South Africa), January 8, 1997 (article originally published in the *New York Times*).

United Nations press release. "Kofi Annan: Seventh United Nations Secretary-General," January 1997.

Nnamdi Azikiwe

Born November 16, 1904
Zungeru, northern Nigeria
Died May 13, 1996
Lagos, Nigeria

First president of Nigeria

Nnamdi Azikiwe (*ah-zee-KEE-weh*) initiated the campaign for nationalism in British West Africa, a movement that led the way to African independence after World War II (1939-45). He discovered and nurtured radical African nationalists, including the most famous, Kwame Nkrumah (1909-1972; see entry) of Ghana. A colorful, rousing political leader, Azikiwe was also a newspaper publisher, scholar, poet, athlete, and enterprising businessman. He became the first president of independent Nigeria in 1963 and is often remembered as the "Father of the Nation." Azikiwe also helped settled the Biafran civil war, Nigeria's worst conflict. Between 1967 and 1970, this war caused the death of a million of his Ibo people.

A striking and magnetic figure standing more than six feet tall, Azikiwe stirred fierce nationalistic feelings—a strong loyalty to African culture and identity and the desire for self-governed

African nations—among Nigerians seeking to throw off European colonialism. (Colonialism is a nation's control of a territory that lies beyond its own borders—in this case, Britain's control over its territories in West Africa.) As the grandson of an Ibo chief, he advocated African self-rule and self-sufficiency. He also promoted pride in Africans and in their continent's history as the place of human origin, even predicting that black missionaries would one day redeem the world. Azikiwe became known as "Zik of Africa," and at its peak Nigerian nationalism was labeled "Zikism."

Nigeria is Africa's most populous country with more than 100 million people. It is made up of three main West African states that had been at war with one another for centuries until Britain forced them into one nation in 1914. The Fulani-Hausa populate the North, the Ibo live in the Southeast, and the Yoruba are concentrated in the Southwest. Lady Flora Lugard, a former foreign correspondent for the London *Times* and the wife of British colonial governor-general Frederick Lugard (1858-1945), named Nigeria after the Niger River that flows through the country from west to east.

Influenced by American ideals

When Azikiwe was a young man, Nigerians who were lucky enough to study at higher institutions abroad usually went to England's colleges and universities. Azikiwe viewed the British as oppressors of the African people, so he sought another route to education. At the age of 21 he went to live and study in the United States. His experience there changed the course of Africa's independence movement in the 1950s and 1960s.

When he returned to Africa after nearly a decade in America, Azikiwe began his unyielding attack on the policy of colonialism. He also recruited help in his mission, sending a dozen young radical Africans to study in the States to prepare for the fight. All 12 of these young Africans played inspiring roles in the independence struggle. The most prominent was Nkrumah, who returned from America to become Ghana's first president.

Early years

Azikiwe was born the first son of Obed-Egom and Chinwe Azikiwe on November 16, 1904, in Zungeru, a Muslim town located in northern Nigeria. The town was part of a camp of the Nigeria Regiment of the British colonial army. The British regiment employed Azikiwe's father as a civilian clerk. Both of Azikiwe's parents had been born in Onitsha, an Ibo village on the bank of the lower Niger River in what is now southeast Nigeria. Azikiwe's grandfather was Chief Eze Chima, the founder of the town of Onitsha and one of the first generation of the Ibo people to receive a Western education.

The family sent young Azikiwe to Onitsha to complete his primary schooling. Azikiwe taught for a short time as a pupil teacher before his father enrolled him in the Hope Waddell Training Institution, a school established in 1846 by the Presbyterian Church of Scotland at Calabar, an Ibo town in the southeastern part of the country. Azikiwe soon transferred to Wesleyan Secondary School in Lagos, the British capital on the Atlantic Ocean in southwest Nigeria. A big, strong, and intelligent youth, he distinguished himself in both athletics and academics.

Speech struck his soul

Azikiwe's experiences as a student and later as a treasury clerk in the British civil service for Nigeria left an indelible imprint on his young mind and helped to shape his future. At the Hope Waddell Training Institution in Calabar, he was profoundly surprised when a fellow student, a Liberian, remarked that in his country blacks ruled themselves. Then, while attending school in Lagos, he learned about Jamaican-born radical political leader Marcus Garvey (1887-1940). Garvey had moved to the United States in 1916 to spread his philosophy of black nationalism and solidarity (unity as a group). He is probably best remembered for leading a "back to Africa" movement for blacks in the Americas.

In 1920 Dr. James E. K. Aggrey (1875-1927) visited Lagos as a member of the U. S. Phelps-Stokes Commission to examine education in Africa. Born on the Gold Coast (now Ghana), Aggrey was educated in the States and established himself as a notable teacher and Christian minister. During his visit to Lagos, he preached a sermon at the Tinubu Methodist Church, where Azikiwe sang in the choir. Azikiwe said later that Aggrey's power of speech "struck my soul with the force of a supernatural wand." Impressed by the young man, Aggrey presented Azikiwe with a copy of a book titled *Negro Education: A Study of Private and*

Higher Education for Colored People in the United States. Aggrey and the book whetted Azikiwe's desire to study in the United States. That same year Azikiwe also won an award at his Lagos school, the Boarders' Prize. The award was a book, *From Log Cabin to the White House,* a biography of James A. Garfield, America's twentieth president. The book told how Garfield rose from humble beginnings to occupy the country's highest office. *From Log Cabin* added fuel to Azikiwe's ambitions to visit and study in the States.

As a civil servant (government worker) in Nigeria, young Azikiwe experienced the humiliating reality of colonialism to the colonized. Although the English dominated the upper, better-paying ranks of the civil service, Azikiwe judged some of them to be less qualified than the Nigerians they treated as inferiors. He also saw stark contradictions between the Europeans' professed ideals and the reality of colonial rule. The Christian missions, for instance, preached equality of all people before God but discriminated against Africans even in church appointments. Azikiwe's goal became to right these wrongs. He knew that a good education would be the necessary armor in the battle he planned to conduct.

Sent for Golden Fleece

In 1924 Azikiwe tried but failed in an attempt to stow away on a ship bound for the United States. That same year his family felt the sting of prejudice firsthand, when Azikiwe's father retired early from the civil service after being insulted by a European 20 years his junior. This incident hardened Azikiwe's resolve to fight colonialism and at the same time opened a door to realizing his educational ambition. From his retirement pay, Azikiwe's father gave him a money to finance a journey to the States—and, ultimately, to follow in Dr. Aggrey's footsteps. His father's parting words were prophetic (seeing into the future): "You will succeed. God knows Africa needs more Aggreys. . . . Go and bring back the Golden Fleece." (The reference was to the story of Jason, a great hero of Greek mythology, who won back the Golden Fleece from a dragon in order to regain a kingdom stolen from his father.)

Azikiwe left Nigeria for the United States in 1925 and stayed there for nine years. His student years in America proved to be a nightmare of financial hardship, which he described as "a triumphant struggle with adversity." Enrolling first at Storer College in West Virginia, he later transferred to Howard University in Washington, D.C. But his finances soon dried up. Dogged by persistent poverty, racial discrimination, and threats from U.S. immigration officials, Azikiwe resorted to dishwashing and coalmining to earn money for his education. He even sparred on an empty stomach with a professional boxer for $10—"the hardest money I ever earned in my life," he later recalled. Despair drove him to attempt suicide by lying across railroad tracks, but a passerby foiled the attempt and took Azikiwe to a YMCA hostel. He eventually transferred to Lincoln University in Pennsylvania, completing his degree program with financial assistance from the institution. Appointed a graduate assistant at Lincoln, he earned a master of arts degree and a master of science degree in political science.

In 1934 Azikiwe returned to Nigeria to open a new chapter in the nationalist movement not only in Nigeria but throughout West Africa. The same year he published *Liberia in World Politics,* a book that severely criticized the western powers for their treatment of independent Liberia. Later in the year he moved to Accra, capital of the Gold Coast (now Ghana), and helped establish a newspaper called *African Morning Post.* He served as the newspaper's editor in chief for two and a half years, using the paper to criticize colonial policies in West Africa and awaken political consciousness in the region. The Gold Coast colonial authorities charged him with seditious publishing (using his newspaper to stir up opposition and resistance to a lawful authority). An Accra court convicted him of the charge, but a higher court overturned his conviction, and he escaped imprisonment.

An African hero

After that celebrated case in the Gold Coast, Azikiwe returned in 1937 to Nigeria as a triumphant hero and almost immediately moved to the center stage of the nationalist movement in the country. He joined the Nigerian Youth Movement, an aggressive nationalist organization. On August 26, 1944, Azikiwe founded the party that would serve as his nationalistic vehicle, the National Council for Nigeria and the Cameroons. Meanwhile, he had established a chain of newspapers—the *West African Pilot,* the *Eastern Nigerian Guardian,* the *Daily Comet,* the *Eastern Sentinel,* the *Nigerian Spokesman,* and the *Southern Nigerian Defender.* Azikiwe persistently criticized British colonial policies and prac-

tices in West Africa. He charged that colonialism exploited the people of Africa economically, denied them basic human rights, and created social barriers based on race. Seeking basic rights for his people, he called for an end to discrimination in salaries and in the provision of urban facilities based on race. He also demanded representative government and independence for Nigeria.

Azikiwe ranted against exploitation of African workers, seizing every opportunity to come to their defense. In 1945, when the Nigerian Trade Union Congress members went on strike to protest low wages and poor working conditions, his newspapers stood behind the workers. The government responded by banning two of the papers.

In the midst of this tense situation, rumors circulated that the government was planning to assassinate Azikiwe. The National Committee of Africans was formed in London in his support. The committee sent telegrams to such world leaders as U.S. president Harry S Truman (1884-1972), French president Charles de Gaulle (1890-1970), and Soviet leader Joseph Stalin (1879-1953), imploring them to use their offices to ensure that no harm would come to Azikiwe. Even after the colonial administration dismissed all

Nnamdi Azikiwe (middle) leads a delegation to the colonial office in London to ask for reforms in the Nigerian constitution, 1947.

reports of an assassination plot, most Nigerians remained skeptical. In 1946 radicals strongly opposed to colonialism organized a movement called the Zikist Movement—named after Azikiwe.

The government ban on Azikiwe's newspapers, the assassination rumors, and Azikiwe's staunch support of the African cause combined to make him ever more popular in Nigeria and one of the best known Africans in the world. Parents named their children after him. A church—the National Church of Nigeria—was established in his honor. Passages from his 1937 book *Renascent Africa* were read at Sunday sermons. Nigerian writer Gabriel Olusanya wrote that wherever Azikiwe went, the cry of "Zeek, Zeek" cut through the air. "Whatever he wrote and said was taken as gospel truth."

"There is no orator in Nigeria like the dynamic, magnificent-looking Zik," wrote bestselling American author John Gunther after visiting Nigeria in the mid-1950s to write his book *Inside Africa.* "Mobs spring up anywhere in southern Nigeria to hear him speak. They sing 'Zee-ee-ek. . . Zee-ee-ek. . .' like a chant."

In 1949 at a coal mine at Enugu in eastern Nigeria, a European police officer ordered his men to open fire on a group of demonstrating miners. The shooting killed 18 demonstrators and wounded 31 others. Azikiwe, along with his press, condemned the incident in strong terms. Zikists went on a rampage in several Nigerian towns. Government officials clamped down on the Zikists, jailing the leaders and banning the movement. Always insistent that constitutional means be used to achieve political objectives, Azikiwe eventually separated himself from the militant radicalism of the movement that bore his name. This move cost him some of his wide popularity.

Rivals arise in North and West

Rival political parties soon began to challenge Azikiwe. The Fulani-Hausa coalition formed the Northern People's Congress in 1949, and two years later the Yoruba from southwest Nigeria founded the Action Group. Azikiwe's party tried to keep its broad, national outlook, but when he was elected president of the Ibo Union in 1948 his political opponents accused him of favoritism toward the Ibo people. He hardly helped counter charges of being a tribal politician when he stated: "It would appear that the God of Africa has created the Ibo nation to lead the children of Africa from the bondage of the ages. . . ." The harsh reality was that

Nigeria was being divided politically—and that these political divisions were being drawn along ethnic lines.

When the British created an Eastern House of Assembly, Azikiwe campaigned for a seat in his home region. He won the seat in the 1954 elections, then became premier of the Eastern Region. Azikiwe's motives fell into question when he allowed 2 million British pounds of government money to be deposited in the African Continental Bank (ACB), in which he was a major shareholder. A committee appointed to look into the issue decided that the premier's conduct had fallen "short of the expectations of honest reasonable people." The legislature was subsequently dissolved. But the voters rejected the committee's findings by electing Azikiwe and his party with an overwhelming majority. Azikiwe's supporters interpreted the banking affair as a conspiracy by the British colonial office to discredit him.

With the approach of Nigerian independence, Azikiwe shifted the arena of his politics to the new federal legislature. He was elected president of the Senate on January 11, 1960. His party joined in a coalition (a union of different parties for the purposes of taking joint actions) with the Northern People's Congress, the majority party, in the first federal legislature. On October 1, 1960, the coalition appointed him governor-general of independent Nigeria. In 1963, when Nigeria became a republic, he accepted the coalition's appointment as Nigeria's first president. Though these offices carry with them a high degree of constitutional influence, Azikiwe still lacked the executive policy-making power held by the prime minister, Abubakar Tafawa Balewa (see entry) of the majority National People's Congress.

Nigeria's first military coups

On the night of January 14-15, 1966, young military officers killed Balewa in the first of many Nigerian coups (the overthrow of the existing government by force). Major General Johnson Aguiyi-Ironsi, an Ibo and the head of the army, took over the government. Ironsi's actions raised fear among Northerners that Southerners intended to control Nigeria. Northern Fulani-Hausa officers killed Ironsi in a coup staged in July 1966. Massacres against Ibos in northern Nigeria followed. Despite Azikiwe's attempts to stop the Ibos, the people from his region seceded, or broke away from, the Nigerian federation and declared the formation of the Republic of Biafra in 1967. Civil war erupted between Biafra and the rest of the Nigerian federation.

The first coup displaced Azikiwe as president in 1966. He remained an adviser to the Biafran regime until he saw the hopelessness of the civil war. Many of the estimated million deaths in the war, most of them Ibo, resulted from starvation. Azikiwe returned to the federal side and pushed negotiations to end the war. Biafran leaders accused Azikiwe of selling out—of betraying his people and the cause of freedom. The war ended in 1970, and Biafra returned to the Nigerian federation.

The army returned rule to civilians in 1978. With the lifting of a ban on political organization, three leading parties emerged: the National Party of Nigeria (NPN) led by Shehu Shagari, the Nigerian People's Party (NPP) led by Azikiwe, and the Unity Party of Nigeria (UPN) led by Obafemi Awolowo. The NPN drew the bulk of its support from the Muslim North, the NPP from the Christian East, and UPN from the Christian West.

Azikiwe, his party's presidential candidate in the 1979 and 1983 elections, lost both times to Shagari. But Azikiwe continued to be the most popular politician among his Ibo people. After the 1983 elections, he bade a sad farewell to active politics. In his "History Will Vindicate the Just," an open letter to the new generation of Nigerian politicians, he worried about the ugly trends in Nigerian affairs. He warned of politicians whose unchecked ambition for political power "motivates them to believe that it is their manifest destiny to control the levers of power at all cost, no matter the consequences. . . . As one patriot who struggled alongside other compatriots to make Nigeria free, I see my country on the brink of dictatorship because of the arrogance of power exhibited by the party in power."

On December 31, 1983, barely four months after Shagari was elected to a second term as president, the military removed him from office. For the remainder of the twentieth century Nigeria continued its struggle for democracy and attempted to put down dictatorial military rule.

Further Reading

Azikiwe, Nnamdi. *My Odyssey*. Hurst, 1970.

Crowder, Michael. *The Story of Nigeria*. Winchester, MA: Faber, 1978.

Gunther, John. *Inside Africa.* North Pomfret, VT: Hamish Hamilton, 1955.

Ikeotuonye, V. C. *Zik of New Africa.* New York: Macmillan, 1961.

Njoku, O. N. "Nnamdi Azikiwe." In *Historic World Leaders.* Edited by Anne Commire. Volume 1. Detroit: Gale, 1994.

Oliver, Roland, and Anthony Atmore. *Africa since 1800.* 2nd ed. New York/UK: Cambridge University Press, 1972.

Olusanya, Gabriel. *The Second World War and Nigerian Politics, 1939-1953.* London, 1973.

Abubakar Tafawa Balewa

Born 1912
Fulani-Hausa area (northern Nigeria)
Died c. June 14, 1966
Nigeria

First prime minister of Nigeria

Sir Abubakar Tafawa Balewa played a leading role in creating the federation of Nigeria out of three warring ethnic groups.

As Nigeria's prime minister from 1960 to 1966, Abubakar Tafawa Balewa (*ba-LAY-wah*) was the most powerful political leader in Africa's giant western republic during its first years of independence from Britain. He played a leading role in creating the federation of Nigeria out of three warring ethnic groups. But Balewa failed to keep ethnic differences in the new country from tearing his government apart. In the end, it cost him and most of Nigeria's political leadership their lives in a 1966 military coup (overthrow of a government).

Part of Balewa's downfall stemmed from his strong pro-Western views in the 1960s, when radical African nationalism—a sense of pride in all things African and a movement to secure independence—prevailed among black revolutionaries. Many African radicals were outraged when Balewa was knighted by Britain's Queen Elizabeth II. Elizabeth stood as a symbol of repression to many

Nigerians who opposed Britain's policy of colonialism (a nation's control of a territory that lies beyond its own borders). The breakdown of Balewa's government and the resulting coup led Nigeria toward disaster. The bloody 1967 Biafran civil war was followed by a series of military dictatorships and the collapse of social and political systems in Nigeria by the end of the twentieth century.

Nigeria

An agent of change

Born to Muslim parents in what is now northern Nigeria, Balewa was among the first Northerners to get a Western education. He became a schoolteacher, then embarked on a career as a successful politician. In the early nineteenth century Fulani-Hausa Muslims had created a landlocked empire that stretched across most of today's northern Nigeria. The empire, based at Sokoto (located in present-day northwest Nigeria), kept out Western Christian and commercial influences. This isolation deprived the North of educational advances, technology, and new ideas brought in by Europeans who invaded Nigeria's southern Atlantic coastal regions toward the end of the nineteenth century. Meanwhile, Christian missionaries established schools in the South and began to teach African students how to cope with the rapidly changing twentieth century.

As a smart, Western-educated Muslim, Balewa emerged from the North's isolation as an agent of change in the Fulani-Hausa region. He supported Nigeria's move toward independence after World War II (1939-45) and soon gained respect in the debate about the region's future. In 1947 he was elected to Nigeria's Northern Region's House of Assembly. When the British created the federal House of Representatives in 1951, he held a seat in that national legislature. As prospects for independence increased in the 1950s, Balewa favored dividing the British-created Nigeria into two countries, thus separating the Fulani-Hausa Northerners and the Christian Southerners. (The Ibos were the most populous people in the Southeast, while the Yoruba was the largest group in the Southwest.) But eventually, perhaps because of his exposure to people and changing times outside the North, Balewa became convinced that a national federation of the three groups was the best course for Nigeria as it set out to gain independence. He also believed the North, which claimed more than half of Nigeria's population, could dominate an independent Nigeria.

Being a founder and deputy president of the Northern People's Congress enabled Balewa to guide his fellow Muslims toward federation with the Christians. His position as minister of the Department of Works and Transport in the pre-independence House of Representatives gave him nationwide political contacts at the time of transition from British rule.

Role in independence

Nigeria achieved independence in 1960. In elections held that year, Balewa's Northern People's Congress won the most votes but fell short of a majority. Balewa's party entered into a coalition, or union, with Nnamdi Azikiwe's (see entry) National Council for Nigeria and the Cameroons, which drew most of its support from the Ibos in the Southeast. That left the Yoruba party from the Southwest—the Action Group headed by Chief Obafemi Awolowo—as the opposition without power in the government. The coalition government elected Balewa as prime minister with executive power (the power to guide domestic and foreign policy and enforce legislation). Azikiwe agreed to take the presidency, largely a ceremonial post, meaning he would be a figurehead with little real power.

By the end of 1965 Balewa was presiding over a corrupt, arrogant government. The administration ignored Nigeria's constitution adopted at independence. If the document's provisions conflicted with his northern party's wishes, the government simply ignored the constitution. The rich elite got richer, while the workers became even poorer.

Balewa's foreign policy was strongly favorable to the capitalist West and contrary to popular anticolonial sentiment among the educated elite and students, who favored socialism. (Socialism is a political and economic system based on government control of the production and distribution of goods. Socialists champion the removal of private property in a quest to attain a classless society. This philosophy clashes with the American ideal of capitalism, which is based on private ownership and a free market system.) Balewa played a decisive role in founding the Organization of African Unity (OAU) in 1963. In doing so, he helped convince other African leaders to accept their colonial borders after independence. The OAU thus rejected the Pan-Africanist (united African) movement headed by Ghana prime minister Kwame

Balewa visits a shipyard in Ohio hoping to pick up ideas for developing transportation in Nigeria, 1955.

Nkrumah (see entry) and other African radicals who wanted to establish a "United States of Africa." As head of the first sub-Saharan African country to get independence in 1957, Nkrumah had launched a campaign championing elimination of colonial boundaries in order to create "one Africa." Radicals had expected Balewa to replace Nkrumah at the forefront of the campaign to rid the rest of Africa of white minority rule, especially in Rhodesia (now Zimbabwe) and South Africa. Instead, Balewa tended to concentrate on affairs at home. And it was domestic discontent that brought him and Nigeria down.

Balewa's administration is known to have conducted voter fraud that favored the electoral interests of the Northerners. His party's candidates won election because election officials simply refused to list the names of opposition candidates on ballots. And census results that found a majority of Nigerian people living in the North caused Southerners to fear they would be forever at the mercy of corrupt Northerners. A census taken in 1952-53 reported Nigeria's population to be 31 million, Africa's largest. The census found 52 percent lived in the North. A 1962 census reported that more than half of Nigeria's population still lived in the North, a belief disputed by Southerners. Because of the uproar over the 1962 census, Balewa ordered a new one only two years later. In 1964 the census showed Nigeria's population had increased to 55 million, with 54 percent of the people living in the North.

Down the slippery slope

Throughout the mid-1960s Nigeria descended into chaos. It soon became unsafe even in the day to drive along the nation's highways. The country was torn by ethnic violence, much of it directed at Ibos, Southerners who had managed to gain key influence in Nigeria's bureaucracy and military. During the night of June 14-15, 1966, young officers spread across the country, assassinating Balewa, two regional premiers, and the federal finance minister. Significantly, the Ibo eastern region's prime minister escaped the coup. Major General Johnson Aguiyi-Ironsi, the army's commander in chief, took over as head of a military regime (the government in power). Ironsi, an Ibo, appointed mostly young Ibo officers to run the government. In July officers from the North staged a second coup, killing Ironsi. Massacres of up to 20,000 Ibos followed in the North. Hundreds of thousands of Ibos fled the North to their homes in the Southeast.

Led by popular Lieutenant Colonel Odumegwu Ojukwu, the Christian Ibos announced separation from Nigeria and the establishment of independent Biafra in early 1967. Not only did Biafra's secession shatter Nigeria's federation as a nation, it also deprived the rest of the country of its major source of oil. Nigeria had emerged as one of the world's largest oil producers. Its oil is located primarily off Nigeria's southeastern shore, territory claimed by the newly proclaimed Biafra.

The Yoruba from the Southwest joined with the Northerners to put down the Biafran rebellion. The deaths of an estimated million people, mostly Ibos who died of starvation, have been attributed to the three-year civil war that followed—a bitter legacy to Nigeria's first decade of independence.

Further Reading

Crowder, Michael. *The Story of Nigeria.* Winchester, MA: Faber, 1978.

Gunther, John. *Inside Africa.* North Pomfret, VT: Hamish Hamilton, 1955.

Oliver, Roland, and Atmore, Anthony. *Africa since 1800.* 2nd ed. New York/UK: Cambridge University Press, 1972.

Hastings Banda

February c. 1898
Chiwengo, Nyasaland (now Malawi)
Died December 2, 1997
Johannesburg, South Africa

President of Malawi

So great was Banda's power that in 1971 Malawi's parliament made him president for life.

For nearly a quarter of a century Hastings Kamuzu Banda was life-president of Malawi, a poor country in central Africa lying along the western edge of Lake Malawi. In 1958, when he was about 60 years old, Banda gave up his medical practice and returned to his homeland of Nyasaland (now Malawi) to lead the African nationalist campaign for independence from Great Britain. The nationalists achieved their goal: in 1964 Nyasaland became the independent Republic of Malawi, and Banda became president two years later. So great was his power that in 1971 Malawi's parliament made him president for life. Banda and a small group of supporters controlled virtually every aspect of life in this farming country: its politics, its courts, its military, and its economy. Critics claim that they made themselves rich at the expense of the nation's 8.5 million people, misusing funds that should have been spent on education and clean water. By the end of the twentieth century Malawi was one of the poorest countries in the world.

A long journey to an M.D. degree

Kamuzu Banda was believed to have been born in 1898 in a rural area of central Malawi. (Banda always claimed he was born in 1906, but most records point to an earlier date.) His parents, Mphonongo Banda and Akupinganyama Phiri, were poor peasant farmers who lived on what they grew. They named him "Kamuzu," or "little root," to honor the root-herb potion that enabled his mother to conceive and give birth to him.

Banda was a Chewa, a member of a Bantu-speaking ethnic group that lives in central Malawi and constitutes approximately 28 percent of Malawi's population. At the age of four, following Chewa custom, Banda left his parents' home to live with his maternal grandmother. There he learned basic farming skills and participated in Chewa ritual.

As a result of his parents' separation in 1905, Banda went to live in his father's village at the age of seven. There he attended the Mtunthama Primary School, which had been established by missionaries from Scotland. Under the influence of a Christian-educated uncle, Banda accepted the Christian faith and was baptized into the Church of Scotland. He took "Hastings"—the last name of a missionary he admired—as his Christian name.

When Banda finished primary school he left Nyasaland to go to the Church of Scotland's Lovedale College in South Africa. In 1914, when he was around the age of 16, Banda set out on foot on the 400-mile journey south. On his way he settled for a time in Hartley, a small town in Southern Rhodesia (now Zimbabwe), where he found a job as a sweeper in a local hospital. Banda stayed in Hartley for two years, saving his small earnings to pay for school. While working at the hospital he decided to become a doctor.

In 1916 Banda left Southern Rhodesia for the higher pay given workers in the gold mines of South Africa. He took a job in the Johannesburg area on the Witwatersrand Deep Mine, where he worked below ground. In Johannesburg, Banda was exposed to the ideas of African political activists who called for the establishment of "Africa for the Africans." Banda joined a black separatist church, the African Methodist Episcopal church (AME), in 1922. The church agreed to finance his education in the United States. In 1925 he began studying at the AME's Wilberforce Institute near Xenia, Ohio. Three years later, at about the age of 30, he graduated with a high school diploma. With the help of wealthy friends, he continued his studies in the States.

Banda attended the University of Indiana from 1928 to 1930, and then finished up his undergraduate degree at the University of Chicago. In 1932 he entered Meharry Medical College in Nashville, Tennessee, graduating five years later with his M.D. To return to Nyasaland as a licensed doctor, however, Banda needed to be tested by a British school. He studied at the University of Edinburgh in Scotland and got his license in 1941. Banda planned to return home as a doctor with a church mission, but the mission canceled his contract when white nurses at Livingstonia in Malawi refused to work under an African doctor. Failing to get another mission sponsorship, Banda moved to Liverpool, England, where he set up his own practice. He escaped military service during World War II (1939-45) by declaring himself a conscientious objector, someone who refuses to engage in combat because of moral or religious reasons. Instead, Banda spent two years working at a Tyneside seaman's mission hospital and at a Newcastle hospital.

The question of federation

At the end of World War II Banda moved to the London suburb of Harlesden and became a National Health Service doctor. His practice of nearly 4,000 patients—mainly whites—brought him financial rewards and respect within the community. Banda became active in politics and met African nationalists such as Jomo Kenyatta (see entry) of Kenya, Kwame Nkrumah (see entry) of Ghana, and other Pan-Africanists. He also kept in touch with independence-seeking African nationalist groups at home, like the Nyasaland African Congress, and gave them money and advice.

Banda's hard-won world of respect and wealth was shaken in the early 1950s when his secretary's husband, Major French, said in divorce proceedings that Banda was having an affair with his wife. In August 1953 Banda left his practice and his home in England and traveled to Ghana in West Africa. Mrs. French joined him there, and they lived together in Kumasi for three years.

Around the same time political changes were taking place in Nyasaland. The region's white British settlers—they had established a farming community there at the turn of the twentieth century—supported the formation of a federation, or union, of Nyasaland, Northern Rhodesia (now Zambia) and Southern Rhodesia (now Zimbabwe). In 1953, following pressure from the settler groups in all three regions, Great Britain allowed the territories to form the Federation of Rhodesia and Nyasaland, even though Africans strongly opposed the move. Blacks in Nyasaland were seeking to improve their political, social, and economic standing, not diminish it. They feared that the federation would limit the rights of blacks and ruin any chance for the region's future independence. Regardless of black opposition, though, the Federation remained in tact for 10 years, from 1953 to 1963.

By 1957 Nyasa nationalists were convinced that Britain was planning to make the three federated territories into one state. They asked Banda to return home and lead the Nyasaland African Congress. Black nationalists wanted an elder to lead them, someone who would earn the respect of the older members and the acceptance of the younger members. At the age of 59—after an absence of 43 years—Banda agreed to return to Nyasaland and take over leadership of the Congress. Mrs. French did not accompany him.

The Nyasa people hailed Banda as their savior. He toured the country demanding self-government for the territory and separation from the federation. Even in the hot tropical air of his native land he emerged as a Westernized leader, wearing a three-piece English suit with a black homburg hat and carrying a fly-whisk made of cattle hair. Although he called for peaceful demonstrations, the crowds became violent. In March 1959 the government declared a state of emergency. Government officials sent Banda out of the country to jail in Gwelo (Gweru) in Southern Rhodesia. The white government smashed the Nyasaland African Con-

White Influence Leads to Federation

In 1891 the British government declared a protectorate over the area known as Nyasaland, making it a political unit dependent on Britain. The British wanted to prevent Arab slavers from claiming the areas on and near Africa's East Coast. They also wanted to keep Portuguese adventurers in Mozambique from taking possession of the territory.

A white British settlement was established in Nyasaland in the 1890s. The whites took over farming rights to the land, making black Africans tenants with few rights to the land they farmed. African resistance to white domination was weak and slow to organize. Under the leadership of John Chilembwe (see entry), an African missionary educated in the United States, African nationalists staged an unsuccessful uprising against the British settlers in 1915. After World War II returning African soldiers and others formed the Nyasaland African Congress, linking native associations, independent churches, and other groups of educated Africans.

Despite strong black opposition, British authorities strengthened white power in Nyasaland in 1953. Britain granted permission to white settlers in Northern Rhodesia (Zambia), Southern Rhodesia (Zimbabwe), and Nyasaland (Malawi), to form a self-governing federation, or union, of the three territories. The white-run Federation of Rhodesia and Nyasaland lasted for 10 years, from 1953 to 1963.

gress. Its leaders were either in jail or in exile (forced out of their homeland).

From prison Banda continued to exercise power. With his approval, Orton Chirwa, the first black Malawian to qualify as a lawyer, established a new political party called the Malawi Congress party. The organization grew rapidly. Despite a ban on public meetings, membership increased from more than 8,000 members in October 1959 to 250,000 by March 1960. Pressure was mounting on the federation government, and it released Banda on April 1, 1961, so he could take part in talks in London on a new constitution. When the London conference was over, Banda returned home as leader of the Malawi Congress party. The party made Banda president for life and gave him nearly total power over its members and its policy.

The lion

As leader of the major opposition party (the party that challenged white rule), Banda served in a temporary joint (black-and

white-led) government until 1962, when the demand for full self-government grew even stronger. By the end of 1962 the British federal governor of Nyasaland declared that the territory could pull out of the federation. On February 1, 1963, Banda took the oath of office as the first prime minister of Nyasaland. One year later, on July 6, Nyasaland became the independent state of Malawi. Two years after that, in 1966, the Republic of Malawi was established with Banda was its first president. (*Malawi,* or *Maravi,* is the name of the people who established a kingdom in the region in the fifteenth century.)

Banda took immediate control, seizing power in Malawi with an iron-handed grip. As part of official party policy, followers were told to address him as *Ngwazi* (meaning "lion" and therefore suggestive of a "conqueror," "savior," or "messiah"). Tension had been building between Banda and other party members for some time, but it was silenced during the struggle for independence. After Banda became president of the new republic, though, the conflict between opposing sides was reignited. The president was always known for his quick temper, but he reportedly became

Hastings Banda waves his Homburg hat from the roof of a car while touring the Northern Province in Nyasaland, 1960.

more and more arrogant and unapproachable, treating even his closest advisers and supporters with contempt. Biographer Philip Short quoted him as saying: "I talk to them like children and they shut up. . . . I say a thing and when I say a thing, nobody must say anything else and my ministers must do nothing before I approve of it otherwise there would be confusion."

The Kamuzu sytem

During a cabinet meeting in 1964, some of Banda's ministers voiced their dissatisfaction with the administration. They began to question his decisions and challenge his power. When the ministers criticized Banda for ignoring the advice of his cabinet and then accused him of favoring relatives and friends for jobs, he fired them on the spot. The three ministers fled to a neighboring country.

Banda feared that an anti-Banda movement was developing in Malawi, so he purged the party of (or got rid of) all members he suspected of being disloyal. He also tightened police powers and created a military group called the Malawi Young Pioneers that was loyal to him alone. With the opposition in exile, Banda acted to realize his dream of the "Kamuzu system," or "guided democracy," with himself as guide. Malawi became a one-party state, and in 1971 Banda was made president for life. Malawi never had a first lady because the president did not take a wife. Rather, he had an "official hostess" named Cecilia Kadzimira.

Banda controlled the courts, the press, and the radio waves, and he even outlawed television broadcasts in the country. Women were not allowed to be seen in public wearing short skirts or pants. Long hair on men was against the law. Banda's subordinates were forced to approach him on their knees. Once he gained control of the power in Malawi, Banda used it to make a fortune for himself and his friends. Exerting full control over the Congress party's company, Press Holdings, they snatched profits from the nation's major retailers and farmers.

Banda manipulated officials from different parts of the country and looked after the interests of his own people, the Chewa of central Malawi. He moved the capital of Malawi from Zomba in the South, where most of the nation's people live, to the central provincial town of Lilongwe. In Lilongwe he built all new public works buildings, offices, and an international airport with financial help from South Africa. (Banda was the only black African leader to give diplomatic recognition to the white minority government in South Africa.) He also made Chewa the official language of the country, alongside English. The national treasury paid for his seven palaces. Sanjika Palace in Blantyre cost 1.5 million pounds sterling to build back in 1971.

The Young Pioneers obtained money for Banda's treasury through fear. Anyone wanting to enter a market or ride a bus or train had to purchase a Congress party card. Opponents were harassed and their property was seized. Most ended up fleeing to Mozambique and Zambia. By the early 1980s the Malawi government had created a special secret intelligence section to deal with exiles. Anti-Banda activists in exile were found and then assassinated or kidnapped and returned to Malawi for imprisonment. In the early 1980's three Cabinet ministers and a member of Parliament died in mysterious circumstances when they challenged policies of the Reserve Bank.

Loses control

In the early 1990s internal opposition to Banda's dictatorship hardened, as did international pressure because of alleged human rights abuses taking place in Malawi. For decades Banda had controlled virtually every aspect of the nation's life. He could not be challenged by anyone. Then the Catholic church in Malawi issued a pastoral letter to its congregations in 1992 criticizing the government. When it became widely known that Banda planned to have the Catholic priests killed for issuing the letter, international donor agencies and foreign governments threatened to hold back aid money to Malawi unless the government made real progress on the human rights front.

To dampen foreign criticisms, Banda announced in October 1992 that the government would hold a multiparty referendum (vote) to ask the people if they wanted a multiparty state. The opposition parties united, and the voters answered with an overwhelming "yes." The nation's first multiparty elections took place in May 1994. Banda and the ruling Malawi Congress party were defeated at the polls, receiving only one-third of the vote. Bakili Muluzi, leader of the United Democratic Front, won 47 percent of the vote. He was sworn in as president in late May.

Virtually unstoppable

In October 1993 Banda, aged 95 years plus, had required brain surgery and traveled to South Africa for the operation. With multiparty elections only six months away, he announced in November 1993—only one month after the surgery—that he had resumed the office of president of Malawi. After Banda was voted out of office in the May 1994 elections, his health continued to decline.

In January 1995 Banda, a close aide named John Tembo, and three police officers were implicated in the 1983 deaths of four opposition politicians. They were charged with murder and conspiracy to murder, but Banda never attended the trial because his physicians claimed he was too ill to endure the ordeal. In July Banda, Tembo, and the other defendants were acquitted. In early 1997 Banda resigned as life-president of the Malawi Congress party. Later in the year the former president was taken to a Johannesburg hospital for treatment of pneumonia. He died there, and his body was flown back to Malawi. He was buried in a casket that cost $37,000—a fitting final tribute, some would say, to a man who impoverished his country for his own benefit. At the time of his death Banda was believed to be over 100 years old.

Further Reading

Contemporary Black Biography. Volume 6. Detroit: Gale, 1994.

Crosby, Cynthia. *Historical Dictionary of Malawi.* Metuchen, NJ: Scarecrow Press, 1980.

The Economist, November 29, 1997, p. 104.

Short, Philip. *Banda.* London: Routledge & Kegan Paul, 1974.

Stephen Biko

Born December 18, 1946
King William's Town, South Africa
Died September 12, 1977
Pretoria, South Africa

South African social activist

From the late 1960s until the early 1980s in South Africa, the apartheid policies of the Nationalist government (1948-94) were firmly in place. Apartheid was a system of racial segregation based on white supremacy and political exclusion of blacks. Following the Sharpeville Massacre of 1960, in which police shot and killed 68 unarmed black demonstrators, the all-white government outlawed most of the county's opposition political parties. For the next 20 years, most of the anti-apartheid leaders were in jail, under restriction, or in exile. Without leadership or the freedom to organize, blacks endured a period of hopelessness and oppression. But new groups and new leaders were evolving. Stephen Bantu Biko (*BEE-ko*), a fourteen-year old at the time of Sharpeville, grew into an articulate and vibrant force in South Africa. By the mid-1970s, Biko's black consciousness movement had generated such a sense

"I am against the fact that a settler minority should impose an entire system of values on an indigenous people. A country in Africa, in which the majority of the people are African, must inevitably exhibit African values and be truly African in style."

of pride and strength in the black community that the white-minority government, finding its power threatened, crushed the movement and Biko.

A black political organization in South Africa

Biko was born on December 18, 1946, in King William's Town, in eastern Cape Province. He was one of three children of Mzimgayi Biko and his wife. His father died when Biko was four years old. Biko went to local primary and secondary schools before enrolling at Lovedale Institution in Alice. He did not stay long at Lovedale, transferring to the Roman Catholic Mariannhill High School in Natal Province. After he passed his exams in 1965, the non-European section of the (white) University of Natal accepted him in their medical program.

At university Biko got involved with the National Union of South African Students (NUSAS); he could not become a full member of NUSAS because the government did not permit multiracial organizations. The white membership of NUSAS consisted of liberal, English-speaking university students who opposed the apartheid policies of the government. No matter how worthy its intentions, however, Biko believed that NUSAS was too white to serve the best interests of black South Africans. He broke with NUSAS and formed the all-black South African Students' Association (SASO), becoming its first president. Through SASO Biko spread his philosophy of black consciousness throughout South Africa.

Biko believed that blacks had to disassociate themselves from well-meaning whites and develop their own black political associations. He started the black consciousness movement to build pride and self-assurance in blacks. Similar in many ways to the black power movement in the United States in the 1960s, black consciousness represented a new style of leadership for South Africa. Biko urged black South Africans to break their ties with liberal whites and multiracial organizations and establish a strong, separate identity based on principles of self-worth and self-reliance. Biko is quoted in Allister Sparks' book *The Mind of South Africa,* "I am against the fact that a settler minority should impose an entire system of values on an indigenous people. A country in Africa, in which the majority of the people are African, must inevitably exhibit African values and be truly African in style." In his view, blacks could only accomplish this in isolation from sympathetic whites, whose eagerness to help was more often than not an obstacle to true black achievement. Once black South Africans had overcome the demoralizing effects of racism, they would then be in a better position psychologically to confront the white power structure.

South Africa

Although Biko sought peaceful change, he often expressed fears that the situation in South Africa had deteriorated to the point where violence was probably inevitable. "The biggest mistake the black world ever made was to assume that whoever opposed apartheid was an ally," Biko once wrote. "One has to overhaul the system in South Africa before hoping to get black and white walking hand in hand to oppose a common enemy."

Biko's call for black pride swept like wild fire among South Africa's young blacks. Throughout the country, the black consciousness movement spawned the formation of development groups, literacy training centers, health education programs, and job training centers. Pride in being black, however, was not confined to the young. Black adults throughout the country organized themselves into groups called the Black People's Convention (BPC).

International recognition

In December 1970 Biko married Nontsikeleo (Ntsiki) Mashalaba from the Transkei. They had one son, Nkosinati. In 1972 the university expelled Biko because, it said, his grades were poor. By this time SASO chapters had spread to colored (mixed race), black, and Indian universities, and its *Newsletter* had a circulation of 4,000. Although Biko tried to stay in the background to develop a broad-based leadership, he emerged as a natural spokesperson. He became well known at home and internationally.

After university he began to work with Black Community Programmes (BCP), a group of self-help projects in Durban. He worked with the BCP until March 1973, when the authorities restricted him, telling him he had to stay in King William's Town, a white town about thirty miles inland from the Indian Ocean port of East London. The government banned him from speaking in public or from being quoted in any publication or broadcast. While he was restricted to King William's Town, Biko started an eastern Cape branch of the BCP. In 1975 the government made it illegal for him to associate with the BCP in King William's Town.

In his spare time, Biko studied law through UNISA, the correspondence school (education by mail) of the University of South Africa. He regularly defied the travel ban to visit friends and colleagues in other parts of the country. During his years at medical school, though married, Biko met and fell in love with a young medical student, Mamhela Ramphele. When they expelled him from the university, Ramphele stayed at university to finish her medical degree. After she graduated she joined Biko in King William's Town. There she developed *Zanempilo,* a community project applying Biko's philosophy of self-help.

Soweto uprising

In the mid-1970s the energy and self-confidence generated by the black consciousness movement fueled the uprising of young people in Soweto. (Soweto is an acronym for South West Township, an area designated for blacks working in Johannesburg.) In June 1976 Soweto erupted in violence as school children demonstrated against the school authorities' decision to use Afrikaans as the language for teaching. Afrikaans is the language of the white settlers of Dutch, German, and French descent and was associated with the racist government. Following the Soweto riots, the government declared a state of emergency and outlawed all black consciousness organizations. Security police arrested Biko on August 18, 1976, stopping him at a roadblock and holding him for questioning. This was not the first time they had harassed and detained him, and his friends were not alarmed when he was not immediately released. The police detained Biko for 101 days. Finally, in December, they released him without charging him with any crime.

A brutal end

In August 1977 security police again detained Biko. This time the police took him to Port Elizabeth where they stripped him of all his clothes, handcuffed him, and put him into leg irons. They chained him to an iron grille in an upright, crucifixion-style position to "break his resistance." They interrogated him for twenty-two hours, during which time they tortured and beat him. Although he showed obvious signs of having suffered severe brain damage, Biko received no special care. His jailers claimed they thought he was faking and the prison doctors repeatedly failed to diagnose the extent of his injuries. By September 11 his condition had seriously deteriorated. They loaded him, still naked and unconscious, into the back of a police Land Rover and drove him 700 miles from Port Elizabeth to a prison hospital in Pretoria. Biko died a day later in the prison hospital without medical attention. Justice Minister James Kruger reported that Biko died while on a hunger strike. The official autopsy showed that he died of massive brain damage. Biko was the twentieth black South African to die in police custody that year.

Meanwhile, in 1977 the security police had banished Ramphele to a remote tribal village in Lebowa in the northern Transvaal. She knew no one there and barely spoke the language. Ramphele was pregnant with Biko's child when she learned of his death. When the baby was born she named him Hlumelo, a Xhosa language word that means "the shoot from a dead tree."

Government coverup

In announcing the news to the world, South African authorities maintained that their previously healthy 30-year-old prisoner had died after a seven-day hunger strike. After weeks of contradictory statements by South African officials, a likely scenario finally emerged at an inquest (court inquiry) held in November 1977. Because no one who testified, however, was willing to name the person (or persons) who delivered the fatal blows, the judge ruled they could not attribute Biko's death to any criminal act or omission. His head injuries, according to the judge, must have occurred during a scuffle with police. But in a reexamination of the case in 1985, the two government doctors who had examined Biko were found guilty of negligence; one was reprimanded and the other barred from practicing medicine until late 1991, when he submitted a written apology to the South African medical society.

In 1997, 20 years after Biko's death, a commission appointed by the black majority African National Congress government is no closer to the truth of his death. The Truth and Reconciliation Commission, chaired by the former Anglican Archbishop of Cape Town Desmond Tutu (see entry), heard testimony from the five Special Branch officers who conducted the final interrogation of Biko. The five admitted they made up the 1977 version of events, but they each told a different story about his death.

In 1987 a film called *Cry Freedom* was made about Steve Biko. The film was based on the book by South African journalist Donald Woods, describing Biko's life and death and recounting the friendship between Woods and Biko.

Further Reading

Arnold, Millard. *Steve Biko: Black Consciousness in South Africa*. New York: Random House, 1978.

Biko, Steve. *I Write What I Like: A Selection of His Writings*. South Africa: Ravan Press, 1996.

Breaking the Silence (video documentary), 1988.

Sparks, Allister. *The Mind of South Africa*. London: Heinemann, 1990.

UXL Biographies CD. Detroit: Gale, 1995.

Woods, Donald. *Biko*. London: Paddington Press, 1978.

Adelaide Smith Casely Hayford

Born June 2, 1868
Freetown, Sierra Leone
Died January 24, 1960
Freetown, Sierra Leone

Sierra Leonean feminist, educator, and author

"In her life on three continents over nine decades, Mrs. Casely Hayford managed to symbolize the problems of modern women— and of modern black women."

—Adelaide M. Cromwell in
An African Victorian Feminist:
The Life and Times of Adelaide
Smith Casely Hayford, 1868-1960

delaide Smith Casely Hayford was the daughter of the socially prominent Smith family in Freetown, Sierra Leone. Sierra Leone, located along the West Coast of Africa, was unique among African countries. In the late 1700s British philanthropists (people who try to help other people in need) established an experimental settler colony there for whites and freed blacks from England and later from Nova Scotia and Jamaica. The experiment failed. Then, when Britain outlawed the trade in slavery in 1807, its ships began to patrol the West African coast looking for ships carrying slaves. The British ships rescued the captives from the slave ships and brought the recaptured slaves to Freetown, Sierra Leone, where they were settled. In 1808 the British government assumed responsibility for the area, and Sierra Leone became a colony of the British crown.

From the interesting blend of settlers and rescued captives in Sierra Leone, a culture developed that was a true mix of Africa and Europe. Casely Hayford, born in Sierra Leone in the late nineteenth century, spent much of her life in Europe. She struggled for years with being both African and European, black and white. She also struggled with being a woman with ambitions in a male-dominated society. In the 1920s, Casely Hayford opened a school for girls in Sierra Leone. She hoped to help her students feel more at home with who they were and give them the skills they would need to find their place in society. Above all, her school encouraged African girls to have pride in being African. Perhaps more than anything, Casely Hayford stands as an example of someone who overcame feelings of being a misfit in Africa as well as Europe, and went on to achieve her dreams and realize her own identity.

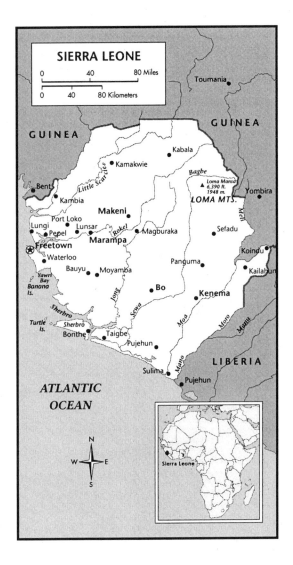

European or African?

Casely Hayford was one of seven children born to William Smith Jr. and his second wife, Anne. William Smith was the son of an English man and an African woman. Anne, her mother, was the daughter of a recaptured slave and a returned slave from Nova Scotia. Casely Hayford writes in her memoirs that her three brothers and three sisters were all of a lighter complexion than she. While they lived in the Creole society in Freetown, her skin coloring was not important.

The Smith family was among the Creole elite in Freetown, having achieved both social prominence and wealth. The *Krios* or Creole culture there developed over time as a combination of customs brought in by the recaptured slaves, who were mainly Yoruba from Nigeria, and the customs of the settlers in Freetown from Europe. The recaptured slaves became property-owners, were generally Christians, and often married European settlers.

The move to England

Casely Hayford's family moved to England in 1872 when she was four years old. As a teenager she felt herself different from her family members and from her schoolmates. She is quoted in Adelaide Cromwell's biography describing herself as looking like her mother, "dark—a real Sambo—and my father was exceptionally fair. . . . I was terribly shy—probably because I was too race conscious. In a white country I felt so conspicuous that I always wanted to hide my diminished head."

In June 1876 when Casely Hayford was seven years old, her mother died. Her death at a young age deprived her children of someone to look after them, and it also deprived the family of her mother's inheritance from a trust fund. Adelaide's father had retired from government service when they left for England and he received a pension. William and his first wife had also had seven children and some of their offspring had come to England to live with their grandfather William Smith. The reduction in income put a severe strain on the growing family. Casely Hayford and her sisters looked after the family's home.

Casely Hayford went to school on the Isle of Jersey, where the family was living in 1881. (Jersey is a British island in the English Channel, off the northwest coast of France.) After her father became a member of the committee of the Jersey Ladies' College, he enrolled his children in the school. Casely Hayford earned her junior certificate from the school in 1882, when she was 14 years old. In 1883 William Smith remarried. Casely Hayford and her stepmother, Elizabeth Jewell, a white English woman, did not get on well together. Young Adelaide attributed some of this ill feeling to the fact that she was darker skinned than her sisters.

One of her teachers suggested that she study in Germany for her German language test (and possibly to get away from her stepmother), and Casely Hayford left for Germany in 1885. In Germany, she stood out even more. Germany, unlike Great Britain, had not had colonies in Africa and the Germans were unaccustomed to seeing black people. They made her feel different.

In 1888 she returned to England. Her sister Nettie was planning to get married and her sister Bea had already left home. In their absence, Casely Hayford decided to go back to Sierra Leone and earn her living by teaching.

Returns to Africa

On her return to Freetown, Casely Hayford took a part-time teaching job at the Methodist School, then known as the Wesleyan Female Institution. She lived with her sister Bea, who had married William Awoonor Renner, a surgeon from the Gold Coast (Ghana) practicing in Freetown. Casely Hayford had a hard time adjusting to the narrow confines of Freetown society. The society did not accept her as a real European or as a real African. Later she would describe herself as a "black white woman."

When her stepmother died in 1894, Casely Hayford returned to England. Her father's health deteriorated after his wife's death and he died in August 1895. Reluctantly, the Smith family left England and returned to Freetown in 1897. Casely Hayford and her sister Emma decided to use their small inheritance from their father to start their own school. Freetown society offered the two unmarried women a cool reception. "Most of the educated Africans were definitely hostile. They shunned us, snubbed us, ostracized us . . . . in six months we lived down all this black prejudice."

Later that year, the two sisters accepted their first pupil. Within six months their enrollment reached 12 girls who were 15 years of age and older. The Smith sisters set up the school in the old Smith family home, the first private secondary school for girls in Sierra Leone. At its peak, the school had 50 students, who received instruction in reading, writing, arithmetic, physical culture, and music.

Sierra Leone society in London

Again family demands influenced Casely Hayford's attempts to become independent. Her sister Nettie's husband, John Farrell Easmon, died at the age of 44 leaving his 28-year-old wife with two small children. Casely Hayford had also been ill and she decided to close the school and return to England. The three sisters, Adelaide, Nettie, and Emma, along with Nettie's two children, again embarked on a month-long sea voyage. They rented a small house in London and took in "paying guests," to help them with the finances.

Through one of their guests they met some prominent members of the Sierra Leone society living in London. Among them was Samuel Coleridge-Taylor (1875-1912), an English musician whose father was from Freetown. Coleridge-Taylor was the first black man to give a concert in New York City's Mendelssohn Hall and at the New England Conservatory of Music in Boston. Impressed with the way the Americans had accepted him, Casely Hayford decided she too would try her luck in America. But before she made her U.S. tour, she met and married Joseph Ephraim Casely Hayford (1866-1930), a prominent lawyer from the Gold Coast (Ghana).

Marriage

J. E. Casely Hayford was well known in England and the United States for his support of African nationalism—the movement to end European rule and form self-governed African nations. He and an associate founded the National Congress of British West Africa in 1920, the major political movement in West Africa in the early 1900s. His first wife died in 1901 and left him with a son, Archibald. In her memoirs, Casely Hayford says that when he proposed marriage to her he told her his wife had died two years ago and that "he had but a second-best affection" to offer her. Nevertheless, they married after a short courtship and left London in 1907 for Axim in the Gold Coast. She writes that they had three happy years together, during which time their daughter Gladys was born.

The Casely Hayfords' daughter Gladys was born with a malformed hip. When she was young, she and her mother sailed for England for medical help, where they stayed for nearly three years. Casely Hayford's long absence from her husband appears to have put too great a burden on her marriage. Although she became pregnant on her return to the Gold Coast (the child was still born), she and her husband separated.

An independent woman

Casely Hayford returned to Sierra Leone in 1914 and took a job as a music mistress at the Annie Walsh Memorial School in Freetown. She also became active in community affairs and gave lectures on the rights of women. For the first time in her life, she was an independent woman, neither any man's daughter nor any man's wife. She served as president of the Freetown Young

Women's Christian Association (YWCA) for a short time and then became president of the Women's League of the local branch of the Universal Negro Improvement Association founded by Jamaican Marcus Garvey (1887-1940).

During this time Casely Hayford began planning to open a technical training school for girls. Underpinning her desire to run a school for girls was her belief that girls should be taught how to function well in society. She personally had been forced into taking responsibility for herself after her family's finances dried up and when her marriage failed, and knew the struggle firsthand. As part of this effort, she and her niece Kathleen Easmon decided that after the end of World War I (1914-18) they would go to the United States, both to learn how Afro-American girls were educated and to raise money for the school. They left in mid-1920. Not until Casely Hayford arrived in the United States did she realize how important and well known her husband had become. Since this helped her in meeting the right people, she wrote him letters asking him not to reveal that they were no longer living as a married couple.

Casely Hayford with students and faculty at her school.

With various church denominations and African women's groups providing financial support, she and her niece traveled throughout the South, Midwest, and Northeast giving lectures about Africa and raising funds. Dressed in traditional cloth from the Gold Coast (Ghana), she attracted large audiences when she spoke to various church groups and Christian associations. As a woman representing Africans in the United States, Casely Hayford began to identify herself as an African. She wrote that she was no longer "a real Sambo" as she had described herself before.

At the end of her trip, after almost three years, she returned to Sierra Leone. She opened the Girls' Vocational and Industrial Training School in 1923 with a partner, Ejesa Osora. But the next year she and Osora had a falling out; Osora left to start her own school. Casely Hayford closed her school for several years, but reopened it in 1926 when her daughter Gladys agreed to help her. Casely Hayford made another fundraising trip to the United States in 1926 and 1927, but it was not nearly as successful as her first trip.

From 1927 until 1940 Casely Hayford ran her school for girls in Freetown. She closed the school at the age of 72 in 1940, because of her old age. In 1949 King George VI of England awarded her an MBE (Member of the British Empire).

Adelaide Smith Casely Hayford died in 1960 at the age of 88 years. Her biographer, Adelaide Cromwell, says of her life:

> In her life on three continents over nine decades, Mrs. Casely Hayford managed to symbolize the problems of modern women—and of modern black women. Identity (cultural and racial), marriage, motherhood, widowhood, career goals, community responsibility are all reflected in the life of this remarkable woman. Perhaps the most important conclusion that can be drawn from knowing Adelaide Smith Casely Hayford . . . is that not only was she a survivor but she was an achiever as well.

Further Reading

Cromwell, Adelaide M. *An African Victorian Feminist: The Life and Times of Adelaide Smith Casely Hayford, 1868-1960.* Washington, DC: Howard University Press, 1992.

Encyclopaedia Africana, Dictionary of African Biography. Vol. 2. Sierra Leone-Zaire: Reference Publications, 1977.

Cetshwayo

Born c. 1826
Zululand (now part of
KwaZulu-Natal province, South Africa)
Died 1884
Zululand

King of the Zulu nation

etshwayo (*Set-SHWIE-o,*) nephew of the Zulu warrior chief Shaka (see entry), succeeded his father as leader of the Zulu kingdom in 1872. At this time, the Zulus were the most powerful African state south of the Limpopo River, which borders present-day Zimbabwe and South Africa. Cetshwayo was a competent and stable ruler, and the kingdom was more united during his reign than it had ever been before. Under his leadership the Zulus fought their victorious battle against the British military at Isandlwana in 1879. But despite this Zulu victory against the British, Cetshwayo ultimately could not shield his kingdom from the internal pressures and external demands. He was the last great king of the Zulu nation.

Cetshwayo was the third ruler of the Zulus after Shaka (1787-1828). Following Shaka's assassination in 1828 by his half-brother Dingane, the Zulu kingdom passed through a violent and

"Sensitive and intelligent, Cetshwayo displayed a considerably better grasp of political reality than his father [Mpande] had."

—Donald Morris, in *The Washing of the Spears*

turbulent period. Dingane, who reigned from 1828 to 1840, did not maintain the strict and rigid discipline over the Zulu warriors that had been Shaka's hallmark. Instead, he stocked up on firearms that he could purchase from traders in neighboring Natal. Dingane had to keep a watchful eye on others who sought to challenge him as leader. In his efforts to eliminate potential competition, Dingane grew more repressive and aggressive. Many groups fled the kingdom for sanctuary in the white-settler colony of Natal.

Shaka's heritage

Dingane also came up against Afrikaner farmers (Boers) who had moved north out of the Cape Colony in the early eighteenth century in search of political freedom and land for their cattle. (An Afrikaner is a white South African of Dutch-German-French descent. The Afrikaners are known historically for their strong dislike of control by government). The Boers wanted to settle on the edge of the Zulu kingdom; their leader, Piet Retief, approached Dingane for permission. In 1838 Dingane agreed to allow them to settle, provided Retief returned some cattle stolen from Dingane. When Retief and his party brought the cattle to Dingane's capital at Emgungundlovu, Dingane went back on their agreement. He gave an order for the Zulus to turn on the Afrikaners and murder every one of them. Later that year, though, the Afrikaners had their revenge. They challenged the Zulu army at Blood River and killed more than 3,000 Zulu people. The Boers then withdrew to Natal and joined forces with Dingane's half-brother, Mpande, to unseat Dingane. In 1840 the two forces invaded Zululand and overthrew Dingane. Dingane fled and was killed.

Mpande, Cetshwayo's father, ruled the Zulu nation for 32 years, from 1840 until 1872. Mpande followed a policy of peaceful coexistence with his white neighbors and his kingdom thrived. At the time of his death, the kingdom had a population of about 300,000. The problem was land. White-controlled territory encircled Zululand, and there was no place left for the kingdom to expand: to the south were the British in Natal, to the west and northwest were the Afrikaners of Transvaal, and to the east was the Indian Ocean.

The "place of bones"

Through his unwillingness to appoint one of his many wives as an official wife or a so-called "Great Wife," Mpande created problems that would take 40 years and much bloodshed to resolve. (Many African societies practice polygamy. Men may take as many wives as they can afford. A chief or king might take 50 or 60 wives. By marrying the wives or daughters of powerful chiefs, he could solidify his personal control and secure the unity of his kingdom.) Traditionally, a Zulu chief marries several women and designates one, usually as he gets older, as his Great Wife. It is from their union that the chief names his successor. Mpande, however, never selected a Great Wife, and his indecision brought disorder to the kingdom. In 1856 two of Mpande's eldest sons—Cetshwayo, son of Ngqumbhazi, and Mbulazi, son of Monase—fought it out on the battlefield. At this time Cetshwayo was about 30 years old.

South Africa

Each man summoned his supporters. Cetshwayo's 20,000 warriors far outnumbered Mbulazi's 7,000 troops. Mbulazi knew he couldn't defeat Cetshwayo, so he told all the families of his supporters—about 30,000 men, women and children—to flee toward the Tugela River on the eastern coast. Even with some support from his father, Mpande, and from six of Mpande's other sons, Mbulazi and his people were completely overwhelmed by Cetshwayo's forces. Few of Mbulazi's faction survived. The stream at Ndondakusuka where the slaughter occurred is known as the *Mathambo,* the "place of bones."

Although Mpande remained the official head of the Zulus, Cetshwayo held the real power after defeating Mbulazi. Mpande had become so inactive that he grew unbelievably fat—so fat that he could not walk and had to be pulled around by an attendant in a little cart especially made for him. Mpande died in 1872; the next year Cetshwayo became the official leader of the Zulu nation.

Succeeds his father

Donald Morris, writing in his book *The Washing of the Spears,* described Cetshwayo:

> [He was] tall and muscular, with finely chiseled features and a regal air. He inherited the royal tendency to fat, but he led an active life and managed to avoid the gross obesity which had over taken his father and Dingane, his uncle. Sensitive and intelligent, he displayed a con-

siderably better grasp of political reality than his father had. . . . He could, however, only deal with immediate situations, and the complexities of European civilization were too great for him to extrapolate with certainty.

Cetshwayo intended to maintain his father's good relations with the English-speaking Natal whites as protection against the Afrikaners living in the Transvaal (a former province in what is now the northeastern section of the Republic of South Africa). In a move designed to win white approval, he invited Natal Secretary for Native Affairs Theophilus Shepstone to come and "crown" him in 1873. Shepstone was a British official who had been in Natal for a long time, and Cetshwayo regarded him as his protector against land grabs by the Boers.

During Cetshwayo's rule the chief homestead was moved to Ulundi, and it became the political and administrative capital of the kingdom. Cetshwayo revitalized the army that had weakened under Mpande, and he established a council of state, which he consulted before making major state decisions.

Outside factors affect kingdom

In 1877 foreign policy decisions made in Britain had an impact on the Zulus. The British colonial office transferred Shepstone from Natal colony to the Transvaal, which the British government had recently taken over. Britain hoped to create a federation of the two British colonies, Natal and Cape, and the two Afrikaans-speaking colonies, the Transvaal and the Orange Free State. The Transvaal had financial problems, and Shepstone argued that it could not defend itself against the Zulu and therefore should become a British colony—a decision to which the Transvaal reluctantly agreed. As representative from Transvaal, Shepstone abandoned the Zulus' cause and sided with the Transvaal.

The Zulus and the Boers in Transvaal had a long-standing disagreement about land boundaries on the eastern side of Blood River. To settle the issue, the lieutenant governor of Natal, Henry Bulwer, commissioned an independent report to examine each party's claims. In June 1878 Bulwer's commission ruled in favor of the Zulus, but the new British High Commissioner in Natal, Bartle Frere, kept the results of the report to himself, hoping he could change the outcome. In his new capacity in the Transvaal, Shepstone had persuaded the newcomer Frere that the Zulus were a menace to European civilization in southern Africa and had to be removed. Frere did not send the report on the land issue to London until he had received additional troops.

Preparing for war

When everything was in place, Frere gave Cetshwayo the results of the report. He also gave Cetshwayo 30 days to disband the Zulu army. Cetshwayo could not possibly comply with this order and retain his position as king. Realizing the consequences of his refusal to obey, he ordered 30,000 warriors to assemble at Ulundi to prepare for war. According to Thomas Pakenham in *The Scramble for Africa,* Cetshwayo addressed his warriors with these words:

> I am sending you out against the whites, who have invaded Zulu-land and driven away our cattle. You are to go against the column at Rorke's Drift, and drive it back into Natal. . . .You will attack by daylight, as there are enough of you to "eat it up" and you will march slowly so as not to tire yourselves. [The capital city of Ulundi was about 70 miles away from the battle site.]

Meanwhile, Lord Chelmsford, his 7,000 British soldiers, and about 7,000 African troops invaded Zululand at three places. On January 22, 1879, the Zulu army concentrated on the central British column at Isandlwana. Taken by surprise as tens of thousands of Zulu warriors rose up from the ridge and streamed across the plain, the British forces were overwhelmed. Of the 800 white soldiers in camp at Isandlwana in the morning, all but one was killed. Of the 907 black soldiers fighting with the British, 471 were killed. Approximately 1,000 Zulu died. The British army had been humiliated by an army whose weaponry consisted mostly of *assegais* (short stabbing spears) and some firearms. This was the greatest defeat of British forces since the turn of the century.

Taken captive

The British army regrouped and made its way to Ulundi in July. Firing shells into the huts of the capital, the British advance met with little resistance. The royal house was burned to the ground. More than 1,000 Zulu warriors died at Ulundi, compared with 13 British. The final death toll was high: at the end of the war against the British, 6,000 Zulus, about 1,080 white soldiers, and

Cetshwayo photographed in London, 1882.

570 Natal Zulu soldiers had been killed. Cetshwayo and his wives escaped and moved to the North. He remained in hiding until late August 1879, when British troops found him and took him captive. They exiled him to Cape Town Castle, a fortress built in the seventeenth century.

Shortly afterward, the British announced that the position of king of the Zulus was being abolished along with the nation's army. In place of the king, they created 13 individual chiefdoms with no loyalty to a central figure. The British officials appointed the chiefs, and the chiefs were not permitted to raise an army. The new arrangement created the potential for conflict between the old Zulu royal order (the *Usuthu*) and the new British-appointed chiefs.

Three appointed chiefs in particular were so ruthless in the way they treated their subjects that Cetshwayo's supporters started a campaign to have him restored to the throne. In 1882 a Zulu group of about 2,000 people went to Natal to complain about the situation. As the campaign built momentum among the public, the authorities agreed to release Cetshwayo temporarily so that he might take his case to the imperial authorities in England. Cetshwayo traveled by boat to England, where he presented his case to the Colonial Office and had an audience with Queen Victoria.

From exile to war

Only when he returned to South Africa did he learn that the British planned to divide Zululand into smaller portions. In exchange, Cetshwayo could return as king—but with limited authority over a reduced area. He returned to Zululand in 1883, and Shepstone installed him as king. The partition did nothing to settle the warring groups. In March 1883 the old royal order—the

Usuthu—gathered forces to invade the northern part of Zululand. This northern area had been partitioned by British officials and made independent of the royal house. As the Usuthu attacked, the people of the North (the Mandlakazi) ambushed the invaders and destroyed their forces. More Zulu lost their lives in this battle than in any other in Zulu history. Three months later the Mandlakazi attacked Ulundi. Taking the king by surprise, they burned and sacked the capital and killed most of the men who had ruled the Zulu kingdom, thus destroying the old order.

Cetshwayo sought protection from the British resident commissioner, and he died the next year at Eshowe in Zululand. Cetshwayo's officials proclaimed his young son Dinuzulu king of the Zulus. Although Dinuzulu was still a child and too young to rule, he served as a symbol of unity in the kingdom. Cetshwayo, like other African rulers up against the advancement of European forces and modern technology, ultimately could not defend his kingdom and preserve his people's traditional ways.

Further Reading

Guy, Jeff. *The Destruction of the Zulu Kingdom: The Civil War in Zululand, 1879-1884.* University of Natal Press, 1994.

Maylam, Paul. *A History of the African People of South Africa: From the Early Iron Age to the 1970s.* New York: St. Martin's, 1986.

Morris, Donald R. *The Washing of the Spears: The Rise and Fall of the Great Zulu Nation.* Abacus, 1992.

Pakenham, Thomas. *The Scramble for Africa: 1876-1912.* Jonathan Ball Publishers, 1991.

Taylor, Stephen. *Shaka's Children: A History of the Zulu People.* New York: HarperCollins, 1994.

Wilson, Monica, and Leonard Thompson, eds. *The Oxford History of South Africa.* Volume 2. New York/UK: Oxford University Press, 1975.

John Chilembwe

Born c. 1872
Chiradzulu, Nyasaland (now Malawi)
Died 1915
Nyasaland (now Malawi)

Christian leader and political activist

> *"The poor Africans who have nothing to win in this present world . . . are invited to die for a cause which is not theirs."*
>
> **—Chilembwe, in a letter to the Nyasaland Times expressing opposition to African involvement in World War I**

ohn Chilembwe (*CHE-lem-bway*) was an African Christian leader who led a revolt against British settlers in Nyasaland (present-day Malawi). The "Rising" organized by Chilembwe against the colonial government and white settlers failed miserably, but he became a folk hero to the people of Nyasaland, a symbol of resistance to white rule. Chilembwe's impact on his followers was so strong that even after his death many held out the hope that he would return from the grave to deliver them from British rule.

Educated in the United States as a Baptist missionary, Chilembwe returned to Nyasaland and established a mission to educate and minister to his people. He worked hard for 14 years building up the church and congregation, all the while maintaining peaceful relations with his white neighbors and colonial authorities. He was respected by the community, and as a man of the church he preached compliance with the laws and obedience to the authorities. No single event seems to have triggered a change in his behavior, but Chilembwe suddenly turned from his priestly vows and organized a militant uprising (an armed, aggressive rebellion).

Educated overseas

Chilembwe was born in Chiradzulu in the southern part of Nyasaland. His parents were Yao and raised their son according to their traditional culture. In 1892, when Chilembwe was about 20 years old, he made friends with a rather unconventional missionary named John Booth. Booth hired Chilembwe as his house servant and converted him to Christianity. Booth went to Nyasaland independent of any church or mission and set out to train Africans to rule their own lives and countries. He established a self-supporting, African-led mission, angering the Scottish missionaries and settlers in the area. Booth defied all the European conventions toward Africans at the time by treating them as equals, paying them fair wages, and taking them into projects as partners.

In 1897 Booth took Chilembwe with him on a trip to the United States. He helped get Chilembwe enrolled in the newly founded Virginia Theological Seminary and College. In the United States, Chilembwe heard discussions and arguments by black intellectuals about the best way for blacks to advance in society. For the first time Chilembwe met self-assured, educated black Americans and Africans. He learned about the history of slavery in America and about the slave revolts before the American Civil War (1861-65).

The turn of the twentieth century marked a period of turmoil and unrest in the black American community. Black churches were breaking away from the established Christian churches and forming their own independent sects. Two well-educated African Americans, Booker T. Washington and W. E. B. Du Bois, were debating about the best path to progress for blacks. Washington argued for gradual social advancement through education and hard work; Du Bois urged militant political activism to gain black rights.

Three years after his arrival in the States, Chilembwe was forced to go back to Nyasaland when he developed asthma, a potentially serious respiratory condition. In 1900 he returned home as a missionary for the Foreign Mission Board of the black National Baptist Convention. The Baptist Convention was interested in

Chilembwe with his family.

showing white America that a black man could spread the gospel as well as a white. Chilembwe was way ahead of the times in his own country—it would be another 10 years before the Scottish missions in Nyasaland ordained an African minister. Chilembwe brought a sense of pride to the people of his country. He was black, intelligent, educated, and the equal of the Europeans.

Between 1900 and 1914 Chilembwe worked hard to build his mission, which he called the Providence Industrial Mission, located near Blantyre. He and his church members built a brick church as big as the Scottish mission headquarters in Blantyre. Chilembwe modeled his church's philosophy along the ideas of his benefactor, John Booth. He taught self-sufficiency and encouraged the members of his congregation to improve themselves so they could succeed, emphasizing the importance of cleanliness, an acceptable physical appearance, education, reading, writing, and manual skills. His wife worked with young girls, teaching them the advantages of delaying marriage until they were older.

Growing frustration

Gradually Chilembwe began to resent the white settler government. Nyasaland was a small country with a very dense population. In 1891 the British government declared Nyasaland a protectorate (a region that is ruled by another power; in this case, Nyasaland was ruled by Great Britain). The British gave the whites a small grant to pay for the running of the territory—an amount much too small to pay all the costs. To raise additional money, the settler government imposed a hut tax on the African population in 1912. An African could pay half this tax by working for a white settler for a month—without pay. The other half was payable in cash. The Africans deeply resented this taxation. They were being asked to pay rent on land that belonged to them and to work the land that the whites had taken from them. The hut tax also forced many Nyasa men out of their village life and into the wage economy. The young men were forced to work on white farms or go south to work in the mines in South Africa for money.

Although Chilembwe had never openly opposed the government, he secretly urged his mission people not to pay the hut tax. The tax caused severe hardship for African families, especially when the rains failed in 1913. To meet their tax that year, many African families switched from growing crops for themselves to growing crops they could sell for cash.

Churches take a stand

Influences from outside Nyasaland added to Chilembwe's growing frustrations. Around him, educated Africans were forming their own separatist churches (advocating separation of blacks from whites). In 1908 Eliot Kamwana had established a millenarian religious group called the Watch Tower Movement (known in the United States as Jehovah's Witnesses) in Nyasaland. (The term *millenarian* refers to the Christian prophecy of the *millenium,* a 1,000-year period of time during which holiness is expected to reign on Earth.) The Watch Tower Movement also preached against foreign domination. Predicting that British rule would end in Nyasaland, Kamwana went around pointing at the offices of the local British administrators and predicting that they would soon be gone. In response, the British arrested him and forced him to leave the country. Nevertheless, Kamwana succeeded in stirring up the Africans and provoking them to consider resisting foreign rule.

Reaching the boiling point

As the beginning of World War I (1914-18) approached, restlessness and anxiety grew among the people of Nyasaland. The separatist preachers raised hopes that the present system of British rule would end. But when the order did not change, Chilembwe's followers probably turned to him to take action. The most likely basis of Chilembwe's sudden rebellious stand occurred at the beginning of World War I, when British and German forces were fighting along the border in northern Nyasaland. Nyasa men were fighting in the battle between the two European countries and were suffering many deaths and injuries. Chilembwe was outraged that African men were dying in a war that was not theirs. In his anger he composed a bitterly sarcastic letter for publication in the *Nyasaland Times,* asking why the Africans should be expected to fight for the whites: "Let the rich men, bankers, title men, storekeepers, farmers and landlords go to war and get shot," he wrote. "Instead the poor Africans who have nothing to win in this present world . . . are invited to die for a cause which is not theirs."

Authorities immediately withdrew the edition of the newspaper in which his letter appeared. Chilembwe was infuriated over the censoring of his opinions on politics in his homeland. Believing that nonviolent means would never bring significant change to Nyasaland, he apparently resorted to militant means. The British government did not arrest him right away but rather planned to deport him in several months' time. Chilembwe probably knew of the plan, felt he didn't have much to lose, and warned his congregation of impending trouble. Chilembwe realized that any revolt at that time would most likely be more symbolic than effective. He is quoted by Robin Hallet in *Africa since 1895,* as telling his followers: "You are to go and strike the blow and then die. You must not think that with that blow you are going to defeat white men and then become kings of your own country."

The "Rising"

Chilembwe's timing was good. The British had moved their troops from Blantyre to the northern border to deal with the German troops, leaving the government offices and settlers unprotected. Chilembwe and his followers spent nearly four months planning their rebellion. In the South they would attack government offices and the farms of the white settlers. Meanwhile, northern African forces would strike on their home turf and then march south to join up with Chilembwe.

Overall, the plan for the "Rising" failed miserably. The group raiding the trading store near Blantyre failed to get the guns. One group, however, did succeed in killing a much-hated manager of a nearby farm, A. L. Bruce, who had a reputation for treating his workers and tenants badly. When Chilembwe protested against Bruce's actions, Bruce tried to silence him by burning down some of his mission's churches. Chilembwe's forces responded by attacking the farm, cutting off Bruce's head, and displaying it in the church. They also killed two other Europeans in the "Rising." Chilembwe eluded the police for two weeks before African police shot and killed him as he was trying to escape across the border to Mozambique.

Further Reading

Hallet, Robin. *Africa since 1895*. Ann Arbor: University of Michigan Press, 1974.

Ray, Benjamin C. *African Religions: Symbol, Ritual, and Community*. Englewood Cliffs, NJ: Prentice Hall, 1976.

Shepperson, George, and Thomas Price. *Independent African*. 1958.

Wilson, Derek. *A History of South and Central Africa*. New York/UK: Cambridge University Press, 1975.

Joaquim Chissano

Born 1939
Malehice, Chibuto district, Gaza, Mozambique

President of Mozambique

Joaquim Chissano was a central figure in Mozambique's struggle for independence from the Portuguese.

oaquim Alberto Chissano (*wa-KEEM chi-SAH-no*) became president of southeast Africa's People's Republic of Mozambique on November 3, 1986. He was elected to office following the death of the nation's former president, Samora Machel, in a plane crash the month before. Chissano was not well known in the West until he became his country's president. He had, however, been a central figure in Mozambique's military struggle for independence from the Portuguese: he was a founder of the ruling party FRELIMO, the Front for the Liberation of Mozambique, in 1962, served as defense minister from 1964 to 1974, and then as minister of foreign affairs. As president he made sweeping changes in the country's political and economic systems and established sound relations with the leading powerholders in the West. Most importantly, he helped end the 16-year-long civil war in Mozambique and brought the rebel group headed by Afonso Dhlakama into the government through the country's first multi-party elections.

Joins the fight for freedom

Chissano was born in 1939 in Mozambique's southerly Gaza province, where his father was a Methodist minister. He attended Gaza primary schools and became one of the first African students to attend the main secondary school in Lourenço Marques (the capital city of Maputo). From high school Chissano went to Lisbon, Portugal, to study medicine. After only one year, though, he headed for France to join exiled Mozambican nationalist and poet Marcelino dos Santos in the struggle for their homeland's independence. By 1962 he was in the eastern African republic of Tanzania with Eduardo Mondlane (see entry), the driving force behind opposition to Portuguese rule in Mozambique.

The Portuguese had been in Mozambique for about 400 years, but they had settled primarily along the East Coast because of its thriving trade. In the 1890s, as European powers consolidated—or unified—their territories in Africa, Portuguese explorers began journeying into Mozambique's interior. Soon the Portuguese sought to control the entire region. Mozambique became an overseas province of Portugal in 1951.

The first real resistance to Portuguese rule came from the workers in the Mozambican towns. In the 1940s and 1950s they called general strikes in Lourenço Marques, but the police brutally put them down. In June 1960 soldiers fired on a crowd of peaceful demonstrators at Mueda in Cabo Delgado province, killing about 600 people. Resistance hardened after this tragedy. As the Portuguese put pressure on political opponents, Mozambican nationalists came to realize that they had to offer organized, military resistance to the Portuguese and not rely only on sudden, unplanned protests.

Mozambican nationalists went to Dar es Salaam in Tanganyika (now Tanzania), where they joined two other nationalist groups that had formed around tribal and regional lines. When Mondlane returned to Africa from the United States in 1962, he persuaded the three groups to form a united group, the Front for the Liberation of Mozambique (FRELIMO). In 1963 Chissano became secretary to Mondlane, who was president of FRELIMO.

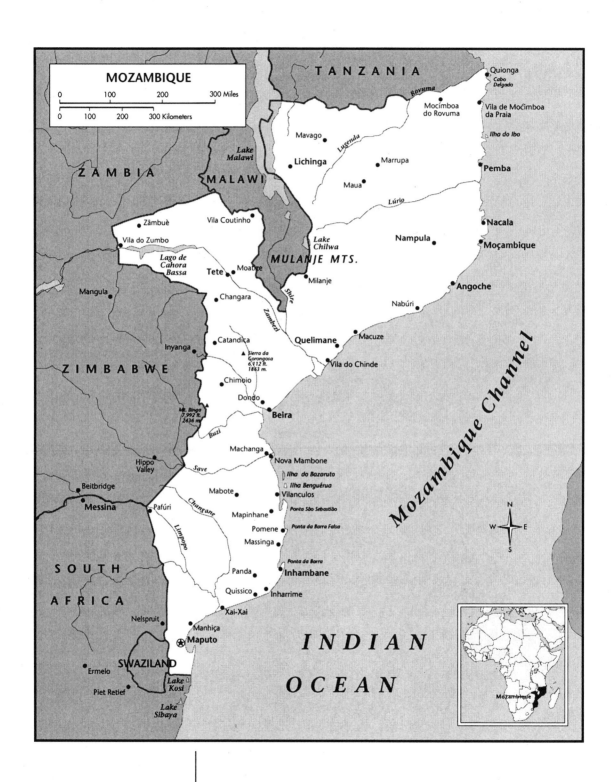

MOZAMBIQUE

| 0 | 100 | 200 | 300 Miles |
| 0 | 100 | 200 | 300 Kilometers |

TANZANIA

Quionga
Cabo Delgado

Rovuma

Moçímboa
do Rovuma

Vila de Moçímboa
da Praia

ZAMBIA

Mavago

Lugenda

Ilha do Ibo

Lichinga

Marrupa

*Lake
Malawi*

MALAWI

Maua

Pemba

Zâmbuè

Vila Coutinho

Nampula

Nacala

Vila do Zumbo

*Lake
Chilwa*

Moçambique

MULANJE MTS.

*Lago de
Cahora
Bassa*

Tete

Moatize

Milanje

Mangula

Changara

Zambezi

Shire

Lúrio

Nabúri

Angoche

ZIMBABWE

Catandica

Quelimane

Macuze

Inyanga

▲ *Sierra da
Gorongosa
6,112 ft.
1863 m.*

Vila do Chinde

Chimoio

Dondo

Mt. Binga
*7,992 ft.
2436 m.*

Beira

Machanga

Buzi

Nova Mambone

Save

Ilha do Bazaruto

Hippo
Valley

Mabote

Ilha Benguérua
Vilanculos

Beitbridge

Changane

Mapinhane

Ponta São Sebastião

Messina

Pafúri

Pomene

Ponta da Barra Falsa

Limpopo

Massinga

SOUTH

Panda

Ponta da Barra

Inhambane

AFRICA

Quissico

Inharrime

Nelspruit

Xai-Xai

Manhiça

Maputo

INDIAN

Ermelo

SWAZILAND

Mozambique Channel

Piet Retief

*Lake
Kosi*

OCEAN

*Lake
Sibaya*

N
W   E
S

Mozambique

Mondlane was killed in 1969 when a parcel he opened exploded. His death caused divisions within FRELIMO's ranks. Some of the more radical members wanted a militant black state—armed and willing to fight for its ideals—to replace the white government. Others were more moderate. Eventually, the moderates won out over the more revolutionary members. Chissano, Machel, and dos Santos took control of the liberation party.

International involvement

In the early years of the war against the Portuguese, African sources furnished FRELIMO with most of its weapons. At the height of the war, the FRELIMO fighters needed more ammunition, and the party's leaders turned to China and Eastern European countries for supplies. By the late 1960s the former Soviet Union supplied most of FRELIMO's needs. China, the Eastern Bloc nations, and the Soviet Union were at this point all Communist countries (they followed a system of government in which the state controls the means of production and the distribution of goods). Before the collapse of the Soviet Union in 1989, control of the Indian Ocean ports on Africa's East Coast were important both to Europe's Communist nations and to anti-Communist countries in the West. Mozambique's four deepwater ports and 1,500-mile-long coastline made it strategically important. Nationalists in the landlocked southern African states fighting for independence turned to Mozambique for an outlet to the sea.

Chissano coordinated FRELIMO forces from his base in neighboring Tanzania throughout the late 1960s. The army moved farther south, crossing the Zambezi River, and spread out from Cabo Delgado, to Niassa in the Northwest, to the provinces of Tete, Zambézia, Manica, and Sofala. In late 1973 and early 1974 FRELIMO attacked settlements as far as 100 miles south of the Zambezi River, almost to Beira. For the first time, the white settler community felt threatened by the war. Frightened and losing money, they asked the government in Portugal for help. The disgruntled Portuguese army—tired of the endless wars they were sent to fight in Africa and desiring a democratic system at home—overthrew the government of Marcello Caetano in 1974.

The new government in Portugal wanted to end its involvement in its colonies. It held a series of meetings with nationalist political leaders and worked out a plan for independence. The

Members of the women's detachment of FRELIMO, the Mozambique Liberation Front, resting during a stop in a village, 1971.

struggle for Mozambique's freedom ended much sooner than anyone anticipated. In September 1974 fighting between FRE-LIMO and the Portuguese government stopped. A temporary government headed by Chissano took office until independence on June 25, 1975. Samora Machel became president, Marcelino dos Santos became vice president, and Joaquim Chissano served as foreign minister.

Independence is not smooth sailing

Freedom brought serious problems. Mozambique came to rely on Soviet help as other sources of financial aid dried up. Because of Mozambique's relationship with the Soviet Union and its support of the African National Congress (ANC; the leading organization opposed to white minority rule in South Africa), the anti-Communist white minority government in South Africa started putting pressure on the Mozambican government. Over the years South Africa's gold mines had employed workers from Mozam-

Faced with an enemy government on its borders, in the late 1970s the Rhodesians created RENAMO to gather information on Zimbabwe nationalists in Mozambique. In 1980 Robert Mugabe came to power in Zimbabwe (the name given to Southern Rhodesia after independence was achieved). After that, South African military operatives took over RENAMO, moving its base from Zimbabwe to South Africa. Rhodesian agents recruited Afonso Dhlakama and persuaded him to join RENAMO in Rhodesia.

RENAMO activities disrupted Mozambique's social, political, and economic structure. The nation was plunged into a brutal civil war. RENAMO forces were blamed for the destruction of the pumps for the oil pipeline that ran from Beira, Mozambique, to the Zimbabwe border. The FRELIMO government was unable to stop the chaos or protect its citizens. They half jokingly called rebel leader Dhlakama "the circuit breaker" because RENAMO continually destroyed the pylons for the electric lines servicing Maputo and Beira.

By 1990 RENAMO attacks and acts of sabotage (deliberate acts of destruction aimed at a government) had displaced nearly 2 million rural Mozambicans. Another million people had fled their homes and sought safety in refugee camps in Malawi and Zimbabwe. Earlier the South African government offered to end its support for RENAMO if Mozambique would expel members of the African National Congress (ANC) who operated from within its borders. The ANC had been getting both guerrillas (independent fighting units) and arms into South Africa from Mozambique. The two governments signed the Nkomati Accord on March 16, 1984, but the South African government did not honor its promise. Instead, it continued to supply RENAMO.

For some years in the 1980s right-wing conservatives (people who generally oppose political change and resist movements perceived as potentially socialist or communist) in the United States actually raised money and bought supplies for RENAMO. As the extent of RENAMO atrocities became known, however, that support fell away, and RENAMO began dealing in ivory and gemstones to support itself. The politics of the region had changed. Eventually, when Dhlakama lost the support of his traditional sponsors, he agreed to come to the conference table.

bique. The mines stopped hiring Mozambican workers, leading to economic turmoil in Mozambique.

South Africa also gave help to the staunchly anti-Communist white government of Ian Smith (see entry) in Rhodesia (now Zimbabwe), which was trying to put down black nationalists fighting for independence. The Mozambican government gave Rhodesian black rights leader Robert Mugabe (see entry) and his fighters the right to set up bases in Mozambique. (Mugabe would later become the first president of the black-majority-led government in Zimbabwe.)

In response, the white-run Rhodesian and South African governments supplied funds and weapons to an anti-Communist rebel group, the Mozambique National Resistance (MNR or RENAMO), led by Afonso Dhlakama. RENAMO devastated the Mozambican countryside during a 16-year-long civil war, destroying schools and clinics, kidnapping young women and men, frightening the farmers, and cutting off normal road and rail lines.

Drastic measures

Within a year of its independence Mozambique closed its borders with Rhodesia—a move that cost the Mozambican government nearly $100 million in just two years. Terrible floods and then drought threatened the lives of hundreds of thousands of people. Poor government planning made the economy even worse. In 1977 FRELIMO had agreed on a five-year economic plan to build up the country's industries and chose not to worry about the farmers. The plan failed. In addition, nearly all of Mozambique's 250,000 whites left the country when the Machel government took over most privately owned property.

When Rhodesia became the independent nation of Zimbabwe in 1980, the people of Mozambique hoped that the border reopening would help boost the economy at home. It didn't. Mozambique became the base for ANC headquarters, and an angry South African government began using RENAMO against the Mozambican government.

In 1981 South African jets attacked ANC headquarters in Maputo. In a show of support the Soviets sent two warships to aid the Mozambicans, but Chissano—then serving as his nation's foreign minister—felt it was necessary to turn to the West for a lasting solution to the violence and the economic woes plaguing Mozambique. The country needed military training and economic aid, and only the West could provide that kind of help. Despite Mozambique's ties with the Soviets, the anti-Communist Western countries were willing to aid Mozambique's fight against RENAMO.

A slow step forward

By 1984 the economy in Mozambique had collapsed. The Machel government had no choice but to cut a deal with the South African government. Mozambique agreed to tell the ANC it had to leave Mozambique; in exchange South Africa promised to end its support of RENAMO and bring business into the country. Foreign Minister Chissano was opposed to the agreement and took no public part in the signing at Nkomati. Two years later, in October 1986, Machel died when his plane crashed along the border of Mozambique and South Africa. Chissano assumed the office of the presidency of Mozambique the next month. In his first press conference as president, Chissano stated that Mozambique would continue to adhere to the Nkomati accord—but only if South Africa did the same.

In 1987 Chissano launched a campaign that would steer Mozambique back onto a peaceful path. The civil war between the government and RENAMO finally ended in 1992. The adoption of a new democratic constitution made the Mozambican dream of

Chissano receives decoration from Mozambique president Samora Machel, 1985.

| Joaquim Chissano

"government by the people" a reality. RENAMO became a legitimate political party. In November 1994 Mozambique held its first multiparty elections. FRELIMO won a majority of the seats and Chissano was elected president.

Further Reading

Africa Watch staff. *Conspicuous Destruction: War, Famine, and the Reform Process in Mozambique.* New York: Africa Watch/Human Rights Watch, 1992.

Contemporary Black Biography. Volume 7. Detroit: Gale, 1994.

Ellert, H. *The Rhodesian Front War.* Mambo, 1989.

Gersony, Robert. *Summary of Mozambican Refugee Accounts of Principally Conflict-Related Experience in Mozambique.* Washington, DC: U.S. State Department, 1988.

Hoile, David. *Mozambique: A Nation in Crisis.* Claridge Press, 1989.

Kaplan, Irving, Howard Blutstein, Peter Just, and others. *Area Handbook for Mozambique.* American University Press, 1977.

Mondlane, Eduardo. *The Struggle for Mozambique.* Zed Press, 1969.

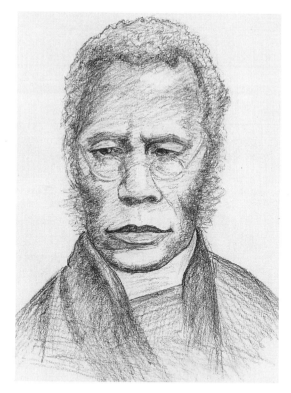

Samuel Ajayi Crowther

Born c. 1806
Osogun, Ibarapa District, Yorubaland (Nigeria)
Died December 31, 1891
Nigeria

Translator, linguist, explorer, and Anglican bishop

As a teenager Samuel Ajayi Crowther was abducted by Muslim Oyo slavers from his village in what is now western Nigeria and sold to Portuguese slave traders. He was rescued from a slave ship headed for Brazil by a British patrol boat and taken as a freed slave to Sierra Leone. Saved from a future of slavery, Crowther went on to become a distinguished translator and linguist, a noted explorer, and the first black bishop in the Anglican church. He established churches and schools in southern Nigeria and translated the Bible into his first language, Yoruba.

"When [my mother] saw me she trembled. She could not believe her own eyes. We grasped one another, looking at one another in silence and great astonishment, and . . . tears rolled down her emaciated cheeks."

—Crowther, describing his reunion with his mother 25 years after their family had been torn apart by the slave trade

A remarkable future in peril

Samuel Crowther was born around 1806 in Osogun in the Ibarapa district of what is today western Nigeria. His given name was Ajayi, which—roughly translated—means the "one born with his face to the ground and destined for a remarkable future." His father was Aiyemi, a descendant of a leading family of skilled weavers from Ketu. His mother, Afala, a priestess of Obatala, also came from a distinguished family. Her grandmother was said to be the daughter of the *alafin* ("king") Abiodun (1770-1789), the last great ruler of Old Oyo (a Yoruba kingdom). Her father was the highest ranking councillor to the king of Osogun. Aiyemi and Afala had four children.

Early in the 1800s the authority of the alafin of Oyo over the smaller kingdoms and states that normally paid him tribute had weakened. The Oyo no longer had access to the western areas for taking slaves, and it turned south toward the Yoruba provinces. Crowther and his family were victims of this turn of events.

Sierra Leone: The British experiment

Around the time Crowther was born, the British government had made it illegal for any British citizen to participate in the slave trade. The British also attempted to prohibit others from engaging in the trade by setting up naval bases along the Gulf of Guinea on the Atlantic coast of West Africa to patrol the waters. One such patrol rescued Crowther from a Portuguese ship headed for Brazil. The British ship took Crowther and the other captives to Sierra Leone, a small colony on the West Coast of Africa. British abolitionists, humanitarians, and church groups had established a community for freed slaves there in 1787.

The Sierra Leone Company started as an experimental colony with 411 freed slaves repatriated (restored to their country of origin) from Britain. Its goals were to "introduce civilisation among the natives and to cultivate the soil by means of free labour." Twelve hundred former slaves who had served the British military in the American Revolution (1775-83) joined the small colony at Sierra Leone when they failed to get land that had been promised them in Nova Scotia, Canada. Later, 500 people of mixed descent from Jamaica settled there, but many people died of fever and other diseases. The colony eventually failed. But when the British parliament outlawed slavery in 1807, it made Freetown, Sierra Leone, its headquarters for the West African Slave Squadron. By the mid-1800s the colony supported 70,000 African refugees or repatriated Africans.

"A most sorrowful scene"

Crowther wrote a narrative about his experiences, relating in detail the slave raid that rocked his village in March 1821. He was in his early teens at the time. The family was preparing breakfast about 9:00 A.M. when word came that an enemy force was outside the palisade (fencing). The village was about four miles in circumference and housed about 12,000 people. No one was prepared for the assault. Within three or four hours the enemy forced its way through the palisade and into the village. Crowther's description of the scene is reprinted in Philip Curtin's collection *Africa Remembered:*

> [It was] a most sorrowful scene imaginable. . . . Women, some with three, four or six children clinging to their arms, with the infants on their backs, and such baggage as they could carry on their heads, running as fast as they could through prickly shrubs, which, hooking their . . . loads, drew them down from the heads of the bearers. . . . While they were endeavouring to disentangle themselves from the ropy shrubs, they were overtaken and caught by the enemies with a noose of rope thrown over the neck of every individual, to be led in the manner of goats tied together. . . . In many cases a family was violently divided between three or four enemies, who each led his away, to see one another no more. . . . Your humble servant was thus caught—with his mother, two sisters (one an infant about ten months old) and a cousin. . . . The last view I had of my father was when he came from the fight. . . . Hence I never saw him more. I learned sometime afterward that he was killed in another battle.

Crowther's captors took him to Iseyin and gave him to the local chief, who traded him for a horse. For two months he was the slave of the horse merchant until the chief decided to return the horse and take Crowther back. Shortly thereafter the chief sold him to an Oyo woman trader in exchange for the local currency, cowrie shells. The trader used Crowther for several months as her household slave, and then, in November 1821, she put him up for sale at the market where professional slave traders bought him. Crowther's memory about these times is understandably hazy: he traveled extensively, lived in virtual isolation, and knew nothing of the people who held him captive. Eventually, however, he was taken across the lagoon to Lagos and left with Portuguese traders.

In his memoir Crowther relates how the men came for him and chained him by the neck to five other men and boys:

> In this situation the boys suffered the most; the men sometimes, getting angry, would draw the chain so violently [that it would leave] bruises on their poor little necks. . . . [At night the men] drew the chain

so close to ease themselves of its weight, in order to be able to lie more conveniently, that we were almost suffocated, or bruised to death. . . .

Rescue at sea

Several months passed in Lagos before the captors put Crowther aboard a ship bound for the plantations of Brazil. On the night of April 8, 1822, after just a short time at sea, a British man-of-war stopped the Portuguese ship and searched it. The British tied up the Portuguese captain and most of his crew, took the 187 African captives on board their warship, and towed the Portuguese slave ship behind them. Several months later the British ship arrived at Sierra Leone. The freed slaves went to Bathurst, where the British Church Missionary Society gave them protection. They housed and fed them and taught them to read and write. (The British Church Missionary Society was a recognized offshoot of the Anglican church.)

Crowther proved an especially quick learner; he claims that within six months he could read the New Testament. On December 11, 1824, he was baptized into the Christian church and took the name Samuel Crowther after a patron of the Church Missionary Society. In 1826 and 1827 Crowther spent a few months in England at a parish school in Islington, north London. He had hoped to study there, but the Church Mission Society asked him to return to Sierra Leone. To continue his study, Crowther attended the newly opened Fourah Bay College. (He was the college's first and only qualified student.

In 1829 Crowther left school to marry his first wife, Susan Asano Thompson, a former slave rescued by His Majesty's Ship *Bann* in 1822. She was a trained schoolteacher and later opened her own school near Lagos. Crowther got an appointment as a government schoolteacher in 1830. After a few years teaching he returned to Fourah Bay as a tutor. He and his wife had three children: a son and two daughters. Samuel Crowther Jr. became an architect; Abigail Crowther was educated in England and married the Reverend T. B. Macaulay (their son Herbert Macaulay was a prominent Nigerian politician in the early 1920s); Susan Crowther married Reverend G. C. Nicol, government chaplain at Bathurst in the Gambia. Crowther later fathered three more children with his second wife, having remarried after the death of Susan Thompson in 1880.

Goes on Niger expedition

Many British humanitarian (social reform) and abolitionist (antislavery) groups believed that if slavery were to be abolished completely, Africans themselves would have to stop trading in slaves and find other goods to sell. At the same time British manufacturers were seeking out new markets for their products and looking for ways to cut out African middlemen who transported their goods inland from the coast. After 1830, when explorers discovered where the Niger River emptied into the Atlantic along the coast of Nigeria, British manufacturers and church groups organized an expedition to sail up the Niger to the continent's interior, looking, among other things, for new avenues of trade.

Meanwhile, freed slaves educated at missions in Sierra Leone were moving back to their original homes. By the early 1840s some 500 ex-slaves had moved to Abeokuta in southwestern Nigeria. They petitioned the Church Missionary Society to set up a mission for them. The society planned to establish a model farm and bought some land for the project from the powerful Ata of Idah. Crowther and another missionary joined the expedition, which received favorable attention in Britain as a "Bible and plough" project. Queen Victoria's husband, Prince Albert, gave the expedition an official send off. But the trip was a failure. Of the 145 Europeans who set out, one-third died of malaria. In addition, the model farm failed and the expedition returned to England with little to show. One positive consequence of the expedition, however, was the realization that Africans—not whites—should be educating and preaching to Africans. Sierra Leone had a pool of trained African evangelists ready to go to the interior.

After he returned from the Niger expedition in 1842, Crowther published his journal of the trip. Impressed by the publication, the Church Missionary Society sent Crowther back to England to continue his training in Islington. While there he was ordained a deacon and later a priest.

In response to African requests for missions in Yoruba territory, the Church Missionary Society decided to establish a mission in Abeokuta with Crowther in charge. For several political and strategic reasons, the setup of the Abeokuta mission was delayed while Crowther went to the town of Badagry. There, he began a church, had schools built, established an experimental farm, and started a grinding mill for corn. In 1846 he moved to Abeokuta and

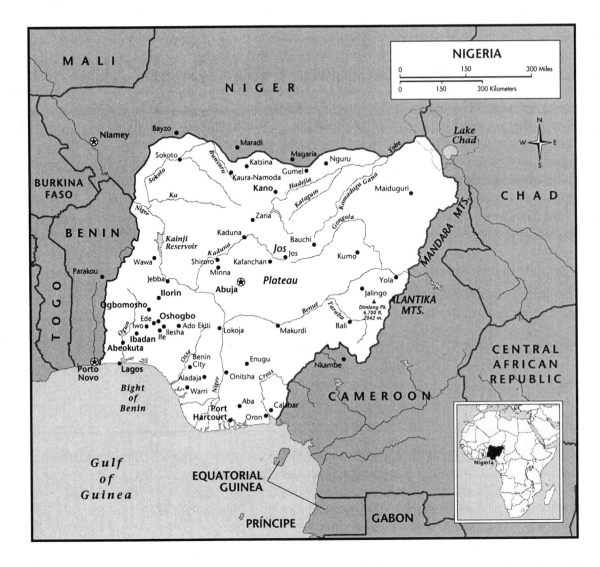

set up another church and more schools. British factories and traders followed. The local inhabitants welcomed the missionaries because they brought schools and commerce to the region.

Reunited with his family

When Crowther arrived in Abeokuta he heard that his mother and sisters were living there. Crowther describes his reunion with his family after 25 years:

> When [my mother] saw me she trembled. She could not believe her own eyes. We grasped one another, looking at one another in

silence and great astonishment, and . . . tears rolled down her emaciated cheeks. She trembled as she held me by the hand and called me by the familiar names which I well remember I used to be called by my grandmother who has since died in slavery. We could not say much, but sat still, casting many an affectionate look towards each other, a look which violence and oppression had long checked, an affection which twenty-five years had not extinguished. She trembled in silence and great astonishment.

Crowther's mother went to live with her newfound extended family. She converted to Christianity 18 months later and took the Christian name Hannah.

More expeditions and expanding trade

Between 1854 and 1857 Crowther accompanied two more expeditions. The 1854 expedition returned from its 900-mile river journey without losing one European to malaria. Quinine had recently been discovered as a preventive against malaria, and it allowed Europeans safer access to the interior. Nonslave trade was expanding in the interior as oil-palm plantations harvested and shipped oil to ports along the river. Manufacturing industries needed palm oil to lubricate their machinery. African middlemen dominated the palm oil trade by keeping African producers away from the Liverpool traders. The intermediaries took the palm oil and some ivory in exchange for cloths, guns, beads, lead, copper rods, and used clothes. By 1864, 21 British firms had set up operations in the Niger Delta.

The new bishop

That same year, against considerable opposition, the secretary of the Church Missionary Society nominated Crowther as bishop of "Western Equatorial Africa beyond the Queen's Dominions." Opposition to the nomination came mostly from Henry Townsend, a fellow missionary who wanted the appointment for himself.

An increase in missionary activity in southern Nigeria between 1850 and 1865 led to a greater need for training in local languages. Crowther had already made a significant contribution to the study of the Yoruba language when he published 1843's *Vocabulary of the Yoruba Language*. By 1851 he had translated the New Testament into Yoruba, and in 1864 he completed his *Grammar and Vocabulary of the Nupe Language*. African missionaries working in southern Nigeria helped promote Western education. As early as 1859 the Yoruba mission published a newspaper in the Yoruba language.

The Niger Mission

After the successful 1854 expedition up the Niger, Crowther founded the Niger Mission—an all-African venture—for the Church Missionary Society. The Niger Mission was in charge of setting up all new missions for the Society. As the expeditions went farther upriver, missionaries became more dependent on business interests for supplies and transport. Local Africans regarded the missions as partners of the traders. In Onitsha, the people attacked the local factory and burned the Niger Mission station. Despite the confrontational situation, the Niger Mission under Bishop Crowther successfully established 11 stations along the Niger by 1880.

As the nature of British trade changed along the Niger, Crowther found himself at odds with British traders who had organized themselves into the United Africa Company (UAC) under Sir George Goldie. The UAC was gradually replacing the African middlemen with their own people, and they wanted to replace the African missionaries with Europeans. Crowther was forced to resign as bishop in 1890. He died on New Year's Eve 1891.

Further Reading

Crowder, Michael. *The Story of Nigeria.* Winchester, MA: Faber, 1978.

Curtin, Philip, ed. *Africa Remembered: Narratives by West Africans from the Era of the Slave Trade.* Madison: University of Wisconsin Press, 1967.

Davidson, Basil. *Africa in History.* New York: Macmillan, 1974.

Harris, Joseph E. *Africans and Their History.* New York: New American Library, 1974.

Usuman dan Fodio

Born December 15, 1754
Gobir (now northwestern Nigeria)
Died April 20, 1817
Sokoto (Nigeria)

Founder of Islamic Sokoto empire

suman dan Fodio founded an early nineteenth-century Islamic empire in west-central Africa. (Islam is the religion of the people called Muslims who worship Allah.) This powerful Fulani-dominated empire lasted nearly 100 years, until British soldiers defeated it with newly invented heavy machine guns in 1903. In major ways Usuman dan Fodio shaped the future Nigeria, Africa's most populous country. The empire ended years of civil war among the Hausa and Fulani people in today's northern Nigeria, replacing corruption and chaos with a stable system of strict Muslim law. Usuman dan Fodio's dependable state triggered a trade boom across the Sahara Desert. Most important, the Islamic ruler brought about a revolution in reading and writing to a vast, illiterate area in Africa's interior.

Accorded the title of *shehu* ("sheik" or "chief"), Usuman dan Fodio was a Muslim mystic. He believed Allah had chosen him to renew the Islamic faith in order to open the way for the coming of the Mahdi, the messiah or savior. From his youth, the shehu studied ancient Islamic instructions about secrets of mysticism. Once he remained silent and prayed for a year. He engaged in religious exercises and recited prayers that he said enabled him to understand the gift of unusual spiritual powers God had given him. The shehu also claimed to have had visions in which he communicated with Muhammad (c. 570-632), Allah's prophet. Muhammad is said to have written down God's revelations to him in the holy Islamic book known as the Koran.

Nigeria

Power over supernatural beings

Usuman dan Fodio was born December 15, 1754, in the village of Maratta in the ancient kingdom of Gobir. His father, Muhammad Fodio, was a teacher and *imam* (Islamic religious leader) in the village. Soon after Usuman dan Fodio's birth, his family moved to the town of Degel, near the present-day city of Sokoto, where he grew up. Muhammad Fodio taught his son to read and write and to recite the Koran. The Degel community believed that Usuman dan Fodio possessed the power to control *djinns*. (In Muslim folklore, djinns are supernatural beings that can assume the shape of animals or human beings and influence human affairs.)

Ancestors of Usuman dan Fodio were nomadic, light-skinned Fulani people who immigrated from today's Senegal in West Africa along the Atlantic Ocean coast. The Fulani began their movement eastward through central Africa around A.D. 500. A cattle-herding people, they generally followed the Niger River. As they migrated they spread the Islamic faith—a practice for which they were often persecuted. By the fifteenth century one of the Fulani clans—the Torokawa—had settled in the fertile Gobir kingdom, just north of today's Sokoto in Nigeria. Usuman dan Fodio's family was a member of that clan.

In Usuman dan Fodio's youth the Hausa, then rulers of powerful city-states in today's northern Nigeria and now Nigeria's largest ethnic group, controlled the Gobir kingdom. They were conquered by the Fulani early in the nineteenth century. The Tuaregs, warrior nomads who never settled and ranged across the

Sahara Desert, had much in common with the Fulani—Islam, cattle, and connections by marriage. The highly mobile Tuaregs often made pilgrimages to the holy city of Mecca (in west-central Saudi Arabia), returning with tales and literature of the Islamic world. Staunch believers in Allah, the Tuaregs claimed a long line of Islamic scholars. One of them—Shaikh Jibril b. Umar—taught Usuman dan Fodio and had a lasting influence on him.

Usuman dan Fodio was of medium height, slender build, and light complexion. A devout and highly intelligent young man, he attracted disciples as a religious leader and wandering Islamic missionary. He showed no interest in wealth, owning just one pair of trousers, one turban, and one gown. He regarded possessions as corrupting. While studying or teaching, he earned his living by making rope. In this simple way, he was following the example of Muhammad. As was common to most Muslims then, Usuman dan Fodio had slaves to attend to his needs—a right defined in Islamic law so long as the slaves were not Muslims.

Opens way for messiah

Orthodox Muslims believe the Mahdi will appear on Earth to rule justly for 1,000 years until the Day of Judgment. Some of the shehu's followers believed he was the Mahdi, but Usuman dan Fodio published writings to the contrary. He said God chose him only as the "renewer of the faith" just before the Mahdi came forth to rule the Earth.

Incidents in Usuman dan Fodio's life seemed to parallel a pattern of events recorded in Muhammad's battles of the seventh century, in which he fought to spread Islam and convert infidels (nonbelievers of Islam) by the sword. Indeed, Usuman dan Fodio apparently believed he was the nineteenth-century successor to Muhammad.

Life parallel to Muhammad

Similarities between the life of Muhammad and that of the shehu became clear in the mid-1790s. At the age of 40 Usuman dan Fodio wrote that he had a religious experience in which he was presented the Sword of Truth with Allah's blessing to use it against the enemies of God. Around age 50 Muhammad became aware of

When I reached thirty-six years of age, God removed the veil from my sight. . . . And I was able to see the near like the far, and hear the far like the near, and smell the scent of him who worshiped God, sweeter than any sweetness; and the stink of the sinner, more foul than any stench. And I could recognize what was lawful to eat by the taste, before I swallowed it; and likewise what was unlawful to eat. I could pick up what was far away with two hands while I was sitting in my place; and I could travel on my two feet (a distance) that a fleet horse could not cover in the space of years. And I knew my body, limb by limb, bone by bone, sinew by sinew, muscle by muscle, hair by hair, each one by its rank, and what was entrusted to it. Then I found written on my fifth rib, on my right side, by the Pen of Power, "Praise be to God, Lord of the Created Worlds" ten times . . . and I marveled greatly at that.

—Usuman dan Fodio's impressions of his first mystical experiences, reprinted in Mervyn Hiskett's The Sword of Truth: The Life and Times of the Shehu Usuman dan Fodio.

a plan to murder him in his hometown of Mecca (in today's Saudi Arabia) because of Islam's growing appeal to the people. The prophet took flight to the nearby Arabian town of Medina. From there, Muhammad launched a holy war to establish Islam. Usuman dan Fodio had similar experiences at about the same age. In the shehu's home kingdom of Gobir, Hausa king Yunfa tried to murder Usuman dan Fodio. The king felt threatened by the large number of Islamic converts the shehu was winning. In 1804 Usuman dan Fodio led a flight of the Muslim faithful to Gudu, a small town on the western border of Gobir.

Usuman dan Fodio's followers chose him to lead a holy war against King Yunfa and other local rulers. A scholar and a philosopher rather than a soldier, Usuman dan Fodio did not take to the field of battle. Rather, he functioned as the brains behind the four-year holy war, directing the military and overseeing their maneuvers. By the end of the war he had established an empire stretching from today's northwestern Nigeria into western Cameroon. His armies, however, did not capture southern Nigeria, where animal disease spread by blood-sucking tsetse flies would have been fatal to the horses his cavalry depended on in battle.

As Muhammad did 1,200 years earlier at Medina, Usuman dan Fodio established a decentralized Islamic state—one in which power was distributed among well-educated Muslim authorities who would govern fairly and effectively. The head of state, according to Islamic law, had to be head of the Muslim community. That made Usuman dan Fodio the first caliph (successor of Muhammad as head of Islam) of Sokoto, a city in present-day northwest Nigeria that he made capital of his empire.

The shehu's holy war in west-central Africa must be viewed against the eighteenth century decline of the vast Islamic Ottoman Empire, ruled by the caliph of Constantinople in today's Turkey. The Ottoman empire had become corrupt, and infighting among ruling families over the Ottoman's leadership weakened the empire militarily. Christians had driven the Islamic Moors out of Spain and Portugal into northern Africa. Ships sailing from Europe under Christian banners circled the globe, sending Islam into retreat.

The time had come for a "renewer of the faith." Usuman dan Fodio saw himself anointed by God for that role; he would usher in the 1,000-year rule by the Mahdi until the end of the world.

Creates rule by Islam

At the end of his holy war in 1808, the victorious shehu divided rule of the empire between his son, Muhammad Bello, and his brother, Abdullah. The two Fulani generals had led the fight in the field against the infidels. Beneath those two, the shehu appointed *emirs* (local leaders) to oversee the day-to-day affairs of the empire. The emirs were obligated to pay a yearly tribute to the Sokoto caliph and to send soldiers to aid the caliph if necessary. Slave raiding continued in border territories as the emirs carried on the religious-based clash in the region, using profits from slaves to pay their tributes to the caliph.

Usuman dan Fodio also created a civil service (administrative service of a government). He instructed officials to rule by Islamic law as it was defined in Medina by Muhammad and the prophet's "companions"—the elite Islamic scholars who counseled Muhammad. The shehu directed that future rulers of the Sokoto empire would govern by divine right, as Usuman dan Fodio did.

An era of learning began in Usuman dan Fodio's empire, driven by radical intellectuals and reformers. Scholars from the Islamic world journeyed to the court at Sokoto. As a noteworthy reform, Usuman dan Fodio insisted on Islamic education for women. The following is a quote from the shehu, reprinted by Michael Crowder in *The Story of Nigeria,* on the senseless repression of women in kingdoms throughout Africa:

> Men treat these beings [women] like household implements which become broken after long use. . . . This is an abominable crime. Alas, how can they shut up their wives, their daughters, and their captives in the darkness of ignorance while daily they impart knowledge to their students?

Literature and laws written in Arabic and local languages, particularly Hausa, emerged and became available to the common people under Usuman dan Fodio's rule. The reformers issued a code of Islamic law written in local languages, enabling the governed to know their rights. And stable government with legally enforced rights stimulated trade over camel routes across the Sahara Desert between the Sokoto empire and the northern African areas of today's Tunisia and Algeria. Northern Africa had commercial ties with Europe and the Far East, thereby connecting Sokoto to world trade. One of Sokoto's main commodities was slaves captured from southern regions of the empire.

To Usuman dan Fodio, it was unacceptable for Muslims to live under uncertain, unwritten laws of African chiefs. The shehu scoffed at African religions based on worship of ancestors whose spirits sometimes returned to Earth. Islam taught that death was the end of life on Earth. The dead either rose to a paradise of unparalleled happiness or dropped into a fiery hell of eternal punishment. The excesses of wealthy, corrupt African kings and chieftains disgusted the shehu, who practiced self-denial all his life. Usuman dan Fodio even studied Islamic law to determine if the ancient African custom of using drums was legal. Africans beat drums for dancing, at weddings, and during a wide variety of ceremonies. He concluded drumming was illegal under Muslim law except for military purposes.

After Usuman dan Fodio's death

Usuman dan Fodio died at the age of 63 on April 20, 1817. He was about the same age as Muhammad had been when he died. The shehu was buried in Sokoto with his wife, Hawwa.

The virtues Usuman dan Fodio fixed for the Sokoto caliphate withered away into corruption over the years. But his system of government remained firmly in place when the British demanded in 1900 that the Sokoto caliph submit to rule by Britain. For two years the caliph refused to answer demands sent by Frederick Lugard, Britain's representative in Nigeria. Finally, in May 1902, Caliph Abdurrahman answered with a letter in Arabic:

> From us to you. I do not consent that any one from you should ever dwell with us. I will never agree with you. I will have nothing ever to do with you. Between us and you there are no dwellings except as between Mussulmans (Muslims) and Unbelievers. . . . There is no power or strength save in God on high.

Lugard interpreted the letter as a declaration of war and used it as an excuse to take Sokoto by force, incorporating the North with the southern regions of Nigeria. The Fulani army resistance proved so strong that the British were forced to deploy Maxim guns—highly effective automatic machine guns—to defeat Sokoto. The British captured Sokoto on March 14, 1906. The Sokoto caliph and thousands of his followers fled and continued to harass British authorities until chased by a British force more than 600 miles to the North. There, British soldiers killed the caliph.

Legacy persists under British rule

The British soon realized that they could not impose a European-type government on the 15 million people accustomed to the Fulani administration in Nigeria. Rather, Lugard established indirect rule whereby the British set overall policy, but it was administered by African authorities. Notes recorded by a Major Burdon, an early British representative in northern Nigeria, showed admiration for the Fulani system:

> Our aim is to rule through the existing chiefs, to raise them in the administrative scale, to enlist them on our side in the work of progress and good government. We cannot do without them. To rule directly would require an army of British magistrates . . . which both the unhealthiness of the country and the present poverty forbid. My hope is that we may make these born rulers a high type of British official, working for the good of their subjects in accordance with the ideals of the British Empire, but carrying on all that is best in the constitution they have evolved for themselves, the one understood by, and therefore best suited to the people.

Lugard informed British officials:

> The Fulani rule has been maintained as an experiment, for I am anxious to prove to these people that we have no hostility to them, and only insist on good government and justice, and I am anxious to utilize, if possible, their wonderful intelligence for they are born rulers.

After Nigeria gained independence from Britain in 1960, the caliph of Sokoto continued to exert significant influence on the country's affairs. Muslim politicians and soldiers from the North ruled Nigeria mostly during the latter part of the twentieth century. But conditions in the country declined to a point that would have provoked Usuman dan Fodio to declare another holy war. Under self-serving dictators who robbed the oil-rich country of hundreds of billions of dollars, Nigeria's once-prized education system collapsed, as did other government services such as health facilities and roads. Nigeria became one of the worst-governed and poorest countries in the world—and the most corrupt.

Further Reading

Blakely, Thomas D., Walter E. A. van Beek, and Dennis L. Thomson. *Religion in Africa*. Provo, UT: David M. Kennedy Center, 1994.

Crowder, Michael. *The Story of Nigeria*. Winchester, MA: Faber, 1978.

Curtin, Philip, and others, eds. *African History: From Earliest Times to Independence*. 2nd ed. New York: Longman, 1995.

Hiskett, Mervyn. *The Sword of Truth: The Life and Times of the Shehu Usuman dan Fodio*. New York/UK: Oxford University Press, 1973.

Ray, Benjamin C. *African Religions: Symbol, Ritual, and Community*. Englewood Cliffs, NJ: Prentice Hall, 1976.

Frederick Willem de Klerk

Born March 18, 1936
Johannesburg, South Africa

*Former president of South Africa and
Nobel Peace Prize winner*

Frederick Willem de Klerk was South Africa's last white president. He is credited with making democracy possible for the first time in South Africa by releasing black activist Nelson Mandela (see entry) from prison in 1990 and working with him for four grueling years to establish a truly representative government. For that achievement, de Klerk shared the 1993 Nobel Peace Prize with Mandela. Whether he foresaw the consequences of his actions, de Klerk is widely credited with following through in difficult times on his pledge to end apartheid and allow the establishment of representative government in South Africa. (Apartheid is an Afrikaans word meaning apartness. In practical terms it meant government-enforced segregation based on race.)

An Afrikaner background

Nothing in de Klerk's background indicated he would be the political leader who would make black majority rule possible in South Africa. To the contrary, he came from a family and political party upbringing that suggested he would do everything possible to prevent black rule and a democratic process.

De Klerk was born March 18, 1936, in the Johannesburg suburb of Mayfair to Jan and Corrie de Klerk. He had a brother, Willem, eight years older. Going back to his great-grandfather, South African Senator Jan van Rooy, de Klerk's Afrikaner ancestors played leading roles in South Africa's politics. (Afrikaners are descendants of Dutch, German, and French immigrants who moved to South Africa beginning in 1652.) The Afrikaner-dominated National party won power in white-only elections in 1948 and immediately began creating the apartheid system to entrench white domination in South Africa.

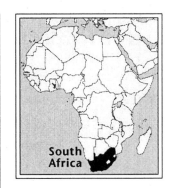

De Klerk's grandfather, Willem, was a national politician and friend of Paul Kruger (see entry), the Afrikaner leader of the South African Republic during the Boer War (1899-1902). The Boer War was fought by the Boers (Afrikaner farmers) and the British for control of the Boer republics of the gold-rich region of the Transvaal and the fertile agricultural lands of the Orange Free State. De Klerk's father, Jan, was a National party leader for 31 years and was one of the designers of apartheid. For 15 years Jan de Klerk served in the cabinets of three hard-line, white supremacist prime ministers. De Klerk's uncle, Johannes Strijdom (1893-1958), was one of those prime ministers. Jan de Klerk also served as president of the South African Senate for seven years.

So when de Klerk arrived in parliament at the age of 36, he brought along with him a family philosophy of white supremacy. Indeed, from the time he was first elected to South Africa's parliament in 1972, de Klerk's actions were those of a white politician dedicated to keeping power in white hands. He differed strongly with his older brother, Willem, an Afrikaans newspaper editor and Afrikaner university professor who began lobbying in the 1960s for more enlightened National party policies.

De Klerk graduated with a law degree in 1958 from Potchefstroom University for Christian Higher Education. (Potchefstroom is near Johannesburg, South Africa's major city.) In religion and politics he followed a rigidly conservative (traditional; opposed to change) path. From 1958 until elected to parliament in 1972, de Klerk practiced law in Klerksdorp, Pretoria, and Vereeniging. In April 1969 he married his college sweetheart, a conservative political activist named Marike Willemse. They have two sons and a daughter. In 1998 de Klerk announced that he would seek a divorce from his wife because he was in love with another woman.

De Klerk won a reputation as a hard-working member of the National party. He was well liked and built up support in the party, particularly in the powerful Transvaal province that included Johannesburg and Pretoria. A close watcher of de Klerk might have been able to detect in 1982 the origins of the important role he would play in South Africa's political transformation. That year, Prime Minister P. W. Botha (1916-) embarked on a program of constitutional change that would give South Africa's Indian and mixed-race populations a separate (but still inferior) role in parliament. Botha's so-called "reforms" did not include the black majority, however.

Emerges as party leader

Transvaal National party leader Andries Treurnicht objected even to Botha's proposed limited changes. Treurnicht split with the National party and formed South Africa's extremist Conservative party. Though Botha never liked him, de Klerk led the Transvaal fight for the prime minister against Treurnicht. De Klerk emerged as the National party's Transvaal leader, a position of power second only to that of Prime Minister Botha.

In 1982 constitutional changes eliminated the position of prime minister and created the more powerful executive office of state president, which Botha filled. An irritable, bad-tempered politician who earned the nickname "Great Crocodile" because of the way he snapped at people, Botha had a stroke in 1989 and resigned as National party leader but retained the presidential post.

Meanwhile, the National party elected de Klerk as its new leader. De Klerk narrowly defeated Botha's candidate, Finance Minister Barend du Plessis. But with Botha as president, de Klerk had no authority to act as anything more than a member of parliament. In 1989, however, Botha's cabinet—led by de Klerk—forced Botha to resign. De Klerk then became South Africa's acting president. After winning a general election, de Klerk was sworn in as full-term president on September 20, 1989. In his inaugural speech he pledged reforms giving full political rights to all South Africans. Henry Kenney noted in *Power, Pride & Prejudice:*

> The former fence-sitter was now taking an outspoken verligte line [meaning "enlightened" in the Afrikaans language]. Whether events pushed him that way, whether it was a matter of intense soul-searching, or whether it was both, F. W. de Klerk had emerged as the Nationalist leader who would finally have to dismantle white supremacy. He was an unlikely choice as a man of destiny, but from unpromising origin he had travelled a long way.

De Klerk said God made him do it. His brother, Willem, described an emotional de Klerk at a gathering of friends and family, quoted here from Allister Sparks's *Tomorrow Is Another Country:*

> In tears he told us we should pray for him—that God was calling him to save all the people of South Africa, that he knew he was going to be rejected by his own people but that he had to walk this road and that we must all help him. He got very emotional, confessing his belief that God had called upon him and that he couldn't ignore the call. I remember, too, that he said, ". . . I don't think I am important in God's eyes, but I believe in God and I believe I am being called upon to perform a specific task at this time in this new situation."

A few months later in February 1990, de Klerk did make a leap of faith to deliver democracy to South Africa. He did it almost singlehandedly, consulting only his cabinet members, then making the final decision himself.

All other achievements by de Klerk will be forever overshadowed by the single event that caught the attention of the world—Mandela's release from prison on February 11, 1990. Mandela was a key figure in the African National Congress's (ANC) campaign of black resistance to white rule in South Africa. (The African National Congress was the leading South African organization opposed to white minority rule.) He had been jailed for more than 27 years for trying to overthrow the white-run government headed by the National party. De Klerk announced plans for Mandela's release and political reforms on February 2, 1990. Journalist Allister Sparks recalled de Klerk's 35-minute speech:

> In that time the new president, short, rotund, balding, . . . head cocked to one side like a sparrow and bobbing on his right foot as he spoke, turned three centuries of his country's history on its head. . . . De Klerk unleashed forces that within four years would sweep away the old South Africa and establish an altogether new and different country in its place.

The big step

It is widely debated whether de Klerk realized the democratic chain reaction he was setting off in 1990 by releasing Mandela and lifting the ban on his African National Congress, the South African Communist Party (SACP), and other political groups. "Don't expect me to negotiate myself out of power," he said shortly after his February 1990 speech. But four years later Mandela would defeat de Klerk for president in South Africa's first democratic election on April 27, 1994. And as a result of the election, the ANC would replace the National party as the majority in government.

In 1990, de Klerk was under strong pressure to end apartheid. International sanctions (multinational agreements to refuse trade with South Africa) had devastated the country's economy. The rising tide of violence by the black majority was almost out of control. And the fall of the Berlin Wall in 1989, signalling the end of socialism in Eastern Europe and, eventually, in the former Soviet Union, removed the threat of a communist-led takeover in South Africa. This allowed de Klerk to embark more easily on reform.

According to Kenney, de Klerk felt that reforms had to be initiated while a white-run government controlled South Africa. This, argued Kenney, would be the only chance for whites to retain their property and play at least a limited political role in the future. As negotiations between the National party and the ANC proceeded, Mandela began to eclipse de Klerk as South Africa's top leader, even though de Klerk remained president for four years.

After Mandela was elected president in 1994, de Klerk led the National party into a government of national unity with the ANC as required under the terms of the transitional constitution. The South African government of national unity had participants in the cabinet from the three major political parties: the ANC, the National party and the Inkatha Freedom Party. But the ANC dominated the new government. De Klerk became Mandela's second vice-president, after first vice-president Thabo Mbeki (1942-). The former president was left with almost no power.

Leaves in disarray

In 1996 South Africa adopted a new constitution. The ANC government composed the document, which called for the elimination of a government of national unity after the next election in 1999. De Klerk led the National party out of the government to become the opposition in parliament. Soon the National party became deeply divided between the conservatives of the past and the young generation. On August 26, 1997, de Klerk resigned as National party leader. Since then he has maintained a low political profile.

Mandela and de Klerk

At the beginning of the negotiations to restructure South Africa's government, Mandela described de Klerk as a "man of integrity" and "a man we could do business with." As the negotiations moved into rougher territory, Mandela often criticized de Klerk. Neither liked the other, but both recognized that, in order to reach an agreement and avoid a civil war between blacks and whites in South Africa, they had to work together.

In his Nobel Peace Prize acceptance speech, Mandela paid tribute to de Klerk: "He had the courage to admit that a terrible wrong had been done to our country and people through the imposition of apartheid," Mandela said. "He had the foresight to understand and accept that all the people of South Africa must, through negotiations and as equal participants in the process, together determine what they want to make of their future." Later Mandela would write in his autobiography: "I was often asked how I could accept the [Nobel] award jointly with Mr. de Klerk after I had criticized him so severely. Although I would not take back my criticisms, I could say that he had made a genuine and indispensable contribution to the peace process."

Further Reading

Adam, H., and K. Moodley. *The Negotiated Revolution.* Jonathan Ball, 1993.

De Klerk, Willem. *The Man in His Time: F. W. De Klerk.* Jonathan Ball, 1991.

Economist, August 30, 1997.

Kenney, Henry. *Power, Pride & Prejudice.* Jonathan Ball, 1991.

Mandela, Nelson. *Long Walk to Freedom.* New York: Abacus, 1995.

O'Meara, Dan. *Forty Lost Years.* Ravan Press, 1996.

Sparks, Allister. *Tomorrow Is Another Country.* Struik, 1994.

Olaudah Equiano (Gustavus Vassa the African)

Born c. 1745
Iboland, West Africa (Nigeria)
Died April 1797
London, England

Freed slave, writer, abolitionist

hen Olaudah Equiano (*ek-wee-AHN-o*) was 10 or 11 years old, kidnappers came into his Ibo village in what is now eastern Nigeria and took him and his sister captive. Sold into slavery in Africa and then shipped to the West Indies on a slave ship, Equiano never returned to his homeland. As a slave he sailed on ships ferrying goods and slaves between the West Indies and North America and Great Britain. On board ship and through the help of kind acquaintances, Equiano learned to read and write. By the time he was 21 years old, in 1766, he had saved enough money through years of shrewd trading to buy his freedom. As a freed slave he worked on sailing ships for several years and traveled throughout the Mediterranean and even to the Arctic. Eventually, he settled in England and became involved in the antislavery movement.

"The shrieks of the women and the groans of the dying rendered the whole a scene of horror almost inconceivable."

—Equiano describing conditions on a slave ship

In 1789 Equiano published a two-volume book, *The Interesting Narrative of the Life of Olaudah Equiano or Gustavus Vassa the Africa.* It is an account of his life, from his childhood in Africa to being a slave and then a free man. His book was famous in its time, running into 17 editions in Great Britain and the United States and translated into Dutch and German. The autobiography provides unique insight into the experiences of an African as a slave and the problems of a freed slave.

Taken captive

Equiano recalls in his narrative how kidnappers stole him and his sister from their family's village when the elders were out working in the fields. He says they traveled about six or seven months before he reached the coast. Some time during the trip, he and his sister were separated from each other. Equiano went from one master to another on the way to the coast; once a master sold him for cowrie shells (small hard white shells from the Indian Ocean used as money by West Africans). Once he arrived at the coast, British slavers bought him for work on the plantations in the West Indies or Caribbean. Equiano says he was put on board by "those white men with horrible looks, red faces and loose hair. . . . I asked them if we were not to be eaten by [them]." The following is his description of the conditions aboard the slave ship:

> The stench of the hold while we were on the coast was so intolerably loathsome that it was dangerous to remain there for any time. . . . The closeness of the place and the heat of the climate, added to the number in the ship, which was so crowded that each had scarcely room to turn himself, almost suffocated us. This produced copious perspirations, so that the air soon became unfit for respiration from a variety of loathsome smells, and brought on a sickness among the slaves, of which many died. . . . This wretched situation was again aggravated by the galling of the chains, now become insupportable, and the filth of the necessary tubs, into which the children often fell and were almost suffocated. The shrieks of the women and the groans of the dying rendered the whole a scene of horror almost inconceivable.

After several months at sea, the ship landed at Bridgetown, Barbados, where the traders sold the surviving slaves to merchants and sugar planters. No one bought Equiano, probably because he was too young to provide much labor. They put him and other unsaleable slaves on board a boat bound for the colony of Virginia. There he worked on a plantation belonging to a Mr. Campbell,

An illustration of slaves being unloaded from a slave ship in the Caribbean in the late eighteenth century.

pulling weeds and collecting stones. Not long after, a lieutenant in the Royal Navy, Michael Henry Pascal, bought him from Campbell for between 30 and 40 pounds sterling. Pascal commanded a merchant ship trading between the colonies and England. He bought Equiano as a present for a friend in England. On board ship Pascal gave him the name Gustavus Vassa. (Why Pascal named Equiano Gustavus Vasa is a mystery. Gustavus Vasa [1496-1560] was one of the greatest Swedish kings. Equiano spelled Vasa with a double *s*.) Luckily for Equiano, a 13-year-old American boy named Richard Baker, only a few years older than he, was on board and the two boys became fast friends. After 13 weeks at sea, the ship landed at Falmouth, England. Equiano remained in England, on the isle of Guernsey, with Richard Baker and a family friend of the captain. In the summer of 1757 Pascal sent for him and for Baker.

Education at sea and in England

In 1754 France and Britain went to war in North America over control of the fur trading posts and land west of the

Appalachian Mountains and over fishing rights off the coast of Canada. The British Royal Navy commissioned Pascal as first lieutenant of the HMS *Roebuck* to fight against France along the Newfoundland coast of Canada. Initially France was successful. But when British General James Wolfe took command of the troops in the New World, the British quickly turned the situation around and conquered all of French Canada. As a slave on board the *Roebuck,* Equiano was present at the siege of Louisbourg in Nova Scotia in 1758.

When they returned to England, Equiano lived with some friends of Pascal's, the two Guerin sisters. They sent him to school, where he had an opportunity to learn to read and write. They also arranged for his baptism in St. Margaret's Church, Westminster, in 1759.

Later that year, Pascal set sail again, this time aboard the *Namur* for the Mediterranean. While the *Namur* was taking on supplies at Gibraltar, the French fleet attacked them. The British eventually repelled them but Pascal suffered some injuries. When he recovered, he was given command of a fire ship called the *Aetna.* Equiano became his steward, a position he says he enjoyed because he had free time to improve on his reading and writing skills.

Cheated of his freedom

Toward the end of 1761 the ship returned to England, to Deptford on the Thames. Although Equiano says he had no specific promise from the captain that he would be given his freedom when they returned to England, he certainly expected it. Instead, the captain forced Equiano onto a barge and later onto a ship sailing for the West Indies. Equiano believed that Pascal had cheated him of his freedom because, he claimed, the law in England held that a baptized man could not be sold. Equiano also accused Pascal of keeping his prize money—his share in the value of the ships captured and their cargoes. Equiano's protests were useless and he soon found himself at sea again, headed for the West Indies.

Under instruction from Pascal, the captain sold Equiano when they got to Montserrat in February 1763 to a Quaker merchant, Robert King. King had a reputation as a kind and charitable man and while working for King, Equiano did a little trading of his own. He would make a small profit by buying an item in the Indies and reselling it for a small profit in North America. Likewise he would purchase something in North America and then sell it in the Indies for a small profit. In this way he earned enough money eventually to buy his freedom from King, who reluctantly agreed to accept 40 pounds sterling and grant Equiano his freedom in 1766.

Equiano soon found, however, that the life of a freed man in the islands was fraught with danger. Blacks had no protection under the law and might easily be kidnapped and taken away on a ship as a slave. To protect himself, Equiano signed on as a sailor for 36 shillings a month on a ship going to England. He learned about sailing on his many voyages between North America and the islands.

Life as a freed slave

Equiano continued as a sailor for several more voyages. Once he had to command the ship himself as the captain and first mate took ill. The captain died on board the ship and Equiano successfully sailed the sloop safely into harbor. He also survived a shipwreck in the Bahamas caused by a self-assured captain who steered an incorrect course.

In 1766 Equiano went to London where he worked for a short time as a hair dresser, a skill he had learned aboard ship. Unable to make ends meet in London, in 1768 he signed up again as a sailor on a ship going to Turkey. He spent several more years sailing in the Mediterranean and made several more trips to the West Indies. In the early 1770s he returned to England and worked for Dr Irving, whose business was purifying salt water into potable or drinkable water. Equiano acted as his assistant, purifying between 26 and 40 gallons a day. When a Captain Phipps asked Equiano to accompany him on an expedition to the Arctic, Irving asked to join Equiano on the trip. Equiano says that in their four-month voyage they explored farther north than any navigation team had done before.

Not long after their return to London, Dr. Irving bought a 150-ton sloop (sailing boat) that he planned to sail to Jamaica to establish a plantation there. In 1775 Equiano accompanied him on this venture. After several months with the doctor along the coast of Nicaragua and Honduras, Equiano left and returned to Jamaica. He planned to go back to England, but in several instances of bad judgement, he put his trust in people who duped, cheated, and enslaved him. Finally, in January 1777, he returned to England.

Joins the antislavery crusade

The final phase of Equiano's life was much more predictable and serene than the years leading up to it. He became involved in the antislavery movement and began work on his autobiography. Because of his activities in the abolitionist movement, the naval authorities in England appointed him Commissary for Provisions and Stores for the Black Poor going to Sierra Leone. In 1787 British abolitionists, humanitarians and church groups had established a community for freed slaves in Sierra Leone, a small British colony on the West Coast of Africa. The Sierra Leone Company started as an experimental colony with 411 freed slaves repatriated from Britain. Its goals were to "introduce civilisation among the natives and to cultivate the soil by means of free labour."

Equiano never made the trip back to Africa. He quarrelled constantly with the agent and wrote a public letter to the newspaper accusing the promoters of the expedition of corruption and deception. In retaliation the agent accused him of insubordination (disobedience to authority) and insolent behavior toward his superiors. The Navy dismissed Equiano from his post and the expedition went ahead, although slightly delayed.

After his dismissal from the expedition, Equiano completed his book. When it was published in 1789 he traveled throughout England promoting it and making speeches against the slave trade. In 1792 , at the age of 47, he married Susan (or Susanna) Cullen. Historians disagree as to whether he had a son or a daughter. It seems fairly certain, however, that he and his wife had a daughter who died while a young child. Equiano died only four months after his daughter, in late April or early May 1797. Although Equiano did not live to see the abolition of slavery, his narrative made the public aware of the horrors of the trade.

Further Reading

Equiano's Travels: His Autobiography: The Interesting Narrative of the Life of Olaudah Equiano or Gustavus Vassa the African Life. Paul Edwards, editor. London: Heinemann, 1967.

Jones, G. I. "Olaudah Equiano of the Niger Ibo," *Africa Remembered: Narratives by West Africans from the Era of the Slave Trade.* Philip D. Curtin, ed. Madison: University of Wisconsin Press, 1977.

Nadine Gordimer

Born November 20, 1923
Springs, South Africa

Writer and Nobel Prize winner

 adine Gordimer is a white South African author of novels, short stories, and plays. She began writing as a young girl growing up in the early years of South Africa's Nationalist government (1948-94)—a government that divided society unjustly with its program of *apartheid,* or racial separateness. Under the race-based laws of apartheid, people's skin color determined almost every aspect of their lives. The Nationalist policy clearly favored whites, giving only limited power to people of mixed race and denying virtually all rights to urban blacks. The Nationalist government was also referred to as the white minority government because whites made up only a fraction of South Africa's population. While white rule existed in South Africa, blacks—the nation's majority—were unempowered socially, politically, and economically. Without access to quality education, most of the black population lingered in the nation's labor class, serving the needs of the white minority.

> *"She has mapped out the social, political and emotional geography of that troubled land [South Africa] with extraordinary passion and precision."*
>
> **—Literary critic Michiko Kakutani,** commenting on Gordimer's work in a *New York Times* review

Selected Works by Nadine Gordimer

- *The Soft Voice of the Serpent and Other Stories* (1952), short stories
- *The Lying Days* (1953), novel
- *Six Feet of the Country* (1956), short stories
- *A World of Strangers* (1958), novel
- *Friday's Footprint and Other Stories* (1960), short stories
- *Not for Publication and Other Stories* (1965), short stories
- *The Late Bourgeois World (1966)*, novella
- *A Guest of Honor* (1970), novel
- *Livingstone's Companions* (1971), short stories
- *The Conservationist* (1974), novel
- *Burger's Daughter* (1979), novel
- *A Soldier's Embrace* (1980), short stories
- *July's People* (1981), novel
- *Something Out There* (1981), short stories
- *A Sport of Nature* (1987), novel
- *The Essential Gesture: Writing, Politics, and Places* (1989), essays
- *My Son's Story* (1990)
- *Jump: And Other Stories* (1991) short stories
- *Why Haven't You Written? Selected Stories* (1993), short stories
- *Crimes of Conscience: Selected Short Stories* (1991), short stories
- *None to Accompany Me* (1994)
- *Occasion for Loving* (1994)
- *House Gun* (1998), novel

Gordimer claims that she began writing to try "to make sense out of the mystery of life." Her fiction mirrors South Africa's social history. The author's characters live in the apartheid environment: they cannot escape it or the impact it has on their daily lives. With unparalleled honesty and a keen, penetrating eye, Gordimer crafts stories that document the political and social changes occurring in

South Africa through the Nationalist period and beyond. "She has mapped out the social, political and emotional geography of that troubled land with extraordinary passion and precision," noted Michiko Kakutani in the *New York Times*. Another critic once stated that "to read her stories is to know Africa." In 1974 Gordimer won the prestigious British Booker Prize for her novel *The Conservationist*. In 1991 the Nobel Committee recognized the body of her work and awarded her the Nobel Prize for literature.

Early Life

The daughter of Jewish immigrants, Gordimer was born on November 20, 1923, in Springs, a mining town near Johannesburg on the eastern portion of the Witwatersrand (or "The Rand," a huge ridge of rock that runs through northeastern South Africa.) Her mother, Nan Myers, was from England, and her father, Isidore, had been born in the northern European country of Lithuania (a part of the United Soviet Socialist Republic, or USSR, from 1940 to 1991). After arriving in South Africa, Isidore Gordimer worked in the nation's rich gold mines. Once he established himself in his adopted country, he became a jeweler.

Describes the world around her

Gordimer began to write when she was only nine. She says she read widely as a young girl, partly to relieve the loneliness of her white middle-class childhood and the isolation of a childhood illness. She went to a Catholic school as a day student, but, as the author told a *Los Angeles Times* interviewer, she was "like a pig in clover" at her local library. Her first published story, "Come Again Tomorrow," appeared in *The Forum,* a South African magazine, when she was just 15 years old.

Gordimer recalls a childhood incident that made her question the very structure of the world around her—a questioning that continued throughout her writing career. In an interview in the *Boston Globe* she described visiting the shops set up for black miners just outside her hometown of Springs:

> My mother and I would go into them to shop sometimes, and I was curious that the shopkeepers treated the miners so rudely. The miners would have to point to what they wanted, and the shopkeepers

would take it down and would grab the money. I was disturbed at the way they were treated, it stuck in my mind. One of the first of my stories came from that experience, "The Defeated." My way of dealing with it was to explore it in writing."

Gordimer gradually came to see her own social world as a great lie, a lie based directly on apartheid. In her interview with the *Boston Globe* she explained the effects the racist system had on a thoughtful young girl:

> You were being taught as a child that it's wrong to tell lies, but the whole society was a lie, the life you were living was a lie. The convent school I went to was for whites only. When I got my pocket money on Saturday, and I went to the movies, only whites could go. Most important, the local public library—I would never have been a writer without it—was open only to white people.

> So wasn't this privilege a big lie? There was this enormous lie and all the little lies that justified it: "Blacks don't really need the things that we need." So the more you grew up in that society, the more you started to question, the more you fell through one layer of lies to the next. And to find the bits of truth that were there, you had to dig into yourself, pass judgment on your parents, on everything that makes your life stable, the very structure of your life.

Life as a writer

At the age of 21 Gordimer studied for one year at the University of Witwatersrand in Johannesburg. There she met other artists and intellectuals. In 1949 she married Gerald Gavronsky. They had one child and divorced in 1952. Two years later she married Reinhold H. Cassiere, owner and director of an art gallery, and they had a son.

During this time, Gordimer set to work as a writer. *Face to Face,* her first collection of short stories, was published the same year as her first marriage in 1949, and her first novel, *The Lying Days,* appeared in 1953. *The Lying Days* tells the story of a white South African girl, Helen Shaw, growing up in a mining town.

A World of Strangers, Gordimer's 1958 novel, describes the Johannesburg world of the mid-1950s as viewed by a young English reporter named Toby Hood. This novel is set during the brief period of time before the South African government clamped down on multiracial political parties and limited social contact between blacks and whites. In post-World War II South Africa (after 1945), the conservative and racist Nationalist party gained

The following quote from Gordimer's *A Soldier's Embrace* (1980) illustrates the gulf that existed between blacks and whites in the old South Africa:

> The farm children play together when they are small; but once the white children go away to school they soon don't play together any more, even in the holidays. Although most of the black children get some sort of schooling, they drop every year farther behind the grade passed by the white children; the childish vocabulary, the child's exploration of the adventurous possibilities of dam, koppies [rocky hills], mealie [corn] lands and veld [pasture]—there comes a time when the white children have surpassed these with the vocabulary of boarding-school and the possibilities of inter-school sports matches and the kind of adventures seen at the cinema. This usefully coincides with the age of twelve or thirteen; so that by the time early adolescence is reached, the black children are making, along with the bodily changes common to all, an easy transition to adult forms of address, beginning to call their old playmates *missus* and *baasie*—little master.

control of the government with a small minority of votes. As its support increased, the Nationalist government pushed through repressive legislation that raised the economic and social position of whites while insuring that blacks remained a source of cheap labor. The one thing that Gordimer never questioned was the absolute evil of racism; she joined the African National Congress (ANC), the foremost group fighting for black rights, and wrote and gave public lectures against apartheid.

The dilemma of the white South African

In the mid-1960s Gordimer expressed the isolation she felt as a white writer in Africa. "When you're born white in South Africa, you're peeling like an onion. You're sloughing off all the conditioning that you've had since you were a child," the author told a *Ms* magazine interviewer. By the 1970s Gordimer had become much more radical than the typical members of South Africa's white liberal community. In her writing, she went beyond racial conflicts, tackling issues of class and class conflict in such works as *Burger's Daughter* (1979), which is set in France and England as well as in South Africa. This and several other novels by

Nadine Gordimer (left) with nationalist Albertina Sisulu giving black power salute to open a writers' conference for an apartheid-free South Africa, 1987.

Gordimer were banned by South Africa's censorship board because of their political and sexual content.

In 1981's *July's People,* the author confronts the question of the future for whites in South Africa. The novel tells the story of a white family that takes refuge from a revolution with the family of July, their servant of 15 years. Other works by Gordimer were published in the 1980s, including a collection of short stories titled *Something Out There* and another novel of South Africa's people, *A Sport of Nature.* With the dawn of democracy in South Africa in 1993 (the nation's first multiparty elections were held the next year), Gordimer penned *None to Accompany Me,* which looks at the new South Africa of majority rule. "Taken chronologically," concluded Kakutani in the *New York Times,* "her work not only reflects her own evolving political consciousness and maturation as an artist . . . but it also charts changes in South Africa's social climate."

Gordimer's fictional account of the history and people of the country continued with her 1998 novel, *The House Gun,* the story of a white couple in post-apartheid South Africa who desperately seek the help of a black attorney to defend their son from murder charges. The novel was purchased by Granada Productions with plans to make it into a feature film.

Gordimer received the Alfred B. Nobel Prize for literature in 1991. Apart from a brief period in the south-central African nation of Zambia in the middle 1960s, she spent most of her life in South Africa, mainly in the Johannesburg area. Although she has traveled extensively throughout Africa, Europe, and North America, often undertaking lecture tours along the way, she continues to live in a suburb of Johannesburg.

Further Reading

Contemporary Authors: New Revision Series. Volume 28. Detroit: Gale, 1990.

Garner, Dwight, "The Salon Interview: Nadine Gordimer," March 1998: www.salonmagazine.com/books/int/1998/03/cov_si_90int.html

Gray, Stephen. *Southern African Literature: An Introduction.* 1979.

Landeg, White, and Tim Couzens, eds. *Literature and Society in South Africa.* 1984.

Los Angeles Times, July 31, 1984; December 7, 1986.

Major Twentieth-Century Writers. Detroit: Gale, 1991.

Mehegan, David, "Nadine Gordimer's Next Chapter," *Boston Globe,* November 29, 1994, p. 69.

Ms., July 1975; September 1987.

New York Times, May 27, 1981; July 9, 1984; January 14, 1986; April 22, 1987; December 28, 1987.

Paris Review, summer 1983.

Parker, Kenneth, ed. *The South African Novel in English.* 1978.

Peck, Richard. "Nadine Gordimer: A Bibliography of Primary and Secondary Sources 1938-1992." In *Research in African Literatures,* March 1, 1995.

Sparks, Allister. *The Mind of South Africa.* North Pomfret, VT: Heinemann, 1990.

Guezo

Born 1797
Kingdom of Dahomey (Benin)
Died 1858
Kingdom of Dahomey (Benin)

King of Dahomey

Guezo's bedroom was paved with the heads of his opponents. Interspersed on the supporting slats of his throne were the polished skulls of his enemies.

During the reign of King Guezo (1818-1858), the kingdom of Dahomey developed into one of the most highly centralized systems of government in sub-Saharan Africa. (To be centralized means that power is concentrated in one place.) Dahomey was also a formidable military state and used its power to grow rich on the slave trade. European traders with access to its capital, Abomey, returned with vivid descriptions of the enormous wealth of the king's court and chilling tales of human sacrifices.

Located along the Atlantic Coast of West Africa, the area once known as Dahomey is now the country of Benin. The creation of the Dahomean kingdom was a direct response to the growth in slave trade in West Africa throughout the sixteenth and seventeenth centuries. Several small African states existed along the coast and inland when Portuguese slavers began taking slaves from the West Coast to plantations in South America and the Caribbean. The

Portuguese maintained their exclusive control on the slave trade until the mid-1600s, when the British, the French, and the Danes entered the trade. By the eighteenth century the slave trade had grown to enormous proportions, with European traders exporting more than 100,000 slaves a year—more than 15 times the amount traded earlier by the Portuguese.

Establishes a powerful state

King Guezo ruled Dahomey for 40 years, from 1818 until his death in 1858. Under his rule the kingdom flourished because of its disciplined military force. In 1863 British explorer Richard Burton described the Dahomean army as "black Spartans" (meaning the warriors were courageous and self-disciplined, as the Spartans of ancient Greece were). The Dahomean state is famous for its use of women in the military. Male and female soldiers raided their weaker neighbors to the north and the west for the purpose of taking captives. Some of these captives served the Dahomean state as slaves; others were sold to European traders as slaves.

The Dahomean state grew strong enough to defy its former overlords—the Oyo from the East—and declare itself independent in 1818. Toward the end of Guezo's long rule he dealt with the consequences of the declining slave trade and substituted other goods for trade with Europe.

Guezo ruled over a territory slightly smaller than the state of West Virginia, approximately 22,000 square miles in size. Like his predecessors, he ruled with absolute power. In the Dahomean kingdom, the king personally appointed and dismissed all his counselors and advisers as well as the administrators of the kingdom's six districts. To watch over the administrators of the districts, the king appointed six women as his official "eyes and ears," another indication of the high regard he held for women.

Ganyehessou, founder of kingdom		Kpingla	1774-1789
Dakodonou	1625-1645	Agonglo	1789-1797
Houegbadja	1645-1685	Guezo	1818-1858
Akuba	1685-1708	Gelele	1858-1889
Agadja	1708-1740	Behanzin	1889-1894
Tegebessou	1740-1774	Agoli-Agbo	1894-1900

Magnificence and barbarity

British commander Frederick Forbes visited King Guezo's court in 1850. In a series of descriptions of the court, he listed all the people who attended the king. He said he counted between 6,000 and 7,000 courtiers, among them:

> 6 Amazons [female warriors], richly dressed, being a part of the harem police
>
> 8 bands playing on elephants' tusk horns
>
> 1019 in single file, with articles on their heads
>
> 1 of the Royal wives in a slouched black hat, crimson robe. . .
>
> [and] 6 ladies of the chamber dressed most magnificently in scarlet-and-gold tunics, slashed with green silk and satin, with slashes and handkerchiefs of silk, satin, and velvet of every colour; coral and bead necklaces, silver ornaments and wristbands.

Commander Forbes also described the king's moral perversion. He noted, as quoted by Nicholas Mosely in *African Switchback:*

> When we arrived at the palace square. at the foot of the ladder leading to the palaver-house [conference room], on each side were three human heads recently decapitated [cut off] with the blood still oozing. . . . In the centre of the courtyard stood a crimson tent or pavilion forty-feet high, ornamented with emblems of human and bullocks' heads, skulls and other devices equally barbarous and disgusting.

The court made human sacrifices at regular intervals in honor of dead kings or as gifts to the people from the kings. When Guezo's grandfather died, 1,300 slaves were sacrificed to accompany him in the next world. The ceremonies were part of the people's traditions, so they did not view them with horror. Guezo's bedroom was paved with the heads of his opponents. Interspersed on the supporting slats of his throne were the polished skulls of his enemies.

The kingdom becomes organized

The rich and lavish kingdom of Dahomey developed as it did in response to the presence of the Europeans and the slave trade. It collapsed because of rivalry between European nations for influence in West Africa. When the slave trade began, the people living along the coast acted as middlemen, taking captives from inland chiefs and trading them to European buyers. The Europeans exchanged manufactured goods, trinkets, and guns for slaves. As the European demand for slaves increased, the coastal traders sent agents deeper and deeper into the African interior. There they came into conflict with the Fon, a loose union of small chiefs who found themselves under pressure from both the coastal people and the Oyo of the East, both of whom were looking for slaves. The Fon paid tribute (or taxes) to the much stronger Yoruba empire of the Oyo, who dominated the area. The Oyo were superior to those around them because they had horses, an enormous advantage for raiding in open country.

To withstand these outside forces, the Fon chiefs organized themselves around military leaders. Sometime around 1650 a new state called Dahomey emerged, primarily for self-defense. Dahomey was based on a strong military force, supplemented by several thousand women. These women held high military rank and took part in slave raiding and fighting. The Europeans called these female fighters Amazons.

Dahomey did not have the gold resources of its neighboring state, the Ashanti, on which to build its empire. Instead, Dahomey built its wealth on slaves. The only way Dahomey could protect itself was to acquire adequate firearms. And the only way it could get the firearms was to trade captives to the coastal people in exchange for arms. With the newly acquired firearms, they captured more slaves.

Controls the trade

Over the years, the middlemen on the coast strengthened their monopoly on the trade with the European buyers and forced the Dahomeans to trade through them. Although they charged high prices for imported goods, the buyers had no alternative but to pay the prices they demanded. In 1727 Dahomean king Agadja (reigned 1708-1740) went to war against the middlemen and put them out of business. He seized their towns and began to trade directly with the European traders. Agadja took control of the coastal markets of Whydah (Ouidah) and Allada.

At first Agadja limited the Europeans to the port area, but gradually they became visitors at Abomey, the capital, located about 80 miles inland. Dahomey exported about 20,000 slaves a year and bought guns and ammunition from England. At the height of the slave trade, the gunsmiths in Birmingham, England, exported about 150,000 muskets a year to the Atlantic Coast of West Africa. Although the British worried about the increasing numbers of guns held by the Africans, they knew that if they did not sell to them, other European powers would.

By 1818 the Dahomean kingdom had become strong enough militarily for Guezo to officially declare it independent of Oyo. The Oyo empire was already collapsing from internal disputes, and Guezo announced that he would no longer pay tribute to them. With the weakened Oyo state, the Dahomean army now turned eastward in its relentless pursuit of slaves. They attacked Abeokuta in present-day Nigeria, the capital of the Egba established after the fall of the Oyo. The Egba of Abeokuta beat back the Dahomeans in all three of their attacks. Despite these setbacks, the Dahomean state continued for another 30 years.

Britain ends trade in slaves

In Britain, the movement to abolish slavery gained momentum in the 1800s. To stop the slaves coming from the Atlantic Coast, the British established a protectorate in 1851 at the port city of Lagos (Nigeria), to the east of Dahomey. British ships patrolled the coast, searched merchant ships for slaves, and effectively ended the trade in slaves from this area of West Africa. Guezo and his successor, Gelele (reigned 1858-1889), found themselves without their major source of income; they could no longer export slaves. In Europe at this time, however, the Industrial Revolution was underway, and factories needed lubricants for their machinery. (The Industrial Revolution was a period of fast-paced economic change that began in Great Britain at the end of the eighteenth century.)

With the end of the slave trade, Guezo was left with a surplus of slaves that he could not export. Recognizing the growing need for oil in European factories, he put the slaves to work on palm tree plantations. Palm oil is a fat pressed from the fruit of palm trees. It is used as a lubricant and in the manufacture of soap. Palm oil soon replaced slaves as the major export from Dahomey. Guezo also introduced cotton plantations in the region and began the manufacture of textiles (cloth).

Guezo's successors are defeated

By 1889, Guezo's successor, Gelele, had ruled for 30 years. He handed the chieftaincy over to his son, Behanzin (reigned 1889-1894), a young and energetic man who set out to restore Dahomey's previous glory by reviving the slave trade. King Behanzin bought arms from the Germans in exchange for slaves, which the Germans then shipped to the Congo (in west-central Africa) and the Cameroons (in West Africa). When Behanzin challenged France's claim to two port cities, Cotonou and Porto Novo, the French retaliated. Britain's hold on the coastal area already worried French traders who feared a British monopoly and thus high tariffs. In 1892 the French landed 2,000 men at Port Novo and invaded the country. They attacked Abomey and forced Behanzin to surrender in 1894. Behanzin went into exile in Martinique, and the French proclaimed his brother, Agoli-Agbo, the king under French rule. The French weakened the kingdom by dividing it into two protectorates (dependent political units). In 1900 they abolished the kingdom and deposed the king.

Further Reading

Davidson, Basil. *Africa in History.* New York: Collier, 1974.

Hallett, Robin. *Africa since 1875.* Ann Arbor: University of Michigan Press, 1974.

Mosely, Nicholas. *African Switchback.* Travel Book Club, 1958.

Oliver, Roland, and Anthony Atmore. *Africa since 1800.* 2nd ed. New York/UK: Cambridge University Press, 1972.

Haile Selassie I

Born July 23, 1892
Harar province, Ethiopia
Died August 27, 1975
Addis Ababa, Ethiopia

Emperor of Ethiopia

"If a strong Government finds it can . . . destroy a weak people, then the hour has struck for that weak people to appeal to the League of Nations to give judgment in all freedom. God and history will remember your judgment."

—Haile Selassie, addressing the League of Nations in 1936

aile Selassie I (*HI-leh seh-LAS-ee*) ruled the northeast African kingdom of Ethiopia for 57 years, 30 of them as emperor. He is best remembered for his attempts to modernize his ancient, feudal country. Selassie's pre-World War II (1939-45) resistance to invading Italian fascists made him an important international moral figure. (Fascists believe in the superiority of their nation and race and are usually ruled by a dictator.) When Italy invaded Ethiopia in 1935, fearful European leaders sought to accommodate Benito Mussolini (1883-1945), Italy's fascist leader, rather than support Selassie.

The Ethiopian emperor abolished slavery, instituted tax reform, promoted education, and created a constitution. He played a dominant role in the formation of the Organization of African Unity (OAU). His coronation as emperor in 1930 gave birth to the Rastafarian religious-cultural movement in Jamaica. Haile

Selassie is considered by Rastafarians to be the spiritual leader of blacks worldwide.

But Selassie's insistence on absolute rule defeated his attempts to cope with a rapidly changing world after World War II. Conflicts generated in the Horn of Africa by the Cold War triggered his doom. (The Cold War—meaning uneasy political relations that fall just short of actual armed combat—is a term used to describe the political and economic struggle between capitalistic, democratic countries on the one hand and the Communist-led Soviet Union and Eastern European countries on the other. Communism is a system of government in which the state controls the means of production and the distribution of goods. It clashes with the American ideal of capitalism, which is based on private ownership and a free market system. The Cold War lasted from the end of World War II until the collapse of communism in Europe in 1989.)

As an ill-fated, aging monarch, possibly suffering from Alzheimer's disease (a progressive illness that deprives a person of memory), Selassie lost touch with political reality. By the end of his reign, Ethiopia was collapsing into famine, poverty, and chaos, soon to be engulfed by communism and war that cost millions of lives.

Ends Solomonic line

The emperor's tragic demise marked the end of Ethiopia's monarchy and the Solomonic dynasty that had ruled, with only a few interruptions, for 3,000 years. The dynasty grew out of Ethiopia's strongest myth—the myth that began with the Queen of Sheba, then Ethiopia's virginal ruler, visiting King Solomon at Jerusalem early in the first century B.C. She is said to have become pregnant by the Israeli king and upon return home gave birth to his son. The son, Menelik I, became Ethiopia's first male ruler and founder of the Solomonic dynasty. Thereafter, Ethiopia's ruler took the title Conquering Lion of Judah, in reference to the Jewish kingdom of the House of David and Solomon's lineage.

Selassie was a short, frail-looking man. When he sat on his throne, he perched his feet on a pillow because they would not reach the floor. He had a light complexion, a chiseled nose, close-cropped hair, and a curly black beard and mustache. Selassie's deceptively slight stature and seemingly unassertive nature may have actually helped him to emerge as a near-mythic emperor of

Ethiopia: following a palace coup in 1916, he was able to convince powerful government ministers that they would be able to dominate him if he were named regent and heir to the nation's throne. In his maneuvering for supreme power, Selassie easily rid himself of competition from provincial governor Dejazmatch Balcha, a warlord who at one time threatened his rise to the throne. From his place of captivity, Balcha observed: "Don't underestimate the power of Tafari [as Selassie was named until he became emperor]. He creeps like a mouse, but he has jaws like a lion."

Early in life Selassie favored Chihuahuas as pets. Later, Great Danes accompanied him around his palaces. Lions roared from cages where he kept them in the center of imperial grounds. The lions symbolized his lineage from Judah.

Complex imperial personality

John H. Spencer, an American graduate of Harvard Law School, served as an adviser to the emperor from 1936 until his disgraceful fall from power in 1974. Spencer described his first-hand observations of Haile Selassie's years in a definitive book on that Ethiopian era:

> As a man, the Emperor was a bundle of contradictions: courageous, cowardly, generous, avaricious, intuitively sensitive to the needs, thoughts and designs of others, suspicious, trusting, loyal, jealous, cynical, romantic and idealistic. He was fundamentally an intensely self-centered person for whom the lives of others counted for little beside his own.

In domestic and foreign affairs, Selassie believed in playing both sides against the middle. Often operating like a local politician, he had a remarkable memory for favors he had given and for enemy actions taken against him—some intended to overthrow his regime and end his life. This emperor of such a complicated and calculating personality came from powerful political and military ancestors. They had exercised power in four important Ethiopian provinces and the nation as a whole. His forebears had one thing in common: they were fascinated with foreigners and modern technology at times when isolated Ethiopians were lucky to own a mule and live within a day's walk of a road. Haile Selassie inherited that important family curiosity.

The emperor's great-grandfather, Sahle Selassie (1795-1847), gained control over Shoa (the fertile central highlands province in which the capital Addis Ababa is located) and declared Shoa an independent kingdom in 1830. Sahle Selassie crowned himself Shoa's king. He had ambitions to reconquer the ancient Ethiopian empire that once stretched from southern Arabia across the Red Sea to the Horn of Africa.

Family intrigued by foreigners

Haile Selassie's father was Makonnen Walda Mikael (1852-1908). Makonnen served as a leading frontline general and influential European diplomat in the court of Menelik II (1845-1913; see entry), founder of modern Ethiopia. Makonnen and Menelik II were cousins, both grandsons of the ambitious Shoa king Sahle Selassie.

The emperor's mother was Wayzaro Yeshimbet, the daughter of a provincial chief. She bore 10 children by her husband, Makonnen. The first nine died shortly after birth. The tenth was born July 23, 1892, in Harar, a hostile province in eastern Ethiopia that was being ruled by Makonnen. The boy survived and was named Tafari Makonnen. He lived to become emperor (under the name Haile Selassie) from 1930 to 1974.

Makonnen, away from home fighting battles and representing Menelik II in Italy and England, wanted to educate his son to exercise power in the modern world. Young Tafari was schooled in European thought and ideas by a French missionary priest. Tafari also learned Amharic, the language of the imperial court in Addis Ababa; French, then the language of diplomats; and the tenets of the Coptic church, Ethiopia's official religion. He was ordained a bishop at the age of eight.

When Tafari was 13, his father appointed him *dejazmatch,* the second rank after *ras* ("prince"), and made him governor of a region in Harar. Diplomats and other foreign officials often stopped in Harar to pay calls on Makonnen and his son. Some diplomats thought Emperor Menelik II would designate Makonnen as his successor. But Makonnen died in 1907, while Menelik II was still alive. Tafari was summoned to Addis Ababa for further education in a modern school and in Menelik II's imperial court.

On July 31, 1913, Tafari married Wayzaro Manan Asfaw, the daughter of an aristocratic family from the northern Wallo province. They had three sons and daughters. Menelik II died that

December. His grandson, Lej Iyasu (1896-1935), succeeded him to the throne. A playboy who paid little attention to palace duties, Iyasu leaned away from the Ethiopian Christian church toward Islam (the religious faith of Muslims). He also sided with Germany against England and France in World War I (1914-18). On September 27, 1916, conservative (those who favor tradition over change) ministers and Coptic church officials deposed the young ruler, then only 20 years old. Five months later the ministers put Menelik II's daughter, Zawditu (1876-1930), on the throne as empress. They also promoted Tafari to the title of ras and designated him prince regent and heir-apparent.

Looks are deceiving

In the Ethiopian tradition that the strongest in battle shall rule, Tafari's supporters killed off or jailed Iyasu and his followers when they attempted to take the throne back by force. Ras Tafari became Ethiopia's ruler, though opponents continued to contest for power. He crowned himself king October 7, 1928. Victory in a final battle against Menelik II's relatives on March 31, 1930, made Tafari the country's uncontested ruler. Empress Zawditu died two days later. Tafari ascended to the throne November 2, 1930, as Emperor Haile Selassie I.

He ruled the only African country to have escaped colonization by Europeans. Because of that, Jamaicans of African descent established a movement that proclaimed Selassie as the messiah, or savior. They named their movement Rastafarianism, after his title of Ras Tafari. The movement now has several hundred thousand members throughout the world. It was given a boost in the 1960s when Bob Marley and the Wailers emerged from the poor quarters of Kingston, Jamaica, to make reggae music popular by drawing on American "soul" and the highly political tenets of Rastafarianism.

Within five years of his coronation, Selassie found his country under attack by a modern Italian army. Mussolini, Italy's insecure fascist leader, wanted to expand his country's colonies so he could preside over an entire empire. Mussolini also sought to impress Germany's Nazi leader, Adolf Hitler (1889-1945), whose aggressive movements were turning Europe upside down.

The only country nearby that was unoccupied by Europeans was Ethiopia. Italy already controlled part of Somaliland, adjoin-

ing Ethiopia on the southeast, and Eritrea, a coastal region on Ethiopia's north. Creating a boundary dispute as an excuse to invade Ethiopia, Mussolini ordered his well-armed troops to move against Selassie's poorly equipped forces in 1935. France and England, the two other major powers with influence in the Red Sea arena, had imposed an arms boycott against Italy and Ethiopia. That deprived Ethiopia of imported arms. But Italy's booming arms industry supplied its own army with the latest weapons.

Haile Selassie and attendants on the balcony of the palace in Addis Ababa.

League of Nations refuses Ethiopian pleas

Selassie appealed to the League of Nations (the forerunner to the United Nations established after World War I) for help to stop the Italian invaders. England and France had disarmed after World War I. They were unprepared militarily when Hitler began rearming Germany and Mussolini began increasing the power of the Italian army. As a result, England and France adopted policies of appeasement, hoping to avoid another world war by yielding to

Hitler's demands. When Mussolini's army invaded Ethiopia, England and France refused to back up the League of Nations' covenant (agreement). They hoped that by not opposing the attack they could prevent Mussolini from joining an alliance with Hitler. England and France also hoped to keep Mussolini from sending arms and troops to Spain to aid Francisco Franco's fascists against the Spanish army.

By the end of March 1936, the Italians advanced on Addis Ababa. Without giving notice to the country, Selassie, his family, and court fled the capital on the night of April 2, 1936, taking a train through the eastern part of Ethiopia to the port of Djibouti, a French colony on the Red Sea. Many Ethiopians accused Selassie of cowardice, criticizing him for sneaking away in the night rather than staying to fight to the death.

Selassie's choices were to stay and die, or go to the League of Nations' forum in Geneva to try to rouse the world's conscience, hopefully prompting action against the Italians. He chose to live to fight another day. Summoning all his majesty of presence as he rose to speak in Geneva on June 30, 1936, the frail African emperor told representatives of the nations of the world that they were facing a question of the League's survival:

> It is not merely a question of a settlement in the matter of Italian aggression; it is a question of collective security; of the very existence of the League; of the trust placed by States in international treaties; of the value of promises made to small states that their integrity and their independence shall be respected and assured. It is the choice between the principle of the equality of States and the imposition upon small Powers of the bonds of vassalage. If a strong Government finds it can, with impunity, destroy a weak people, then the hour has struck for that weak people to appeal to the League of Nations to give judgment in all freedom. God and history will remember your judgment.

History remembers England and France ignored Selassie's appeal. Italy occupied Ethiopia with hardly a protest. Mussolini promptly sent large shipments of arms and soldiers to Spain. He entered into a pact with Hitler to dominate the world even if it meant another world war.

Emperor returns a hero

Selassie went into exile in England. After Italy entered World War II (1939-45) on Hitler's side in 1940, the British sent forces—

mainly South African troops entering from Kenya—into Ethiopia to oust the Italians. Selassie returned triumphantly to Addis Ababa on May 5, 1941, a popular leader at home and a moral hero abroad. Ethiopia had been the first victim of World War II, but it was also the first country to be freed from the fascist grasp.

After World War II Selassie embarked on further modernization, putting special emphasis on education. He established a university in Addis Ababa. Ethiopia financed scholarships to the university for students from other African countries. In cooperation with U.S. TransWorld Airline (TWA), Ethiopia founded the first African airline. It remains one of the finest in the world.

Even as Ethiopia gleamed as the star of Africa, a dark cloud descended on Selassie. Trouble brewed in Eritrea to the north and the Ogaden to the southeast. Eritrea wanted independence from Ethiopia; Somalia demanded control of the Ogaden as part of Greater Somaliland. Eritrea's two ports, Assab and Massawa, provided Ethiopia its only outlets to the sea. And Ogaden was viewed as part of Ethiopia's historical empire. To give up either Eritrea or the Ogaden would have been highly unpopular in Ethiopia.

At the same time, Selassie was changing—acting almost like a different person. Upon his heroic return after Ethiopia's liberation from Italy, he became increasingly arrogant and self-important. Prior to the Italian-Ethiopian war and Selassie's exile, the emperor would ride around Addis Ababa on horseback, dropping in unannounced on foreigners for coffee. He often toured the capital without notice. After he returned from England, however, motorcycle outriders and armed soldiers escorted his entourage. Other motorists were required to stop their cars and stand by the roadside until the emperor passed. Selassie forced ministers and other officials to lay flat on the floor, face down, when he received them at the palace. And, as the emperor's long-standing leading officials became elderly and ineffective, corruption took its toll on the government.

Colonial boundaries prevail

Selassie turned to the countries of the developing world, hoping they would help him withstand the demands put on him by Eritrea and Somalia. New Pan-Africanist leaders, including Ghana's Kwame Nkrumah (1909-1972; see entry) and Egypt's

Gamal Nasser (1918-1970), opposed keeping the boundaries decided on by the colonial (European) powers when they carved up Africa in 1885. (Pan-Africanists stressed African unity in dealing with common problems and concerns.) Selassie, however, wanted to keep these colonial borders because they gave him legal authority for keeping Eritrea and the Ogaden. (Eritrea had been a colony of Italy for 57 years. The Italians occupied Eritrea in 1884 and remained in control until defeat in World War II cost the nation its colonies.) After World War II the United Nations (a multinational peacekeeping organization) ordered Eritrea into union with Ethiopia, giving Eritrea substantial self-rule.

At a 1963 conference of African leaders in Addis Ababa, the Organization of African Unity (OAU) established itself with headquarters in Ethiopia's capital. Selassie pushed through a central OAU principle: African countries would keep borders as they were drawn by European colonists. Eritreans, whose national slogan is "Never Kneel Down," began armed resistance. They drew support from Islamic countries from North Africa, Arabia, the former Soviet Union, and China. As Selassie's corrupt government grew more intolerant of Eritrea's self-rule, support for the independence movement swelled. The war in Eritrea drained Ethiopia's treasury.

In addition, a border conflict with Somalia erupted in 1964. The Soviet Union, seeing an opportunity to dominate the Horn of Africa and control access from the Indian Ocean to the Red Sea, began pumping millions of dollars into Somalia. Said Barre (1919-1995), Somalia's dictator, attacked in the Ogaden with modern weapons supplied by the Soviet Union. Haile Selassie tried to negotiate a settlement to the wars squeezing his country, but he failed.

Nation collapses around him

In 1972 and 1974 famines struck in rural Ethiopian regions. Haile Selassie's inept government tried to conceal the disasters from the rest of the world. Tens of thousands starved. The nation's economy was in ruins. The aging emperor could not remember his top ministers when they came to see him. (On one occasion at a state dinner in honor of Zaire's President Mobutu Sese Seko [1930-1997], the emperor asked an aide the name of the guest sitting opposite him.) At times, Selassie could not even speak.

Mengistu Haile Mariam

When Mengistu Haile Mariam (1937-) became president in May 1987, he ended more than 3,000 years of rule by emperors. Mengistu anointed himself president after murdering the last emperor, Haile Selassie I and killing tens of thousands of Ethiopians. He established Ethiopia as a satellite state of the Soviet Union, dependent on Communist countries for arms, economic assistance, and troops. Mengistu fought wars against Eritrea, Somalia, and his own people in the northern province of Tigre.

Mengistu was a leader among a group of military officers who overthrew the senile Selassie in September 1974. General Aman Andom, Ethiopia's minister of defense, emerged as prime minister and head of state. He and Mengistu disagreed on a number of issues and Mengistu ordered the general shot in his villa. Mengistu became known as the Black Stalin, after Soviet political leader Joseph Stalin (1879-1953), a leader of the Russian Revolution of 1917 and later dictator of the Union of Soviet Socialist Republics (U.S.S.R.), who was known for harsh repression and the brutal murders of enemies and allies alike.

Mengistu took command of the Derg, his legislative body, then went on a killing spree. On November 23, 1974, Mengistu ordered floodlights and machine guns set up inside Akaki Prison in Addis Ababa. The prison held officials and generals who served Selassie. Mengistu also ordered movie cameras to record the scene. The cameras rolled as the firing squad opened up with the machine guns. The number executed is in dispute. The Derg announced 59. Others say the number may have been as high as 82.

Mengistu's dictatorship ended with him fleeing for his life as Tigrean soldiers, backed up by Eritreans, marched into Addis Ababa in May 1991 behind Soviet tanks they had captured from Mengistu's army. The new government charged him with mass murder. The Zimbabwe government granted him asylum and he lives there in a guarded compound with his family.

In *Ethiopia at Bay,* Spencer recalls his last meeting in 1974 with the emperor after 38 years of service: "I withdrew with the piercing realization that the curtain of senility had dropped. I had the sensation, still vivid today, that in leaving the private office, I was leaving the cockpit of a 747 after finding both the captain and co-pilot unconscious. How was the craft to keep flying?"

His authority gone, Selassie suffered the fate dealt by Ethiopian tradition. Street mobs demanded he be hanged. A small group of military officers who had taken control of the country by force humiliated the emperor's daughters and granddaughters by imprisoning them in dungeons and shaving their heads. The emperor was accustomed to access to four Rolls Royces, a Cadillac, and 23 Mercedes Benz automobiles. On September 12, 1974, sergeants arrested the emperor at the palace. They took him away in a Volkswagen to prison, where he remained until about August 27, 1975. At that time he disappeared mysteriously.

As it later developed, the emperor had been murdered by the communist regime that succeeded Selassie, headed by mass killer Colonel Haile Mariam Mengistu. Five months after Mengistu's overthrow by another military uprising in May 1991, Emperor Haile Selassie's body was discovered buried 10 feet beneath Mengistu's desk in his office on the Grand Palace grounds.

Ironically, Eritrea declared itself an independent nation in 1993—the first break in the OAU's rule for maintaining colonial boundaries. Somalians and Ethiopians continued to fight over the Ogaden a generation after Haile Selassie's death.

Further Reading

Contemporary Black Biography. Volume 7. Detroit: Gale, 1994.

Dictionary of African Biography. Algonac, MI: Reference Publications, 1977.

Gunther, John. *Inside Africa.* North Pomfret, VT: Hamish Hamilton, 1955.

Mosley, Leonard. *Haile Selassie I: The Conquering Lion.* Englewood Cliffs, NJ: Prentice Hall, 1965.

Spencer, John H. *Ethiopia at Bay: A Personal Account of the Haile Selassie Years.* Algonac, MI: Reference Publications, 1984.

Bessie Head

Born July 6, 1937
Pietermaritzburg, Natal Province, South Africa
Died April 17, 1986
Serowe, Botswana

Exiled South African writer

essie Head was a complex woman whose novels and short stories reflected her traumatic childhood and her life in exile. The circumstances of her birth deprived her of a sense of belonging to a family, and the race-based apartheid laws of South Africa in the 1950s and 1960s alienated her from her own country. Apartheid is an Afrikaans word meaning apartness. In practical terms it meant government-enforced segregation based on race. Despite the hardships in her life and a harsh struggle to maintain mental stability, Head wrote six novels and more than 50 articles and chapters in books. Her works are particularly interesting because they describe the world she came to know—rural African communities and the tensions that filled them. She focused primarily on the role of authority in the community and how individuals responded to it. Head received international attention for her work and was nominated for the prestigious Booker Prize.

"Nothing seems to wash away the horror of this racial business."

—**Bessie Head**, commenting on the discrimination she and her son encountered as Africans of mixed racial heritage

A difficult beginning

Head was born in a mental hospital to a white institutionalized patient and an unknown black father. Her mother, who went by the nickname Toby, had lost her first-born son in an accident for which her husband blamed her. They were divorced 10 years after the tragic incident, and Toby's mental state deteriorated to such an extent that she had to be committed to a hospital in 1933. The authorities released her in 1936, but she was readmitted two months before Bessie was born in July 1937. At the time of Head's birth, extramarital sexual intercourse between white and black people was a punishable offense in South Africa. Head's mother's family put the newborn up for adoption, feeling disgraced and overwhelmed at the prospect of caring for their mixed-race grandchild. At first taken in by a white family, the baby was returned shortly thereafter because, the family's lawyer said, she was "coloured, in fact quite black and native in appearance."

After the white family gave Head back to authorities, George Heathcote, who served on the Child Welfare Committee in Pietermaritzburg, took her home to raise her as his own child. He and his wife Nellie were of mixed race—which was called "coloured" at the time in South Africa. They raised Head from infancy to her teen years, allowing her to believe she was their natural child. (Head would not learn the true circumstances of her birth for some time.) The Heathcotes lived in the poorest section of the city. Bessie's grandmother, Alice, continued to help the Heathcotes raise the child until Toby's death in 1943. George Heathcote died that same year, and the family fell into hard financial times.

Head adored Nellie Heathcote; she was the only mother the young girl had ever really known. A good student and a hard worker, Head later described herself in those years as "scrubbing an eternally dirty house . . . selling bones and bottles for a shilling for meat, and scouring fields around the house for spinach." Head, who loved to read, recalled that her mother was so poor she could afford to buy her only one book, *The Adventures of Fuzzy Wuzzy Bear.*

Head was fortunate enough to get a good elementary education at St. Monica's, an Anglican mission boarding school for coloured (mixed race) girls. Despite the rigid discipline, Head was happy at school because she had access to books and a wide array of friends. But in 1951, a year after she started at St. Monica's, the social welfare authorities decided to remove her from the care of Nellie Heathcote and place her in the custody of the school. During the court procedures Head learned of her family background, having believed until this time that Nellie Heathcote was her natural mother. According to Gillian Stead Eilersen in *Bessie Head: Thunder Behind Her Ears,* it was a very painful time for Head. She later commented:

> The lady [Louie Farmer who headed the school] seemed completely unaware of the appalling cruelty of her words. But for years and years after that I harboured a terrible and blind hatred for missionaries and the Christianity which they represented, and once I left the mission I never set foot in a Christian church again.

Life for Head improved when the new warden, Miss Margaret Cadmore, replaced Farmer as the headmistress. Cadmore was an unconventional woman known for her keen common sense and down-to-earth ways. (Head later named one of her fictional characters after Cadmore.) In 1956 Head graduated from St. Monica's and was out on her own. Nellie Heathcote had moved to a "coloured village" after South African authorities declared the area in which she lived an Indian-businesses-only section. (Indians ranked higher than blacks on the apartheid racial scale.)

Out on her own

Head soon landed a job teaching at the Clairwood Coloured School for girls. She could not use the library in the area because it was reserved for whites, so she found a library that had been established by an Indian merchant. There she learned about Hinduism, an Indian religious tradition that emphasizes the "right way" of living. The Hindu philosophy provided Head with a source of comfort for the rest of her life.

After a brief stint at Clairwood, Head went to Cape Town, South Africa, in 1958 and managed to get a job as a journalist on a black newspaper, the *Golden City Post,* writing an advice column for teenagers. Head moved around a lot during these years and got involved with African politics, especially the Pan-African Congress (PAC). Because of her association with PAC, she became embroiled with the South African authorities and was jailed. Shortly after being released from prison Head tried to commit suicide. The suicide attempt cost her the job on the *City Post.*

Head continued her involvement in politics, but the South African government outlawed both PAC and the African National

The writings of Bessie Head

- *When Rain Clouds Gather* (1969), novel
- *Maru* (1971), novel
- *A Question of Power* (1973), novel
- *The Collector of Treasures and Other Botswana Village Tales* (1977), short stories
- *Serowe: Village of the Rain Wind* (1981), historical chronicle
- *A Bewitched Crossroad: An African Saga* (1984), historical chronicle

Congress (ANC; an organization committed to the advancement of the black South African majority). She joined the Liberal party and met her future husband, Harold Head, a political activist and journalist. In 1961 they married and moved to District 6, an area reserved for "coloureds" in Cape Town. In 1962 their son, Howard, was born.

These were turbulent years in South Africa and in the Head family. Under the terms of the Group Areas Act of the mid-1960s, District 6 became a whites-only area. (The Group Areas Act designated where people were allowed to live, based on their color.) All the buildings in the district were torn down, leaving only mosques standing amid the rubble. The Heads were forced to leave, finally finding housing in the Muslim district of Cape Town. Head did not get along well with her neighbors and soon left Harold to live with his parents. She and her in-laws quarreled, and Head eventually left everyone behind but her two-year-old son, Howard. Together, they headed north.

Even though South African authorities denied Head a passport, she left the country, crossing the border to present-day Botswana illegally. In Botswana, she and her son were stateless. They had no legal standing and no travel documents.

From the late 1800s until 1966 Botswana (Bechuanaland) was considered a British protectorate—a political unit dependent on Britain. Consequently, it never developed the strict racial structure of its South African neighbor. Head and her son settled in the small remote community of Serowe. She worked for a short time as a teacher in a local school but left within a few months because of conflicts with the principal. She also unintentionally alienated the

Bamagwato community because she violated their ways and was insensitive to their values. The Department of Education eventually blacklisted her from teaching in Botswana because of her behavior. They even ordered her to take a sanity test. When she refused, authorities declared she could not teach again.

Rumbles of thunder

With no income, Head and her son lived in poverty. Sometimes they would not have enough money to eat more than once during the week. She began to concentrate on her writing, describing the life around her in the small Botswana village. In the mid-1960s she wrote short pieces such as "The Green Tree," "Summer Sun," and "The Woman from America." Then in 1966 she had an opportunity to work and live on an experimental farm project called Radisele. While she was there, she began having visions and showing disturbing signs of mental illness. Head had become paranoid, suspecting everybody on the farm of being against her. The project organizers received so many complaints about her behavior that they told her to leave. Believing she was not wanted in Serowe, she eventually moved to the much larger community of Francistown.

With Botswana achieving independence in 1966, Head registered with the United Nations (UN) High Commission on Refugees. Unable to find her another place of refuge, they gave her 40 rands a month on which to live (about the equivalent then of $40 a month). Nevertheless, she struggled and continued with her writing. In 1967 she completed a novel, *When Rain Clouds Gather,* which focuses on the impact of tribalism on the community and on women in particular.

In January 1968 Head's son Howard started school in Francistown. Although he had grown up speaking English and the Tswana language, the children at school regarded him as an outsider and treated him horribly, attacking him both psychologically and physically. Head was devastated by the abuse her son was forced to endure: "Perhaps I did not realise how much . . . a mixed breed . . . is really deeply hated by African people." She later admitted, as quoted by Eilersen, that "everything went wrong from that time Howard was assaulted. I never seemed to recover and the nightmare was so persistent and inward-turning in my own mind that nothing seems to wash away the horror of this racial business."

Storm clouds

Bessie Head's 1971 novel *Maru* begins this way:

The rains were so late that year. But throughout that hot, dry summer those black storm clouds clung in thick folds of brooding darkness along the low horizon. There seemed to be a secret in their activity, because each evening they broke the long sullen silence of the day, and sent soft rumbles of thunder and flickering slicks of lightning across the empty sky. They were not promising rain. They were prisoners, pushed back, in trapped coils of boiling cloud.

Ups and downs

For the rest of the school year Head tried to teach Howard herself, but she found this exhausting because she was also trying to write at night. At the beginning of the next school year, in January 1969, Head moved back to Serowe, where Howard entered a local school. In March, *Rain Clouds* was published and received good reviews. With the thousand British pounds she received for the book, she bought a small house on property belonging to the Swaneng Hill School Project. She worked for a short time with a gardening group but her mental health was not good, and she began to show signs of delusions. She claimed to have had a series of visions in which she believed she was Mary Queen of Scots and a monk. Shortly after Christmas of 1970 she was hospitalized.

When Head returned to Serowe in June 1971, the community people were more sympathetic toward her and tolerated her eccentricities. She began work on another novel—this one shorter and more powerful than her first—called *Maru*. The book focuses on racial discrimination and is based on her early experience in Serowe:

> [I know] about the triumphant cohesiveness [of African people] from having loved an African man. You can nearly get killed. The story travels from place to place along the unseen grape-vine and you are tightly surrounded by a net-work of spies. Your every move and word is closely watched and reported. People are deadly faithful to their own, not to you, the outsiders.

Head completed work on a third novel, *A Question of Power,* in April 1972, but it was not published for more than a year. The first part of the book is autobiographical. It describes a South African woman living alone in Botswana and suffering a nervous breakdown. A *New Republic* reviewer said it enlarged "the geographical as well as the symbolic regions of madness." This book received more critical acclaim than any of her other writings.

Before the book was published, Head was again in financial trouble. She appealed to the UN Commission on Refugees to arrange for resettlement in another country. A friend offered her a chance to immigrate to Norway, but as she began to think seriously about leaving Africa and her community at Serowe, she decided that she did indeed belong there.

Chooses to stay

Once Head made the decision to stay in Botswana, she took a closer look around her and wrote a book called *Serowe: Village of the Rain Wind.* It took several years for *Serowe* to be published because Head clashed with her literary agent. She entered another difficult time in her complicated life, cutting ties to her friends and supporters.

As her literary reputation grew, Head was invited to attend a series of workshops for writers. For the first time in years (and with the help of the U.S. State Department) she left Botswana to attend a workshop at the University of Iowa in 1977. In February 1979 the Botswana government gave her citizenship and a passport. After all those years of struggle, hardship, and deprivation, Head began to travel. She went to Berlin for a writers' workshop in 1979 and to Nigeria three years later; she also traveled to Australia. In addition, Head began giving interviews to journalists and academics writing articles about her and her work.

In the 1980s a publishing house gave her money in advance to write an autobiography that focused largely on her childhood years. The publisher gave her a deadline of September 1986, but by March she had not even started the book. The pressure prompted Head to begin drinking excessively. In April she was hospitalized with hepatitis. She died on April 17, 1986, and was buried at the Botolatoe Cemetery near Serowe. Head was only 48 years old at the time of her death.

Further Reading

Contemporary Literary Criticism. Volume 25. Detroit: Gale, 1983.

Eilersen, Gillian Stead. *Bessie Head: Thunder Behind Her Ears.* North Pomfret, VT: Heinemann, 1996.

Ms., January 1987.

New Republic, April 27, 1974.

Nichols, Lee, ed. *Conversations with African Writers.* Washington, DC: Voice of America, 1981.

World Literature Written in English, Volume 17, number 1, 1978; Volume 17, number 2, 1978; Volume 18, number 1, 1979.

Félix Houphouët-Boigny

Born October 18, 1905
Yamoussoukro, Côte d'Ivoire
Died December 7, 1993
Yamoussoukro, Côte d'Ivoire

President of Côte d'Ivoire

élix Houphouët-Boigny (*hoo-foo-AY BWAH-nyee*) was the key figure in Côte d'Ivoire (Ivory Coast) politics for nearly 33 years. A wealthy plantation owner and former Cabinet minister in the French National Assembly, he became president in 1960, when he was 55 years old. Houphouët-Boigny was in many ways a dictator of his West African country, but he did not resort to brutality and physical repression to achieve his goals. Instead, he created a political system where all decision-making powers were in his hands. George B. Ayittey, author of *Africa Betrayed,* quoted him as having said that in the Ivory Coast "there is no number two, three or four. . . . There is only a number one: that's me and I do not share my decisions."

Referred to as "Le Vieux" ("the old man"), he was more of a father figure to his people than a symbol of opression. Unusual for

"There is no number two, three or four. . . . There is only a number one: that's me and I do not share my decisions."

—Houphouët-Boigny, commenting on his method of running the Ivory Coast

The Basilica of Our Lady of Peace

In 1986 Houphouët-Boigny decided to build the tallest Christian church in the world. Three years later, with the use of state funds and without any effective political opposition, he completed construction of a $280 million basilica at Yamoussoukro. He even convinced Pope John Paul II to visit the Ivory Coast to bless the church. Made of gold, ivory, marble, and glass, the building is situated in the middle of a cacao plantation. At his death, Houphouët-Boigny was buried in this lavish building.

most leaders of African countries after World War II (1939-45), Houphouët-Boigny maintained friendly relations with France, the former colonial power in Côte d'Ivoire. (Colonialism is the extension of a nation's power beyond its own borders, usually for economic gain.) In addition, he followed a capitalist, private enterprise-oriented economic program. (In a capitalist system, business and property are owned and controlled by individuals, not by the government.) In the early years the nation's economy was called the Ivorian "miracle."

The French in Africa

France began to exert influence over the native rulers of the Ivory Coast in the early 1800s. In 1893 the region officially became a French colony. By 1914 France claimed control over the largest land mass in Africa, but it ruled over less than half as many people as Great Britain. In West Africa its colonies included Senegal, Mauritania, Mali, Burkina Faso (Upper Volta), Guinea, Côte d'Ivoire (Ivory Coast), Niger, and Benin (Dahomey). Rather than rule indirectly from Paris, the French sent administrators to Dakar, Senegal, to oversee the territories and appointed governors to rule each colony. Such was the political situation in the Ivory Coast when Houphouët-Boigny was growing up.

Born into a wealthy Baoulé family, Félix Houphouët was among the Ivorian upper-class elite. He studied medicine at the Medical School in Dakar, qualified as a doctor in 1925, and then worked with the Medical Assistance Service in the Ivory Coast for more than 15 years. Houphouët was also a successful plantation owner. His political career was a natural outgrowth of his involvement with farmers' issues.

Throughout his years at the forefront of Ivory Coast politics, Houphouët-Boigny looked after the concerns of the plantation owners and cacao bean farmers. The cacao bean is used to make cocoa, the basic ingredient of chocolate. Agricultural products are the major exports of Côte d'Ivoire, and coffee and cocoa are the country's main products. During World War II, the pro-German Vichy government (1940-45) in France favored white French plantation owners in the Ivory Coast over the black African farmers.

When the war ended in 1945, African planters formed the Syndicat Agricole Africain and demanded reversal of the pro-white policies. As leader of the *syndicat,* or union, Houphouët-Boigny became well known and admired throughout the country. He used the union's network of branches to form the base of a new political party called Parti Démocratique de la Côte d'Ivoire (PDCI).

A change in French policy

In 1944 French general Charles de Gaulle called a conference at Brazzaville, Congo, and outlined political, social, and economic reforms for France's territories. These reforms came about partly in response to the support the West African territories had given De Gaulle's Free French Movement during the war. From 1943 to the end of the war, the African territories had provided soldiers and supplies to De Gaulle's forces, which were trying to liberate France from the pro-German government. After the war, France's African possessions became part of Overseas France in what was called the French Union. The constitutional reforms proposed by De Gaulle gave Africans representation in the French National Assembly and the Senate. In 1946 Ivorian voters elected Houphouët to the assembly in Paris, where he participated in the debate on the future structure of the French West African colonies. France was the only colonial government that welcomed black Africans into its political culture.

Caught up in the jubilant reception on his return from Paris, Houphouët celebrated by changing his name. He added *boigny*— a Baoulé word that means "ram" or "irresistible force"—to his family name. As deputies in the French government, the Africans joined into the mainstream of French political life. But at home in Côte d'Ivoire, the French got the jobs rather than the Africans, the education system for Africans remained inferior, and the local legislative assemblies lacked power.

Moves toward independence

In response to the growth of political opportunities in postwar French West Africa, Houphouët-Boigny had formed a territory-wide political party called the Rassemblement Démocratique Africaine (RDA) and had become its president. In the early years of the RDA, French Communists were active members of the party. (Communism is a system of government in which the state controls the means of production and the distribution of goods.) In the late 1940s the Communists organized strikes and boycotts of European imports. The French administration, particularly in the Ivory Coast, came down hard on the demonstrators. They arrested hundreds of people, and in January 1950 police killed 13 Africans.

Realizing just how dangerous and unproductive this confrontational approach was, the more conservative (traditional; resistant to change) elements in the RDA separated themselves from the Communists and asked Houphouët-Boigny to rebuild the weakened party. In the 1951 elections to the French National Assembly, the RDA won only three seats. Much work had to be done in the intervening five years before the next elections. The RDA restructured itself, adopted a new policy of close cooperation with France, and won nine seats in the assembly elections of 1956.

Outside influences

Political observers say that in the 1950s French-speaking Africans were somewhat more content with their status than their British counterparts. A political awakening in French West Africa came, however, with the successful independence movements in Ghana and Nigeria in the late 1950s. France's attitude also changed because of events in Algeria, another of its African colonies. France fought a long and bitter war between 1954 and 1962 with Algerian nationalists who wanted total independence for their country. In the end the French gave in and withdrew their troops. Rather than face this experience in other territories, France negotiated peaceful arrangements for independence with Morocco and Tunisia in 1956.

In 1958 French president Charles de Gaulle proposed to the territories of French West Africa that they form a loosely knit confederation called the French Community, with certain rights and responsibilities to France. The intention of the new policy was to break up the large union of territories and give semi-independence to smaller units. Largely as a result of negotiations between de Gaulle and Houphouët-Boigny, each French territory voted on whether it wanted to join in the French Community.

To establish an outline or procedure of how power would be passed on to all its West African territories, the French assembly

passed the *loi cadre*. Houphouët-Boigny and Léopold Senghor (see entry) of Senegal helped to draft the law, giving France's African colonies full internal decision-making powers except in defense, foreign policy, and economic policy affecting the franc, the currency of France and the territories. As a member of the French Community, then, the Africans would lose their representation in the French Assembly in Paris, but they would receive a degree of independence in return. The territories would become autonomous (self-governing) republics.

The debate over federation or independent development divided the RDA. Houphouët-Boigny advocated self-government within a French-African community in which each country was linked individually to France. Under the *loi cadre,* the concept of a loose community prevailed. With the RDA's influence reduced in this system, Houphouët-Boigny decided to concentrate upon the Parti Démocratique de la Côte d'Ivoire (PDCI) and the Ivory Coast. Two years later, in 1960, all the states of French West Africa gained their independence. The Ivory Coast became independent in August 1960, and in November Houphouët-Boigny was elected president. The members of the legislature were all PDCI members.

Establishes one-man rule

So great was the party's influence that for nearly 30 years no one outside the PDCI had a chance to be heard. When opponents did rise up, the government bought them off by offering them jobs or funding for special projects. Houphouët-Boigny justified his one-party state on the grounds that a multiparty system would create rivalries among the 60 different ethnic groups in the country. Rivalry among groups, he claimed, would jeopardize economic development.

During his early years in power, no one challenged Houphouët-Boigny's leadership. The Ivory Coast prospered, and unrest was minimal. In foreign affairs the president continued to support moves toward greater economic cooperation between states. While opposing any political unification that would diminish the independence of the Ivory Coast, Houphouët-Boigny supported the Organization for African Unity (OAU), which was formed by 30 African states in Addis Ababa, Ethiopia, in 1963.

The cornerstone of Houphouët-Boigny's economic policy was close cooperation with France, believing that "national independence is meaningless in the face of economic underdevelopment." His slow-paced, conciliatory (or agreeing with the French) policy irritated students and trade unionists, who tended to be more radical (supportive of change). Nevertheless, he was popular enough with the public to fend off these criticisms.

French ties vs. Pan-Africanism

Houphouët-Boigny's policies were not universally popular. Kwame Nkrumah (see entry) of Ghana and Sékou Touré (see entry) of Guinea—two close political allies—accused him of fostering a new form of colonialism because of the ties he maintained to France. Nkrumah and Touré took a radical approach to former colonialists, striving for a more unified and independent Africa. In response to their criticism, Houphouët-Boigny organized opposition to Nkrumah and Touré at the 1965 OAU meeting in Accra, Ghana. After Nkrumah's overthrow in 1966, Houphouët-Boigny threatened to call for French military help if Touré tried to restore Nkrumah to office by force.

The Legacy

While in office Houphouët-Boigny spent state funds lavishly, building a new political and administrative capital at Yamoussoukro, his birthplace. The new capital opened in 1983. From the time of independence until the late 1970s, the Ivory Coast's economy grew at a steady pace, raising people's expectations of better living conditions and job opportunities. Houphouët-Boigny applied the resources of that state to agriculture. He made sure the farmers learned and practiced good farming techniques and that they received fair prices for their crops. Despite its lack of mineral resources, the Ivory Coast prospered under his direction. It became the largest cacao producer in the world and the third largest coffee producer.

But the prosperity did not last. The effects of excessive borrowing were compounded by collapsing cacao prices. France had to give the country money. With the failing economy, opposition political parties formed and demanded changes in economic policies. Alarmed by the protest movement, Houphouët-Boigny declared a state of emergency and detained supporters of the opposition. Then, in 1988, in response to international pressure, he announced a general amnesty to all political opponents and exiles (people forced to leave their home country). But not long after their release, the police rounded up the returning exiles and political opponents and rearrested them.

The economy remained poor. Continuing low producer prices on the international markets for cacao threatened to empty the country's treasury. Houphouët-Boigny asked government workers to take a cut in pay to offset the lack of income. The workers refused and took to the streets to protest. (They felt that the president was asking them to take a cut in pay so he could spend government money to build the magnificent basilica that would be his burial place. See box titled "The Basilica of Our Lady of Peace.") The government responded to the 1990 strikes and protests with an extremely heavy hand, arresting teachers and closing schools. France refused to send troops to back the government, and Houphouët-Boigny was forced to give in to the opposition demands. He legalized opposition parties and agreed to hold general presidential elections.

In November 1990, for the first time, voters in the Ivory Coast participated in multiparty elections. At the age of 85, Houphouët-Boigny won a seventh presidential term, although the election was thought by many to have been rigged. Meanwhile, the economic deterioration continued, and students and teachers continued to protest. Even the presidential guard demanded decent pay packages. The president spent more and more time out of the country.

In May 1993, doctors discovered that Houphouët-Boigny had cancer of the prostate (a gland of the male reproductive system). He left the Ivory Coast and spent about six months receiving medical treatment in France before returning home. At dawn on December 7, 1993—the 33rd anniversary of his country's independence from France—Houphouët-Boigny dramatically arranged for his life support system to be turned off. At his death, he had been president of Ivory Coast for 33 years, the longest tenure of any African leader. He was buried in the basilica in Yamoussoukro.

Further Reading

Ayittey, George B. *Africa Betrayed.* New York: St. Martin's Press, 1992.

Contemporary Black Biography. Volume 4. Detroit: Gale, 1993.

Crowder, Michael. "History of French West Africa until Independence." In *Africa South of the Sahara: 1982-83.* London: Europa Publications, 1982.

Harden, Blaine. *Africa: Dispatches from a Fragile Continent.* New York: HarperCollins, 1990.

Phillips, Claude S. *The African Political Dictionary.* Santa Barbara, CA: ABC-CLIO, 1984.

Kenneth Kaunda

Born April 28, 1924
Lubwa, Northern Rhodesia (Zambia)

President of Zambia

Kaunda had stayed too long in power. In the 1991 multiparty elections, the Zambian people voted for change.

enneth David Kaunda (*cow-UN-dah*), Zambia's first president, was one of the early African nationalist leaders (those who fought for independence from European control) to rise to power in the 1960s. He joined the political struggle to free his country from British control in the 1950s. British influence in Zambia began in the 1800s, represented by mining interests and then by white settler farmers. The nationalist movement gathered momentum when, in 1949, British settlers in Nyasaland (now Malawi), Northern Rhodesia (now Zambia), and Southern Rhodesia (now Zimbabwe) asked Britain if they could form a federation, or union, of the three British-held territories. In 1953, following pressure from the white settler groups, Great Britain allowed the territories to form the Federation of Rhodesia and Nyasaland, which lasted for 10 years.

Unlike the nationalist movements in most other African countries, the people of Northern Rhodesia did not have to take up arms against the colonial government to gain the right to self-rule. Following the breakup of the federation in 1963, Great Britain granted Northern Rhodesia its full independence within a year. Kaunda became the new republic's first president and stayed in power for 27 years. While in office he made serious attempts to end racism and emphasize the value and interests of all the nation's people—regardless of their color. Although it hurt Zambia's economy, Kaunda offered help to African nationalists in South Africa, Namibia, Angola, Mozambique, and Zimbabwe in their struggles for independence. Despite his good intentions and his personal integrity, however, Kaunda made serious economic mistakes over the years, and as a result the once-vibrant Zambian economy virtually collapsed.

A rural childhood

Kaunda was born April 28, 1924, at Lubwa in Bembaland in Northern Rhodesia (now Zambia). His father, David Kaunda, was a missionary who came from nearby Nyasaland (now Malawi) and was sent to Northern Rhodesia by the Livingstonia Mission of Nyasaland. David and his wife, Betty, had seven children: six boys and one girl. Kenneth Kaunda grew up at Lubwa, eight miles from Chinsali township in the northern part of Northern Rhodesia. Because his father was a Christian missionary, Kaunda was not raised in the tribal customs and rituals of his people. But the Lubwa mission was a part of the local community, so he was able to learn the values of both the missionary world and the traditional African world.

Kaunda went to school at Lubwa, where the children studied in the open air without the use of books or blackboards. He learned his letters by writing in the sand. In 1941 Kaunda was chosen as one of 29 students who would attend high school in Lusaka, the country's capital. When he finished school, he returned to the Lubwa mission to teach.

For the first 20 years of his life Kaunda lived under his father's authority. When his father died, his mother became the main influence in his life—she even chose his wife for him. On a visit to the Kaweche family, she decided that a girl named Mutinkhe, or Betty Banda, would be a good wife for her son. Kaunda consented and

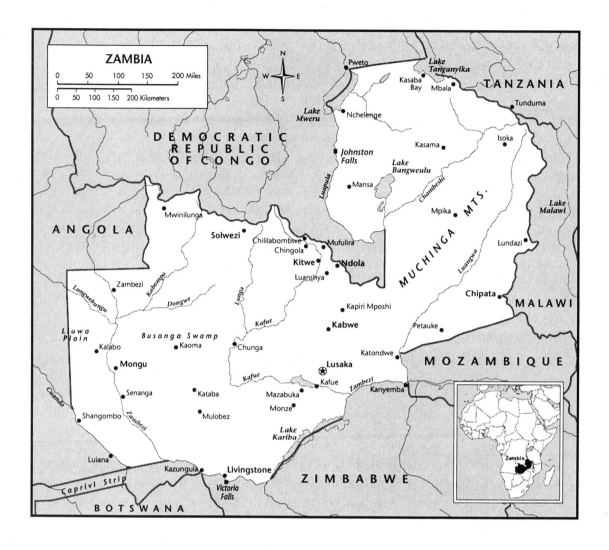

in August 1946 they married. According to the Bemba custom, the couple first celebrated their marriage in the bride's home, in Mpika, and then in the village of the bridegroom, in Lubwa.

Kaunda first experienced blatant racial discrimination when he and two friends—Simon Kapwepwe (later vice president of Zambia) and John Sokoni (a future political leader)—traveled to Salisbury in Southern Rhodesia, where Kaunda intended to take a job at a Salvation Army school. When he arrived, he found that someone else had taken the job. He also found that the law required him, as a black in Southern Rhodesia, to carry a pass at all times. In his autobiography, *Zambia Shall Be Free,* Kaunda describes his anger at being refused entry to stores or restaurants because of his color. He was outraged that Rhodesian Africans, who had fought with the British against the Nazis in World War II (1939-45), could not even eat in a white-owned restaurant.

Settling down

Kaunda returned to Northern Rhodesia and decided to start farming. First, though, he needed to make some money, so he took a job as an assistant welfare officer in the Nchanga Mine in Chingola. Kaunda was unhappy at the mine, partly because he found little opportunity for intellectual or physical stimulation. He changed jobs and went to work as a boarding school master in Mufulira in the copper mining area known as the Copperbelt. On a small scale, he began to practice the self-help ideas he would later urge Zambians to adopt nationally. Kaunda organized his students to grow vegetables for school use, and he paid them so they could save money to pay their way through school. He also set up a cooperative farm outside Lubwa. (A cooperative farm is one that is owned and operated by a group of people who work together to live off the farm's crops.) Kaunda studied all he could about agriculture and earned extra money by selling used clothes.

Political involvement

From 1949 white settlers in the British colonies of Northern and Southern Rhodesia and Nyasaland had been discussing the formation of a central government for the three colonies. The black Africans living in the colonies were strongly against this federation, or union. Kaunda got involved in the protest movement and was active in the Northern Rhodesia African National Congress (ANC) from 1950 onward. Basing his movement on the nonviolent principles of Indian nationalist and spiritual leader Mohandas Gandhi (1869-1948), Kaunda organized the final stages of the freedom struggle in Zambia. He noted in his 1980 book *The Riddle of Violence:* "Gandhi's philosophy deepened and broadened my own thinking which had been based on rather narrow but enthusiastic mission-station Christianity."

By 1952 Kaunda was the chief organizer of the African National Congress for the Northern province. He became secre-

Federation Hurts Black Majority Population

In 1924 the British government declared a protectorate over Northern Rhodesia, making it a political unit dependent on Britain. Despite strong black opposition, British authorities strengthened white power in central southern Africa in the 1950s. Britain granted white settlers in Northern Rhodesia (now Zambia), Southern Rhodesia (Zimbabwe), and Nyasaland (Malawi) permission to form a self-governing federation, or union, of the three territories. The white-run Federation of Rhodesia and Nyasaland lasted for 10 years, from 1953 to 1963.

The white settlers in the three territories wanted to make improvements—to build dams and highways—in the region. Zambia figured prominently in these plans, since it yielded high profits from its rich copper deposits. Among the advances made by the federal government were the construction of the Kariba Dam and electric power stations, completion of a railway line connecting Southern Rhodesia with Mozambique, and the building of a government-supported university in Salisbury (now Harare, Zimbabwe).

The English-speaking whites in the three territories also wanted to form a large political unit—a unit strong enough to become a single, white-controlled independent state. The federation clearly gave whites an unfair advantage over the majority population. In the federal legislature 35 seats were reserved for whites and 6 were set aside for black Africans.

tary general in 1953. For the next five years he helped organize ANC resistance to federation. Disappointed with the party's weak political strategy, Kaunda broke away from the ANC to form his own party, the Zambia African National Congress. The authorities in Lusaka objected to Kaunda's politics. In 1959 they put Kaunda and his colleagues in prison.

The following year Kaunda became the leader of the new United National Independence Party (UNIP). UNIP led a successful, nationwide, nonviolent campaign against federation. After meeting opposition from the black population in all three territories, Britain realized that the union was not going to work. In Northern Rhodesia, Britain agreed to African demands for self-rule and presented a constitution that would give Africans the majority in the government. UNIP agreed. The end of the white-dominated federation in 1963 was a victory for Kaunda and his supporters. He made political tours abroad and visited Sweden, Italy, and the United States, receiving an honorary degree from New York's Fordham University.

A promising start

In the 1964 pre-independence parliamentary elections, UNIP won a decisive victory. As head of the party, Kaunda became the prime minister. When Zambia became fully independent on October 24, 1964, Kaunda was elected the first president of the new republic. At independence, Zambia—like other former colonies—had few African college or university graduates to pilot the government. Generally, former freedom fighters and political leaders achieved high office because of their political commitment; they often lacked the technical skills required for their position.

Kaunda himself directed the course for Zambia's economic reform. He favored a mixed economy in which the central government ran the major enterprises such as the railways and airways. In 1969 the government bought the country's copper mines from the private companies that had been operating them. The government takeover of the mines put many people to work. By 1970 Zambians had more money, more jobs, better educational and health facilities, and possibly the best, most well-organized adult education program in Africa. The government paid for the mines and its social progams from the currency surplus it inherited in 1964 (money left over from the British-controlled government).

Independence brings problems

In the early years the labor unions supported the new government, which paid high wages and provided high quality institutions. But the government began to run out of money by the late 1970s and 1980s, and the high wages would not cover the high cost of imported goods and services. As the cost of living went up, the quality of educational and health systems plummeted. The unions turned against the government. By 1990 Zambia owed $7.8 billion in foreign debt.

As the economy worsened, tribal rivalry grew stronger. In the Western province the Lozi were dissatisfied as were the Bemba in the eastern provinces. Kaunda's vice president and childhood friend Simon Kapwepwe resigned from office, claiming that UNIP was persecuting the Bemba people. Around 1968 Kapwepwe formed his own party, the United Progressive party. According to Bill Saidi, a journalist who worked in Zambia, Kapwepwe had been the second most powerful man in the country.

When he formed his own party, the "ruling party thugs beat him up severely. . . . After this his health rapidly deteriorated. He died a few years later, a broken man."

In 1972 Kaunda declared that only one party—his party—would be allowed to operate in Zambia. He became more authoritative and, as his problems worsened, he began to ignore even his most trusted advisers and make many decisions on his own. UNIP was the dominant party in parliament and no one dared challenge Kaunda. Sikota Wina, a one-time associate of Kaunda's, commented that the president had an "extremely short temper."

Regional politics

Throughout the 1970s Kaunda was involved in the politics of south-central Africa. He was elected chair of the Organization of African Unity in 1970. Zambia sacrificed quite a bit by supporting the nationalists (supporters of independence) in Southern Rhodesia and in Mozambique. Kaunda let the forces of Zimbabwe nationalist Joshua Nkomo (see entry) set up headquarters in Zambia. He also allowed South African ANC exiles (supporters of majority rule in white-run South Africa) to live and work in Zambia. His support made Zambia an obvious target for revenge by agents of South Africa and Southern Rhodesia. In January 1973 the Rhodesian government led by Ian Smith (see entry) closed the border with Zambia along the Zambezi River, cutting off all trade between the two countries. (In 1980 Rhodesia, also called Southern Rhodesia, was granted independence from Great Britain and became Zimbabwe. The formerly white-run government was dismantled, and majority rule was established. Back in the early 1970s, however, Rhodesian military forces were attacking Zimbabwe nationalists, or freedom fighters, stationed in Zambia.)

By 1978 Kaunda was hinting that he might turn to the communist countries of the Soviet Union and Cuba for help if Western nations did not protect him against Rhodesian attacks. (Communism is a system of government in which the state controls the means of production and the distribution of goods.) His relations with communist countries, however, were limited mostly to contact with China, which helped Zambia and Tanzania build the Tanzania-Zambia Railway. The railway helped landlocked Zambia export its copper.

Forced to make changes

Desperate to get new loans from the International Monetary Fund (IMF), a lending agency of the United Nations (an international peace organization), Kaunda agreed to make changes in the economy. Following the IMF's guidelines, the Zambian government sold some small companies to private owners, relaxed price controls, and in 1986 ended government control of the National Agricultural Marketing Board (NAMBOARD), which sold all the corn and fertilizer the country produced. Even after laying off a large number of workers in the mid-1980s, the government was overwhelmed by economic troubles. It had borrowed more money than it could repay.

Repairing Zambia's devastated economy would not be easy. The reforms, or economic changes, that Kaunda sought to enact would hit the nation's poorest people the hardest. After riots broke out in 1987, Kaunda changed his mind and put a stop to the reforms. But by the 1990s popular demand was growing for some sort of political reform—especially as the communist governments in East Europe collapsed. Kaunda moved ahead of the opposition

Kaunda (left) as chair of the Commonwealth Conference, 1979.

and called for a conference on a multiparty state. The March 1990 meeting revealed serious disagreements between party officials and the others, mainly church, labor, and business leaders, students, and industrialists. These groups wanted the government to sell its interests in mining and manufacturing. They also wanted a multiparty system with a fixed term of office for the president.

Kaunda initially refused to hold a vote on the question of establishing a multiparty system. The people who favored a multiparty system formed a separate pressure group, the Movement for Multiparty Democracy (MMD). Finally, after more demonstrations, food riots, and an attempted coup (the overthrow of an existing government), Kaunda agreed to let the Zambian people decide the issue at the polls. In 1991, when the government removed the ban on opposition political parties, 12 new parties registered.

The people's frustration with the Kaunda government was quite evident. Presidential and parliamentary elections were held on October 31, 1991. MMD president Frederick Chiluba, a former labor leader, opposed UNIP candidate Kaunda in the presidential elections. The MMD overwhelmed the opposition, winning 125 of the 150 parliamentary seats. In the presidential race, Chiluba won 79 percent of the vote. So decisive was the vote that Chiluba was sworn in as president before officials announced the final count. Kaunda had stayed too long in power. The people voted for change.

Even though he is out of power, Kaunda has remained active in politics as the head of Zambia's opposition party. He was a candidate for president in the 1996 elections, but the Chiluba government changed the constitution to disqualify him from running. On the surface, Kaunda or "KK," as he is often called, appears a simple man. He usually carries a white handkerchief in his hand and is not embarrassed to weep in public. Kaunda speaks openly of his religious faith. Political observers maintain that he is one of the few African leaders who has not personally enriched himself at the expense of his country. He is also one of the few African leaders to respect the wishes of the voters and turn power over to his rival when he loses an election.

Imprisoned

A brief coup occurred in Zambia on October 28, 1997, in which some military officers broke into a radio station and the

Frederick Chiluba

On November 2, 1991, Frederick Chiluba (1943-) took the oath of office as the second president of the Republic of Zambia. Chiluba and his Movement for a Multiparty Democracy (MMD) had toppled the 27-year-old regime of Kenneth Kaunda in a landslide election victory.

Chiluba, a born-again Christian, self-described "bullfighter," and generally witty speaker, often uses quotes from the Bible in his fiery speeches. During the 1991 election campaign he drew enormous crowds to his rallies, addressing his audiences from makeshift platforms set up in empty soccer fields. For some, this five-foot tall "political dwarf"—as Kaunda referred to him—became the "Black Moses" or the "Liberator," who would deliver his people from the economic impoverishment of the Kaunda years.

Chiluba got into politics through the trade unions. He was first elected chairman of the 300,000 member Zambian Congress of Trade Unions (ZCTU) in 1974. Unlike unions in most other African countries, the Zambian trade unions operate independent of the government and the party. Chiluba had a ready-made national platform independent of the government.

In his first year of office Chiluba made some important changes in Zambia's economy. Gradually, however, corruption charges were leveled against some of his cabinet officials. The government imprisoned journalists working for the independent press, and the economy failed to provide jobs for the majority of the nation's people. Chiluba won reelection in 1996 but failed to stifle the growing opposition in Zambia.

house of a military official and called on Chiluba to surrender the presidency. On Christmas day 1997, Chiluba ordered Kaunda's arrest and detention on charges of plotting the coup, although the evidence against him was very weak. Responding to an international outcry over Kaunda's imprisonment in an overcrowded jail with hardened criminals, Chiluba later placed him under house arrest. Kaunda remained in detention for six months until charges were dropped on June 1, 1998. South African president Nelson Mandela (see entry), who sent his defense minister to negotiate between Kaunda and the Zambian government, was thought to be responsible for Kaunda's release. Hundreds of supporters cheered Kaunda on the courthouse steps in Lusaka after his release. He later announced his retirement from politics.

Further Reading

Anglin, Douglas G., and Timothy M. Shaw. *Zambia's Foreign Policy: Studies in Diplomacy and Dependence.* Boulder, CO: Westview Press, 1979.

Contemporary Black Biography. Volume 2. Detroit: Gale, 1992.

Hatch, John. *Two African Statesmen.* Regnery, 1975.

Kaunda, Kenneth D. *Zambia Shall Be Free: An Autobiography.* New York: Praeger, 1963.

Kaunda, Kenneth D. *The Riddle of Violence.* New York: Harper, 1980.

Historic World Leaders. Edited by Anne Commire. Volume 1. Detroit: Gale, 1994.

MacPherson, Fergus. *Kenneth Kaunda of Zambia: The Times and the Man.* New York/UK: Oxford University Press, 1974.

McNeil, Donald G. Jr. "Coup Charges Dropped, and Zambia's Ex-Leader is Freed," *New York Times,* June 2, 1998.

Saidi, Bill. "How the World Is Always Forgiving KK." *Zimbabwe Independent,* January 16, 1998.

Zolberg, Aristide R. *One-Party Government in the Ivory Coast.* Rev. ed. Princeton, NJ: Princeton University Press, 1969.

Jomo Kenyatta

Born October 20, c. 1891
Ngenda, Kikuyuland, British East Africa (Kenya)
Died August 22, 1978
Mombasa, Kenya

First president of Kenya

omo Kenyatta was the first president of independent Kenya, an eastern African nation that had been a British protectorate since 1895. At the time Kenyatta became a rising political figure, Kenya was one of several British colonies in eastern Africa referred to collectively as British East Africa. (Colonialism is the extension of a nation's power beyond its own borders, usually for economic gain.)

Kenyatta came to prominence through the nationalist (independence-seeking), anticolonial movement that arose in Africa after World War II (1939-45). He rose quickly to the leadership of an influential nationalist organization and became a principal voice in the growing opposition to British colonial rule. In an attempt to silence him, the colonial government arrested and imprisoned him for nearly seven years. When Britain realized that the African people would not submit to colonial rule and agreed to an independent Kenya in the early 1960s, Kenyatta became the

Kenyatta was revered by many as Mzee, the "wise father" of Kenya.

new nation's first president. At first his nationalist government was extremely popular, but as time passed, the Kenyatta regime became increasingly centralized and authoritarian. It also became corrupt, enriching colleagues and families close to the leaders. Opposition parties were either absorbed into the ruling party or silenced. Nonetheless, Kenyatta is remembered by many in eastern Africa as a leader who contributed greatly to the building of an independent new nation.

A beaded belt: *mucibi wa kinyata*

According to most biographers, Jomo Kenyatta was born on October 20, 1891, at Ngenda, Kikuyuland, British East Africa. Questions have always been raised about the his birth date, though, because of the unusual way the Kikuyu kept records. Kenyatta said that even he wasn't sure of his true date of birth.

Kenyatta's father was Muigai, a farmer, and his mother was Wambui. His parents named him Kamau wa Ngengi, but he later took the name "Kenyatta" from the Kikuyu name for the beaded workers' belt that he wore as a youth (*mucibi wa kinyata*). He went to the Church of Scotland Mission near Nairobi for his first five years of schooling. In August 1914 he was baptized as a Presbyterian in the Church of Scotland.

From 1921 to 1926 Kenyatta worked for the Nairobi municipal water board and served as an interpreter of the Kikuyu language for the Kenya Supreme Court. In 1922 he joined the Young Kikuyu Association, a nationalistic organization formed by the Kikuyu, the largest ethnic group in the country. The Africans of British East Africa had been receptive to many aspects of British culture, but gradually they learned to use the institutions of British democracy to achieve their own nationalistic goals.

British colonialism:
Kenya's— and Kenyatta's—background

Back in the late 1800s, the British East Africa Company—a private company backed by the British government—looked after British interests in East Africa. With the opening of the Suez Canal (connecting the Red and Mediterranean seas in northeastern

Africa) in 1869, Britain realized the importance of controlling the headwaters of the world's longest river, the Nile. The White Nile flows out of Lake Victoria and joins the Blue Nile, flowing out of Ethiopia's Lake Tana. The two join at Khartoum in the Sudan to become the Nile River. The southern half of Lake Victoria is in Tanzania and the northern half is mostly in Uganda, with a small portion in the northwest of Kenya.

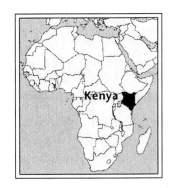

The British government decided to build a rail line from Mombasa, a key port off the southern coast of Kenya, to Lake Victoria and made the surrounding portion of British East Africa a British colony. One of the stops along the rail line, Nairobi in Kenya, became the administrative center and later the country's capital city. Once construction of the railway was under way, the British government began urging its citizens to settle in Kenya and take up farming. Britain was determined to turn Kenya into a "white man's" country.

After World War I (1914-18) nearly 9,000 Europeans had settled in Kenya, and much of the highlands outside Nairobi had been set aside for whites. Close to 7 million acres of African land were taken—mostly from the Maasai and Kikuyu peoples—for European settlement.

The idea of white settlers owning Kikuyu land outraged the Kikuyu. As one of the educated elite among the Kikuyu, Jomo Kenyatta played a leading role in the Young Kikuyu Association's struggle for black rights. From this organization grew the Kikuyu Central Association and the East African Association. In 1928 the Kikuyu Central Association elected Kenyatta its general secretary. He worked hard to broaden the organization's base of support, educating the Kikuyu in the politics of land expropriation (Britain's policy of taking over tribal lands). In 1929, in an effort to reach the distant villages comprising Kikuyu territory, the association started a monthly Kikuyu-language newspaper called the *Muigwithania.* Kenyatta became the editor of *Muigwithania,* the first newspaper produced by Africans in Kenya.

Travels and lives in Europe

In 1928 the British government held meetings to get views on a projected federation, or union, of British East African territories. Kenyatta testified before the Hilton-Young Commission on the topic. The next year the Kikuyu Central Association sent Kenyatta to London to present their land claims and testify against the proposed union of Kenya, Uganda, and Tanganyika. While in Europe, Kenyatta became involved with more radical anticolonial organizations—organizations that favored a more revolutionary approach to achieving their goals.

Kenyatta traveled to various European cities and then spent several weeks in the Soviet Union in August 1929. Returning to Kenya in the fall of 1930, he gained permission for the Kikuyu to control their own schools despite opposition from Christian missionaries in the region. The following spring the Kikuyu Central Association sent Kenyatta to London as a delegate to a parliamentary committee studying the East Africa Federation plans. He stayed there for 15 years before returning home. During this time Kenyatta studied English at the Quaker Woodbrooke College and at Selly Oak in Birmingham. After teaching language courses at the School of African and Oriental Studies in London from 1933 to 1936, he earned a postgraduate degree in anthropology (the study of human societies, origins, racial relationships, and cultures) under Professor Bronislaw Malinowski at the London School of Economics. His thesis, *Facing Mount Kenya,* a study of Kikuyu culture and society, was published in 1938. It is one of the earliest works on cultural nationalism by an African nationalist about his own society.

During World War II (1939-45) Kenyatta worked on a farm in Surrey, England, and served as a lecturer on Africa for the Worker's Educational Association. In 1945 Kenyatta, Kwame Nkrumah (see entry), George Padmore, and other African nationalists established the Pan-African Federation (an organization dedicated to the union of all Africans) and set up the Fifth Pan-African Congress in Manchester with the theme "Africa for the Africans."

Leads nationalists

Kenyatta left England in 1946 to return to Kenya. He was immediately elected president of the Kenya African Union (KAU), a newly formed nationalist organization in his homeland. Kenyatta reignited the feud over Kikuyu land that pitted tribal members against the colonial government and white British settlers. His strong personality, fiery speeches, and well-organized

A Striking Appearance

Jomo Kenyatta was considered a flashy dresser back in the late 1940s. Most photos show him in traditional African dress, usually wearing an animal-skinned or feathered hat. Sometimes he draped a cape of monkey skins around his shoulders, and he wore a heavy red-stoned signet ring on his left hand. In his right hand Kenyatta carried a large ebony walking stick. Africans greeted him with shouts of "Savior," "Great Elder," and "Hero of Our Race."

Pictured here, Kenyatta addresses a cheering crowd of 50,000 Kikuyu in 1952. "I have the British lion by the tail after 40 years of fighting for independence," he told them.

freedom marches captured the attention of other Kenyan tribal leaders and brought new members into the KAU. Its membership soon swelled to more than 100,000 people.

As the 1940s progressed black Africans became increasingly frustrated with the white-dominated government in British East Africa. The KAU had a long-established policy of working for a peaceful change to white-minority rule in Kenya, but the opposition was growing more and more discontented. Militant blacks—black Africans who were ready to fight for their freedom—organized direct challenges to British authority.

Despite his denials, Kenyatta was suspected of heading the fanatical Mau Mau, a secret society whose members had taken an oath to rid Kenya of its white settlers. In October 1952 Kenyatta and five others were arrested on charges of organizing and/or participating in the terrorist movement. By that time nearly 100 Europeans and more than 3,000 Kikuyu had been killed or executed. In a world-famous trial in the remote town of Kapenguria, Kenyatta and his associates were found guilty of the charges leveled against them. In April 1953 they were sentenced to seven years of hard labor. British authorities hoped that by removing Kenyatta from public life, the Mau Mau movement would become disorganized and eventually disappear. But during his six and a half years in prison in the desert of Lokitaung in northwestern Kenya, the terrorism actually increased in violence and frequency. Thousands of Kikuyu militants fled to the forest areas

Terror Stalked the Land: Mau Mau

Mau Mau was a violent rebellion by Kikuyu that broke out during the late 1940s in the European farming area of Kenya. Mau Mau began with the murder of a few British farmers and the destruction of their cattle. The Kikuyu wanted their land back and hoped to frighten the Europeans into leaving the country. The government responded by arresting Jomo Kenyatta and other well-known Kikuyu leaders and rounding up Kikuyu farmers and forcing them to live in guarded compounds. By the end of 1955 the revolt had been put down. About 100 British settlers were killed in the uprising; nearly 3,000 Kikuyu died in the civil war that pitted Kenyan rebels against blacks who were suspected of supporting the white regime.

of Mount Kenya and the Aberdares, where they continued their battle against the government. Britain sent in troops to reinforce the colony's security forces.

While Kenyatta was in prison, the British declared a state of emergency, outlawing all political party activity. The Kenya Federation of Labor under Tom Mboya (see entry) led political activism during the time political parties were outlawed. By 1955 the government was allowing limited, district-level political organizations in the non-Kikuyu areas to start up; these groups began to take up the labor union's political activities.

With Kenyatta's release from prison in 1959, violence in the region subsided. Nevertheless, the government restricted him to an additional two years of house arrest in the Northern Frontier district town of Lodwar. A new generation of Kenyan nationalists continued to agitate for Kenyatta's release. Meanwhile, the British government began to accept the idea that the existing colonial government could no longer control Kenya. Making a firm move toward granting Kenya its independence, Great Britain revised its colonial constitution several times in the late 1950s. Each constitutional step increased African involvement in self-government.

Kenyan leaders insisted on Kenyatta's participation in any government leading to independence. In March 1960 members of the old Kenya African Union (KAU) reorganized themselves as the Kenya African National Union (KANU) and elected Kenyatta as their president, even though he remained under house arrest.

Finally, on August 14, 1961, the British authorities permitted Kenyatta to return to Kikuyuland.

Kenyatta is cheered as he walks through the gates of his home after being released from political detention, 1961.

Forms independent government

KANU took a radical nationalist stand and drew its membership from the groups most affected by colonial rule, especially the Kikuyu and the Luo. The Kenya African Democratic Union (KADU), created in 1960, was more conservative (more traditional and less supportive of change brought on by revolutionary means). Headed by Ronald Ngala and Daniel arap Moi (see entry), KADU represented the interests of the smaller ethnic groups.

On January 12, 1962, voters in the Fort Hall constituency elected Kenyatta to the Kenyan legislative assembly. That April he agreed to serve in a coalition (combination British and African) government as minister of state for constitutional affairs and economic planning. In March 1963 the legislative assembly met for the last time in a colonial form. The election that followed would decide who would lead Kenya into independence. On the heels of KANU's overwhelming victory in the election, Kenyatta became self-governing Kenya's first prime minister on June 1, 1963.

Kenyatta took extraordinary steps to reassure European farmers about their future. He also appealed to the freedom fighters and members of Mau Mau to lay down their arms and join the new nation. On December 12, 1963, Kenya received its independence from Great Britain. The following year it became a republic with Kenyatta as its president. Once in power, Kenyatta continued to build a new nation based on racial and tribal harmony under the old workers' slogan *Harambee,* meaning "pull together." Britain helped Kenya to finance a massive land purchase scheme that permitted the settlers in the "white highlands" to sell their lands to Africans. Most white farmers in the highlands agreed to sell.

Conflicts arise

Kenya's new president was not a firm backer of "African socialism," the political trend of his day. Under the capitalistic system he adopted, Kenya's economy developed rapidly, but some inequities existed in opportunity and distribution of wealth. The Kikuyu people and Kenyatta's immediate family (four wives and seven children) profited the most from the new economic system. At independence, the constitution gave considerable powers to various autonomous (self-governing) regions in Kenya. Kenyatta soon abolished these regional powers and replaced them with a highly centralized and authoritarian system. For instance, in 1964, when the Somali people living in Kenya's North-West province wanted to join the Somali Republic across the border, Kenyatta sent in troops to crush the separatist movement.

Kenyatta persuaded the Kenya African Democratic Union to drop its political opposition and to voluntarily dissolve itself in November 1964. KADU—KANU's greatest rival—supported at least limited regional self-government, while Kenyatta's party argued for the concentration of power in a strong central government. The conflicting views of key figures in the government—mainly friction between Kenyatta and former leaders of KADU—fueled a political crisis in Kenya. Kenyatta's vice president eventually resigned to form an opposition party known as the Kenya Peoples' Union Party (KPU). In response, the ruling party redoubled its efforts to put down the opposition.

On July 5, 1969, Tom Mboya, a popular Luo politician, was assassinated by a Kikuyu. Although the assassin was tried and executed, the Luo were not satisfied. Kenyatta's appearance in Luo country that October set off riots and threatened to divide the country. At first he ignored the problem, but finally he was forced to take action. Kenyatta banned the KPU, making Kenya a virtual one-party state.

Kenyatta's legacy

In foreign policy, Kenyatta accepted aid from communist and capitalist countries while remaining as politically neutral as possible in global affairs. (Communism is a system of government in which the state controls the means of production and the distribution of goods.) His strategy helped Kenya take the lead in economic development in eastern Africa. Kenyatta became the undisputed leader in East Africa and achieved his greatest foreign policy success when he helped to settle a border dispute between Uganda and Tanzania in 1971.

But the 1970s were marred by political violence in Kenya. Alleged attempts to overthrow the Kenyatta regime brought severe government crackdowns. And the 1975 assassination of Josiah Kariuki, an outspoken critic of the government and member of parliament, sparked rumors that the government would resort to murder to stifle the opposition.

All criticisms aside, Kenyatta made independent Kenya a showcase nation among the former African colonial states. He is best remembered for stabilizing relations with whites in the region and turning Kenya into a viable twentieth-century society. Kenyatta was revered by many as *Mzee,* the "wise father" of Kenya. He died in Mombasa on August 22, 1978. As a tribute to Kenya's first president, his successor, Daniel arap Moi, suggested a continuation of Kenyatta's policies by calling his own program *Nyayo* or "footsteps."

Further Reading

Contemporary Black Biography. Volume 5. Detroit: Gale, 1994.

Delf, George. *Jomo Kenyatta: Towards Truth about "The Light of Kenya."* New York: Doubleday, 1961.

Historic World Leaders. Edited by Anne Commire. Volume 1. Detroit: Gale, 1994.

Kenyatta, Jomo. *Facing Mount Kenya.* North Pomfret, VT: Secker & Warburg, 1938.

Kenyatta, Jomo. *Kenya: The Land of Conflict.* International African Service Bureau, 1945.

Kenyatta, Jomo. *Harambee! The Prime Minister of Kenya's Speeches, 1963-1964.* New York/UK: Oxford University Press, 1964.

Murray-Brown, Jeremy. *Kenyatta.* Allen & Unwin, 1979.

Newsweek, September 4, 1978.

Slater, Montague. *The Trial of Jomo Kenyatta.* North Pomfret, VT: Secker & Warburg, 1955.

Time, September 4, 1978.

Wepman, Dennis. *Jomo Kenyatta.* Broomall, PA: Chelsea House, 1989.

Seretse Khama

Born July 1, 1921
Serowe, Bechuanaland Protectorate (Botswana)
Died July 13, 1980
Gaborone, Botswana

*African statesman and
first president of Botswana*

eretse Khama was the first president of independent Botswana. During his nearly 14 years as president (1966-80), he established one of the few competitive democratic (by the people) political systems in sub-Saharan Africa. At the time of his election, Botswana was one of the least populated and poorest countries in Africa. About the size of Texas and mostly desert land, Botswana is landlocked and dependent on its neighbors for manufactured goods and access to the sea. Throughout Khama's presidency, the region was in turmoil. He was constantly juggling his country's interests against those of African nationalists from neighboring countries. Nationalists were fighting for independence from white minority rule in the nearby countries of Rhodesia (now Zimbabwe), South Africa, and South-West Africa (now Namibia). Nationalists were also struggling against Portuguese occupation in Angola and Mozambique. Still, Khama managed to earn a reputation as one of the African continent's leading statesmen.

"We want to see majority rule established throughout southern Africa . . . and we are determined to contribute towards the achievement of that noble goal. We are, however, aware that there is a limit beyond which our contribution cannot go without endangering our very independence."

—Seretse Khama, in a speech to a 1970 meeting of the Non-Aligned States

In 1885 Great Britain declared a protectorate (a political unit dependent on the British) over Ngwato territory to prevent the Germans from annexing it to their territory in southwest Africa. Britain feared Germany would link up with the Afrikaners (people of Dutch, French, and German descent) in the Transvaal, sealing the Cape Colony off from access to the North. (The Transvaal—a former province of northeastern South Africa—ceased to exist in 1994, when it was split into different provinces.) Britain's intervention pleased Khama III because it protected him from encroachment by Afrikaner farmers and mineral prospectors from the Transvaal. Later, Britain considered giving British financier Cecil Rhodes's British South Africa Company permission to administer Ngwato territory. In response, Khama III and two other Tswana chiefs traveled to London to ask Queen Victoria to intervene on their behalf. As a result, the British colonial government partitioned the territory into two regions: one for Rhodes's company and the other for Khama.

A proud tradition

Seretse Khama came from a politically influential family with a history of courage and defiance. His grandfather, Khama the Great or Khama III (1838-1923), was a traditional ruler of the Ngwato, the largest of Botswana's eight major ethnic groups. In defiance of the traditional elders, Khama III became a Christian and established Christianity as the official religion of the Ngwato people.

In 1925, when Seretse Khama was just four years old, his father died after having served as chief for two years. Because Seretse was too young to become chief, his father's brother, Tshekedi Khama (1906-1959) interrupted his studies at Fort Hare College in Cape Province to return home and act as regent (temporary ruler). He remained acting chief until Seretse was ready to take over. Tshekedi was an innovative regent and between 1925 and 1950 accomplished quite a bit for the Ngwato people, especially in the field of education. He formed voluntary work groups to build schools and colleges. By 1966 about 10 elementary schools and the Moeng College, a technical institute, had been constructed.

In 1933 Tshekedi and the British resident commissioner became embroiled in a public dispute. The resident commissioner accused Tshekedi, as acting chief of the Ngwato, of overstepping his bounds by allowing tribal elders to order the flogging (beating) of a white man. Thinking he had an opportunity to strip Tshekedi

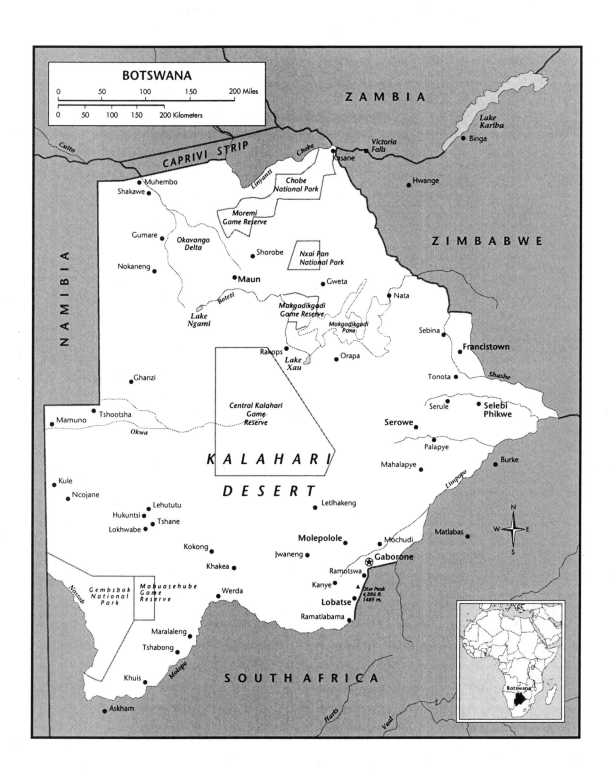

BOTSWANA

| 0 | 50 | 100 | 150 | 200 Miles |
| 0 | 50 | 100 | 150 | 200 Kilometers |

ZAMBIA

Lake Kariba

● Binga

CAPRIVI STRIP

Victoria Falls

Chobe

Kasane

● Hwange

● Muhembo

Shakawe ●

Linyanti

Chobe National Park

Moremi Game Reserve

N A M I B I A

Gumare ●

Okavango Delta

● Shorobe

Nxai Pan National Park

Z I M B A B W E

Nokaneng ●

● Maun

Boteti

● Gweta

● Nata

Lake Ngami

Makgadikgadi Game Reserve

Makgadikgadi Pans

Sebina ●

Francistown

Rakops ●

Lake Xau

● Orapa

Tonota ●

Shashe

Ghanzi ●

Central Kalahari Game Reserve

Serule ●

Selebi Phikwe

Mamuno ●

Tshootsha ●

Okwa

Serowe ●

● Palapye

K A L A H A R I

Mahalapye ●

Limpopo

● Burke

Kule ●

D E S E R T

● Letlhakeng

Matlabas ●

Ncojane ●

Lehututu ●

Molepolole ●

● Mochudi

N

Hukuntsi ●
● Tshane

W E

Lokhwabe ●

Kokong ●

Jwaneng ●

Gaborone

S

Khakea ●

Ramotswa ●

Gembsbok National Park

Mabuasehube Game Reserve

Werda ●

Kanye ●

Otse Peak 4,886 ft. 1489 m.

Nossob

Lobatse

Ramatlabama ●

Maralaleng ●

Tshabong ●

Molopo

Khuis ●

S O U T H   A F R I C A

Harts

● Askham

Vaal

Botswana

of his regency, the resident commissioner called in 200 marines from the British naval base at Simonstown, near Cape Town. But the British public ended up sympathizing with Tshekedi. And the next year, when Tshekedi wrote to the British press to protest the planned incorporation of Bechuanaland (now Botswana) into South Africa, evidence of his popularity with the British public again became evident. He argued that South African control of Bechuanaland would lead to racial inequality throughout the region. He and his people did not want that to happen. The incorporation proposal was set aside because the Tswana people opposed it and the British public supported them.

Personal life sparks public debate

Tshekedi valued education and sent Seretse to South Africa for his secondary school education. Khama went to Tiger Kloof and later to Lovedale College. In 1941 he entered Fort Hare College, graduating with a degree in history in 1944. After the end of World War II (1939-45) Khama went to England to continue his studies. He attended Balliol College at Oxford University and then studied for his law degree at the Middle Temple Inn.

While in England, Seretse Khama met and fell in love with a young Englishwoman named Ruth Williams. They married on September 28, 1948, despite opposition from his uncle and the tribal elders. Khama was in line to become the head chief of the huge Ngwato tribe in Bechuanaland. The elders were afraid that the influence of a white wife would make him forget his traditional values. But when the couple traveled to Bechuanaland and Khama introduced Williams to his people, the elders agreed that she could become their queen. Khama, however, did not win the approval of his uncle.

From the 1880s Great Britain had governed Bechuanaland as a protectorate (dependent political unit) and had ultimate control over tribal matters. Claiming that the internal security of Bechuanaland was being jeopardized by the divisions over Khama's marriage, British authorities intervened in the dispute. With pressure from the South African government, Great Britain banished Khama and his uncle from Bechuanaland for about five years. Seretse Khama and his wife were tricked into leaving by the British government. The government had invited them to London to discuss the matter and then prevented them from returning to

Bechuanaland. British prime minister Sir Winston Churchill later described it as "a very disreputable transaction."

Lives in exile

Khama's marriage to Ruth Williams contradicted the basis of the apartheid state—that people of different races should live separately. For this reason, the neighboring South African government opposed the union. Britain, in turn, was forced to take a hard line against the marriage: if it did not, the South African government threatened to cut off British access to South Africa's uranium.

In exile, Tshekedi and Seretse Khama settled their differences and worked together to organize their return to Bechuanaland. In 1952 the British allowed Tshekedi to go back to his homeland, and four years later Seretse Khama went back as well. But Seretse's return was conditional. He had to give up his right and the rights of his heirs to the chieftaincy. Khama agreed to do this because he had come to recognize the importance of democratic institutions. He saw that the future of his people lay in a democratic system of government—not in the traditional system.

Although Khama was a victim of racial prejudice, he did not become a racist himself. Instead, he became deeply committed to the idea of a society free of racial strife and divisions. Ironically, the conditions imposed on him by the British—that he return to Bechuanaland as an ordinary citizen—led him into active politics and ultimately to the presidency of his home country.

Forming an independent nation

After resettling in Bechuanaland in 1956, Khama got involved with politics cautiously, first as a member of the Tribal Council. As talks got under way with Great Britain about constitutional reform and eventual independence, political parties emerged. The Bechuanaland People's Party (BPP)—formed in 1960 with the slogan, "one man, one vote"—had ties with South Africa's African National Congress (ANC). The BPP split into two factions, or groups, which later became the Botswana Independence Party (BIP) and the Botswana People's Party (BPP). In 1961 Khama won a seat in the legislative council and became a member of the territory's executive council. The next year he

Khama speaks at the opening of the Bechuanaland Independence Conference in London, 1966.

formed the Bechuanaland Democratic Party (BDP). The BDP was popular because it incorporated some traditional practices along with democratic principles.

The British accepted a proposed constitution in 1964 that included universal adult suffrage (the right to vote for all adults) and a parliamentary form of government. In March 1965 the protectorate achieved the right to full internal self-government and held nationwide elections. The BDP won 28 out of 31 seats and formed the first independent government. On September 30, 1966, the protectorate of Bechuanaland became the independent republic of Botswana. Seretse Khama was sworn in as president and received a knighthood from the British crown.

Problems in the region

Shortly after independence, Botswana faced turmoil on its eastern border with the then-British colony of Southern Rhodesia. In November 1965 the prime minister of Southern Rhodesia, Ian

Smith (see entry), declared his country independent of Great Britain. Britain wanted Rhodesia to work toward a democratic system in which blacks had full political representation, but the white minority government (led by Smith) opposed it. Although Khama did not agree with Smith's policies, he could not afford to close Botswana's borders with Rhodesia. Botswana needed access to the Rhodesia-owned rail line that connected it with South Africa. Without the railway, Botswana had no outlet to the sea.

Throughout the region in the late 1960s, African freedom fighters clashed with white governments. In the face of these struggles for liberation, Khama tried to remain neutral, denying guerrillas from South-West Africa (Namibia), South Africa, and Rhodesia military bases in Botswana. He did, however, accept thousands of refugees from the neighboring countries, at great expense to Botswana. And his antiracist speeches acknowledge the precarious position in which he found himself. In 1970 he told the meeting of the Non-Aligned States (neutral powers in the post-World War II conflict between "superpowers"—the United States and the former Soviet Union):

> If we appear reluctant to play an active and prominent part in the struggle for majority rule throughout southern Africa, it is not because we are unconcerned about the plight of our oppressed brothers in the white-ruled states of our region. . . .We want to see majority rule established throughout southern Africa . . . and we are determined to contribute towards the achievement of that noble goal. We are, however, aware that there is a limit beyond which our contribution cannot go without endangering our very independence.

Steering Botswana in its early years

The tiny country of Botswana, with a population under a million when Khama became president, was one of the 20 poorest countries in the world. Botswana is now the third largest diamond producer in Africa. Diamonds were discovered in 1967, a year after independence, and mining began in 1971. Diamonds make up nearly all of Botswana's exports. (Earlier the economy had largely depended on cattle.) Khama returned the money from diamond mining back to the country in development projects and infrastructure, including electrification and the building of schools and hospitals.

Khama had suffered from poor health since the late 1960s. In June 1980 doctors diagnosed him as having cancer of the stomach.

He died in Gaborone on July 13, 1980, leaving his wife, three daughters, and three sons behind. One son, Ian, is the chief lieutenant-general in the Botswana Defense Forces.

Khama had just lived to see the neighboring country of Zimbabwe achieve its independence in 1980. But it would not be until 1994, when multiracial elections took place in South Africa, that the region would stabilize to any significant extent. Until his death, Khama remained genuinely popular with his people. He successfully steered his country through its first 14 years of independence in often difficult and unsettled circumstances. Although he despised the apartheid state and the racist policies of Ian Smith in Rhodesia, he was never bitter about racism. His moderation gave him great standing and respect in Africa and beyond and earned him an undisputed reputation as one of Africa's leading statesmen.

Further Reading

Eilersen, Gillian Stead. *Bessie Head: Thunder Behind Her Ears.* North Pomfret, VT: Heinemann, 1995.

Halpern, Jack. "Botswana: Recent History." In *Africa South of the Sahara, 1981-1982.* London: Europa, 1981.

Wilson, Monica, and Leonard Thompson, eds. *The Oxford History of South Africa: 1870-1966.* New York: Clarendon Press, 1975.

Simon Kimbangu

Born 1889
Mbanza-Ngungu, Congo Free State (now
Democratic Republic of the Congo)
Died October 12, 1951
Belgian Congo (now Democratic
Republic of the Congo)

*Leader of an independent Christian religious
movement in central Africa*

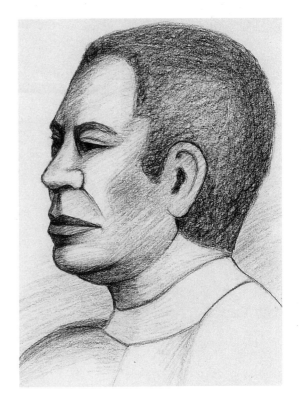

Simon Kimbangu began one of the most important indepen-dent Christian religious movements in central Africa. After he built a new African religion in just a few short months, his preaching became so popular that Belgian colonial authorities in the Congo tried to put a stop to it. (Colonialism is a nation's con-trol of territory that lies beyond its own borders—in this case, Bel-gium's control over the Congo.) They arrested Kimbangu and sent him to prison for the rest of his life. Nevertheless, his movement gained popularity, and the church he founded, the Church of Jesus Christ on Earth through the Prophet Simon Kimbangu, continues today in his name in the new Democratic Republic of the Congo (the country known as Zaire from 1971 to 1997).

Simon Kimbangu was born in 1889 in Nkamba, a small vil-lage near Mbanza-Ngungu in Lower Congo. His parents belonged

Kimbangu's disciples called him the "Savior of the Black People" and compared him to Moses and Jesus, Muhammad and Buddha.

King Leopold II of Belgium

Belgian king Leopold II (1835-1909) ruled Belgium from 1865 to 1909. In his native land he was known for a scandalous private life, a policy of industrial expansion that imposed terrible conditions upon workers, and increasing social unrest. But he was also well known for his avid colonial expansion into Africa. In 1876 he and Henry Morton Stanley organized the International Association for the Exploration and Civilization of the Congo. In a conference in Berlin in 1884-85—in which European powers divided the continent of Africa among themselves—Leopold succeeded in having the Congo Free State placed under his personal rule.

In the 1890s when he took over the area known today as the Democratic Republic of the Congo—with almost unlimited power—Leopold proceeded to exploit the Congo's people and resources. His purpose was to use the area—his own personal kingdom—to his own advantage. The region was rich in rubber, ivory, and minerals, but the Kongo people and others living in the region did not benefit from these resources. Instead, they worked the land for the king, suffering horribly in a hot humid climate where malaria and sleeping sickness thrived. The Belgians recruited the region's people as porters to carry loads on their heads from the estuary (or arm) of the Congo River up and around the massive waterfalls to Stanley Pool (now Malebo Pool). Later the Kongo men were forced to work on the construction of the railway. But conditions on the rubber plantations were the most horrid of all.

Other European powers learned of the devastating conditions in the Congo and sent out an investigator. He reported seeing women chained to sheds with their babies, held hostage until the village met its rubber quota, and men being whipped for failing to bring enough rubber to the collection point. British novelist Joseph Conrad wrote eloquently in *Heart of Darkness* about this dark period of the Congo's history. In 1908, after the terrible conditions of the people in the Congo became known, public pressure forced Leopold to transfer the Congo Free State to Belgium. The Belgian government began to reform the horrid conditions, but it took time. By 1930 the situation for the Congolese had improved somewhat.

to the KiKongo group. They both died when Kimbangu was young, so he was raised by his grandmother. Kimbangu attended primary school at the Baptist Missionary Society station, where he studied the Bible and was baptized into the Christian faith. Afterward he worked as an evangelist, teaching and preaching in local villages. He married Marie Mwilu and they had several children. He did not become a teacher or a pastor because he did not have enough money for further studies.

In 1918 a severe flu epidemic killed thousands of people in the Congo. In the same year many Kongo laborers died while working on the railway. Overwhelmed by the troubles in his homeland,

Kimbangu claimed he had a vision. A voice told him he had been touched by God and been given the power to heal. At first he did not want to answer the call. He left the mission and went to Leopoldville (now Kinshasa) hoping to avoid the responsibility. After three months of difficult labor for which he did not receive his pay, he returned to his home village to farm.

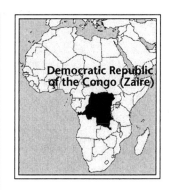

Democratic Republic of the Congo (Zaire)

A prophet to his followers

Several years later, in 1921, Kimbangu began having other visions. Once the voice told him to go to a sick woman in a nearby village and heal her. He traveled to her home, laid his hands on her, and she recovered from her illness. With some successes, Kimbangu began preaching that April. His reputation as a healer spread quickly. People began to flock to his Nkamba village. Word spread that he performed miracles, cured the sick, and even raised the dead. He became known as a prophet with a special mission from God, and his village was called the New Jerusalem.

Kimbangu held his services in a special area in front of his hut. Besides singing, prayer, and Bible reading, Kimbangu gave sermons, urging his followers to abandon some of their traditional ways. He also told his people to give up the practice of polygyny (the practice of marrying two or more women) and to worship only one God. He urged them to destroy their *nkisi* or fetishes (usually carved wooden figurines regarded by the Kongo as having the power to ward off evil caused by witchcraft). In his book *African Religions,* Benjamin Ray says that Kimbangu's denunciation of the fetishes or *nkisi* was so strong that "many people cast them away in heaps by the roadside, a phenomenon which centuries of missionary work had failed to accomplish." As a conservative Christian, Kimbangu opposed the trend toward formation of churches separate from the mission churches. He urged people to obey the laws and pay their taxes to the government. He never pushed for resistance to the government.

Belgian authorities take alarm

Within a few weeks Kimbangu had become a phenomenon. He attracted thousands of people—even Belgian government workers—to his village. Patients left their hospital beds to seek a cure from Kimbangu. Catholic missions began to lose some of their converts. Some reports say as many as 10,000 people had gathered at his village at one time, waiting to be healed.

In addition to being a religious figure with healing powers, Kimbangu became a role model to his people. Before 1950 most Africans were prevented from involvement in politics by the colonial governments. Religion then became one of the few outlets open to educated Africans. Although Kimbangu did not address political issues and did not urge resistance to the Belgian authorities, others used his name to incite rebellion. The Belgian authorities became increasingly alarmed. Kimbangu had started a nationalist movement—a movement he had not intended to create—that the Belgians were afraid they could not control. (Nationalism was a movement for independence from colonial control.)

The Catholic missions grew concerned about Kimbangu's success because they were losing converts, and the plantation owners worried about their loss of labor. These groups put pressure on the Belgian administration to investigate. Unable to stop the thousands of people flocking into his village, the police went to arrest Kimbangu in 1921. Kimbangu fled and went to live in a village near Leopoldville. While he was in hiding, resentment grew toward the government authorities. In September 1921 Kimbangu came out of hiding and returned to his village. The police were waiting for him and arrested him on charges of disturbing the security of the state and the public peace. He was tried and condemned to death. Eleven of his followers received life prison terms. Belgian king Albert changed Kimbangu's sentence to life in prison, then had him transferred to a prison in Elisabethville (now Lubumbashi), all the way across the country, more than a thousand miles away from his home. He spent most of the rest of his life in a cell by himself and died there in 1951.

The momentum continues

After his arrest the authorities did their best to disperse Kimbangu's followers and close down his church. They sent troops to Nkamba, the New Jerusalem, and outlawed any public demonstrations expressing allegiance to Kimbangu. But the Belgian authorities only added to the passionate devotion of his followers by intervening when emotions were at a high pitch. When rumors began to circulate that the authorities had killed Kimbangu after the trial, excitement mounted and the movement grew even larger. To his followers Kimbangu was a martyr, a savior chosen by God to sacrifice himself for his people. They believed that he had appointed apostles (disciples, or people given a mission) to spread his message. The myth that developed around Kimbangu was similar to the Christian belief in the Son of God, Jesus Christ. Kimbangu's disciples called him the "Savior of the Black People" and compared him to Moses and Jesus, Muhammad and Buddha.

Afraid that Kimbanguism would attract more followers, the government made it illegal for the church to hold public services. As a result, the movement went underground and spread throughout the Belgian Congo and to other countries in the region—Congo Brazzaville and Angola. When the Belgian Congo became the independent nation of Congo, the prohibition against the movement was lifted. With independence in 1960, Kimbanguism (as his religion was called) became an important part of national life. The church operated primary and secondary schools and had a seminary (an institution for religious training). It also provided social services, primarily in Lower Congo and Kinshasa. The new government recognized it as a major religious organization, along with Protestantism and Catholicism.

Further Reading

Dictionary of African Biography. Volume 2. Algonac, MI: Reference Publications, 1979.

Hallett, Robin. *Africa since 1875.* Ann Arbor: University of Michigan Press, 1974.

Ray, Benjamin C. *African Religions: Symbol, Ritual, and Community.* Englewood Cliffs, NJ: Prentice Hall, 1976.

Bibliography

Wole Soyinka.

Books

Adam, H., and K. Moodley. *The Negotiated Revolution.* Jonathan Ball, 1993.

Adamolekun, Ladipo. *Sékou Touré's Guinea: An Experiment in Nation Building.* New York: Methuen, 1976.

Africa Watch staff. *Conspicuous Destruction: War, Famine, and the Reform Process in Mozambique.* New York: Africa Watch/Human Rights Watch, 1992.

Africa Watch staff. *Kenya: Taking Liberties.* New York: Africa Watch/Human Rights Watch, 1991.

al-'Umari, Shihab al-Din Ibn Fadi and el Amsar. *Masalik el Absar fi Mamalik.* Traduit par Gaudefroy-Demombynes, Librarie Orientaliste Paul Geuthner, 1927.

Anglin, Douglas G., and Timothy M. Shaw. *Zambia's Foreign Policy: Studies in Diplomacy and Dependence.* Boulder, CO: Westview Press, 1979.

Arhin, Kwame. *Traditional Rule in Ghana, Past and Present.* Sedco Publishing Ltd., 1985.

Arnold, Millard. *Steve Biko: Black Consciousness in South Africa.* New York: Random House, 1978.

Ayittey, George B. *Africa Betrayed.* New York: St. Martin's Press, 1992.

Azikiwe, Nnamdi. *My Odyssey.* Hurst, 1970.

Beach, D. N. *The Shona and Zimbabwe: 900-1850.* Mambo Press, 1980.

Beach, D. N. *Zimbabwe before 1900.* Mambo Press, 1984.

Bender, Gerald J. *Angola under the Portuguese: The Myth and the Reality.* Berkeley: University of California Press, 1978.

Benson, Mary. *African Patriots: The Story of the African National Congress.* 1963.

Benson, M. *Chief Albert Luthuli of South Africa.* 1963.

Benson, M. *South Africa: The Struggle for a Birthright, International Defence, and Aid Fund for Southern Africa.* 1966.

Bermann, Richard A. *The Mahdi of Allah.* 1931.

Biko, Steve. *I Write What I Like: A Selection of His Writings.* South Africa: Ravan Press, 1996.

Binsbergen, W. M. J. van. "Religious Innovation and Political Conflict in Zambia: A Contribution to the Interpretation of the Lumpa Rising." In *African Perspectives: Religious Innovation in Modern African Society.* Volume 2. Leiden: Afrika-Studiecentrum, 1976.

Black Literature Criticism. Detroit: Gale, 1992.

Black Writers. Detroit: Gale, 1989.

Blake, Robert. *A History of Rhodesia.* Eyre Methuen, 1977.

Blakely, Thomas D., Walter E. A. van Beek, and Dennis L. Thomson. *Religion in Africa.* Provo, UT: David M. Kennedy Center, 1994.

Boahen, Adu. *Topics in West African History.* New York: Longman, 1966.

Bond, George C. "A Prophecy That Failed: The Lumpa Church of Uyombe, Zambia." In *African Christianity: Patterns of Religious Continuity.* Academic Press, 1979.

Botman, H. R., and Robin M. Petersen, eds. *To Remember and to Heal: Theological and Psychological Reflections on Truth and Reconciliation.* Human & Rousseau, 1996.

Bourdillon, Michael, *The Shona Peoples,* revised edition. Mambo Press, 1982.

Bouscaren, A. E. *Tshombe.* 1967.

Bradt, Hilary. *Guide to Madagascar.* Bradt Publications, 1988.

Bretton, Henry. *The Rise and Fall of Kwame Nkrumah.* New York: Praeger, 1966.

The Cambridge History of Africa. Vol. 8. Edited by Michael Crowder. New York/UK: Cambridge University Press, 1984.

Cary, Robert, and Diana Mitchell. *African Nationalist Leaders in Rhodesia: Who's Who 1980.* Books of Rhodesia, 1980.

Cary, Robert. *A Time to Die.* 1969.

Churchill, Lord Randolph. *Men, Mines, and Animals in South Africa.* Originally published in 1892. Reprinted. Books of Rhodesia, 1975.

Contemporary Authors. Detroit: Gale, 1990.

Contemporary Black Biography. Detroit: Gale, 1994.

Contemporary Literary Criticism. Detroit: Gale, 1983.

Contemporary Musicians. Detroit: Gale, 1992.

Contemporary Newsmakers. Detroit: Gale, 1989.

Contemporary Novelists. Detroit: St. James Press, 1991.

Cooper-Chadwick, J. *Three Years with Lobengula.* Books of Rhodesia, 1975.

Cromwell, Adelaide M. *An African Victorian Feminist: The Life and Times of Adelaide Smith Casely Hayford, 1868-1960.* Washington, DC: Howard University Press, 1992.

Crosby, Cynthia. *Historical Dictionary of Malawi.* Metuchen, NJ: Scarecrow Press, 1980.

Crowder, Michael. "History of French West Africa until Independence." In *Africa South of the Sahara: 1982-83.* London: Europa Publications, 1982.

Crowder, Michael. *The Story of Nigeria.* Winchester, MA: Faber, 1978.

Curtin, Philip, ed. *Africa Remembered: Narratives by West Africans from the Era of the Slave Trade.* Madison: University of Wisconsin Press, 1967.

Curtin, Philip, and others, eds. *African History: From Earliest Times to Independence.* 2nd ed. New York: Longman, 1995.

Dantzig, Albert van. *Forts and Castles of Ghana.* Sedco Publishing Ltd., 1980.

Davenport, T. R. H. *South Africa: A Modern History.* Toronto, Ontario, Canada: University of Toronto Press, 1987.

Davidson, Basil. *Africa in History.* New York: Macmillan, 1974.

Davidson, Basil. *Africa History, Themes and Outlines.* New rev. ed. New York: Collier Books, 1974.

Davidson, Basil, *The Black Man's Burden: Africa and the Curse of the Nation-State.* James Curry, 1992.

Davidson, Basil. *The Growth of African Civilisation: History of West Africa, 1000-1800.* New York: Longman, 1965.

Davis, Dorothy K. *Race Relations in Rhodesia.* Rex Collings, 1975.

Days, Drew S., et al. *Justice Enjoined: The State of the Judiciary in Kenya.* Robert F. Kennedy Memorial Center for Human Rights, 1992

Decalo, Samuel. *Psychoses of Power: African Personal Dictatorships.* Boulder, CO: Westview Press.

DeKlerk, W. A. *The Puritans in Africa.* Rex Collings, 1975.

De Klerk, Willem. *The Man in His Time: F. W. De Klerk.* Jonathan Ball, 1991.

Delf, George. *Jomo Kenyatta: Towards Truth about "The Light of Kenya."* New York: Doubleday, 1961.

Depelchin, H., and C. Croonenberghs. *Letters of Journey to Gubuluwayo.* Books of Rhodesia, 1979.

Dickie, John, and Alan Rake. *Who's Who in Africa.* Africa Buyer and Trader, 1973.

Dictionary of African Biography. Algonac, MI: Reference Publications, 1977.

Drechsler, Horst. *Let Us Die Fighting.* Akademie-Verlag, 1966.

Du Boulay, Shirley. *Tutu: Voice of the Voiceless.* North Pomfret, VT: Hodder & Stoughton, 1988.

Duerden, Dennis, and Cosmo Pieterse, eds. *African Writers Talking: A Collection of Radio Interviews.* Africana Publishing, 1972.

Duggan, William Redman, and John R. Civille. *Tanzania and Nyerere: A Study of Ujamaa and Nationhood.* London: Orbis Books, 1976.

Eilersen, Gillian Stead. *Bessie Head: Thunder Behind Her Ears.* North Pomfret, VT: Heinemann, 1996.

Ellert H. *Rivers of Gold.* Mambo Press, 1993.

Ellert, H. *The Rhodesian Front War.* Mambo, 1989.

Encyclopaedia Africana, Dictionary of African Biography. Vol. 2. Sierra Leone-Zaire: Reference Publications, 1977.

Equiano's Travels: His Autobiography: The Interesting Narrative of the Life of Olaudah Equiano or Gustavus Vassa the African Life. Paul Edwards, editor. London: Heinemann, 1967.

Farrant, Leda. *Tippu Tip and the East African Slave Trade.* London: Hamish Hamilton, 1975

Farwell, Byron. *Prisoners of the Mahdi: The Story of the Mahdist Revolt Which Frustrated Queen Victoria's Designs on the Sudan.* New York: Norton, 1989.

Fisher, John. *The Afrikaners.* Cassell, 1969.

Forbath, Peter. *The River Congo.* New York: Harper & Row, 1977.

Forrest, Ronald. *An African Reader.* New York: Longman, 1965.

Forster, E. M. *Alexandria: A History and a Guide.* Bath Press, 1922.

Froehlich, Manuel. "The Old and the New UN Secretary-General." In *Aussen Politik,* 48:3, 1997, pp. 301-9.

Gérard-Libois, J. *Sécession au Katanga.* 1963

Gertzel, Cherry. *The Politics of Independent Kenya: 1963-1968.* Northwestern, 1970.

Gertzel, Cherry. "Uganda's Continuing Search for Peace." In *Current History,* May 1990.

Gibbs, James, ed. *Critical Perspectives on Wole Soyinka.* Washington, DC: Three Continents, 1980.

Gossler, Horst. *Portfolio Lalibela.* Africa Environment and Wildlife, 1996.

Graham, Shirley. *Julius K. Nyerere: Teacher of Africa.* New York: Messner, 1975.

Gray, Stephen. *Southern African Literature: An Introduction.* 1979.

Greschat, Hans-Jurgen. "Legends? Frauds? Reality? Alice Lenshina's Prophetic Experience." In *Africana Marburgensia.* Edited by Hans-Jurgen Greschat and Hermann Jungraithmayr. Volume 1. 1968.

Gunther, John. *Inside Africa.* North Pomfret, VT: Hamish Hamilton, 1955.

Guy, Jeff. *The Destruction of the Zulu Kingdom: The Civil War in Zululand, 1879-1884*. University of Natal Press, 1994.

Hallet, Robin. *Africa since 1895*. Ann Arbor: University of Michigan Press, 1974.

Halpern, Jack. "Botswana: Recent History." In *Africa South of the Sahara, 1981-1982*. London: Europa, 1981.

Harden, Blaine. *Africa: Dispatches from a Fragile Continent*. New York: HarperCollins, 1990.

Harris, Joseph E. *Africans and Their History*. New York: New American Library, 1974.

Hatch, John. *Tanzania: A Profile*. New York: Praeger, 1972.

Hatch, John. *Two African Statesmen*. Regnery, 1975.

Helbig, Ludwig, and Werner Hillebrecht. *The Witbooi*. Longman Namibia, 1992.

Hempstone, Smith. *Katanga Report*. Winchester, MA: Faber, 1962.

Hibbert, Christopher. *Africa Explored: Europeans in the Dark Continent, 1769-1889*. New York: Norton, 1982.

Hiskett, Mervyn. *The Sword of Truth: The Life and Times of the Shehu Usuman dan Fodio*. New York/UK: Oxford University Press, 1973.

Historic World Leaders. Edited by Anne Commire. Detroit: Gale, 1994.

Hoile, David. *Mozambique: A Nation in Crisis*. Claridge Press, 1989.

Holt, P. M. *The Mahdist State in the Sudan: 1881-1898*. 1958.

Holt, P. M. *A Modern History of the Sudan*. 1966.

Hymans, Jacques Louis. *Léopold Sédar Senghor: An Intellectual Biography*. Edinburgh University Press, 1971.

James, Lawrence. *The Rise and Fall of the British Empire*. Boston: Little, Brown, 1994.

Jenny, Hans. *South West Africa: Land of Extremes*. Southwest Africa Scientific Society, 1976.

Johnson-Odin, Cheryl. *For Women and the Nation: Funmilayo Ransome-Kuti of Nigeria*. University of Illinois Press, 1997.

Jones, Eldred. *Wole Soyinka*. New York: Twayne, 1973.

Jones, G.I. "Olaudah Equiano of the Niger Ibo," *Africa Remembered: Narratives by West Africans from the Era of the Slave Trade*. Philip D.Curtin, ed. Madison: University of Wisconsin Press, 1977.

Kaplan, Irving, Howard Blutstein, Peter Just, and others. *Area Handbook for Mozambique*. American University Press, 1977.

Katrak, Ketu. *Wole Soyinka and Modern Tragedy: A Study of Dramatic Theory and Practice*. Westport, CT: Greenwood Press, 1986.

Kaunda, Kenneth D. *The Riddle of Violence*. New York: Harper, 1980.

Kaunda, Kenneth D. *Zambia Shall Be Free: An Autobiography*. New York: Praeger, 1963.

Kenney, Henry. *Power, Pride & Prejudice*. Jonathan Ball, 1991.

Kenyatta, Jomo. *Facing Mount Kenya.* North Pomfret, VT: Secker & Warburg, 1938.

Kenyatta, Jomo. *Harambee! The Prime Minister of Kenya's Speeches, 1963-1964.* New York/UK: Oxford University Press, 1964.

Kenyatta, Jomo. *Kenya: The Land of Conflict.* International African Service Bureau, 1945.

Killam, G. D. *The Novels of Chinua Achebe.* Africana Publishing, 1969.

King, Bruce. *Introduction to Nigerian Literature.* Africana Publishing, 1972.

Kuper, Hilda. *Sobhuza II: Ngwenyama and King of Swaziland.* London: Duckworth, 1978.

Lamb, David. *The Africans.* New York: Random House, 1984.

Landeg, White, and Tim Couzens, eds. *Literature and Society in South Africa.* 1984.

Larson, Charles R. *The Emergence of African Fiction.* Bloomington: Indiana University Press, 1972.

Lau, Brigitte. *Namibia in Jonker Afrikaner's Time.* Namibia Archives, 1987.

Laurence, Margaret. *Long Drums and Cannons: Nigerian Dramatists and Novelists.* New York: Praeger, 1968.

Leakey, Louis. *White African: An Early Autobiography.* Originally published in 1937. Reprinted. New York: Ballantine Books, 1973.

Leakey, Louis. *By the Evidence: Memoirs, 1932-1951.* Orlando, FL: Harcourt, 1974.

Leakey, Mary. *Disclosing the Past.* New York: Doubleday, 1984.

Leakey, Richard. *One Life: An Autobiography.* Salem House, 1984.

LeMay, G. H. L. *Black and White in South Africa: The Politics of Survival.* American Heritage Press, 1971.

Levtzion, Nehemia. *Muslims and Chiefs in West Africa.* New York/UK: Oxford University Press, 1968.

Lipschutz, Mark, and R. Kent Rasmussen. *Dictionary of African Historical Biography.* Aldine Publishing, 1978.

Lodge, Tom. *Black Politics in South Africa since 1945.* Ravan Press, 1990.

Lunn, John, and Christopher Saunders. "Recent History of Namibia." In *Africa South of the Sahara: 1994.* 23rd ed. London: Europa, 1994.

Luthuli, Albert. *Let My People Go.* Collins, 1962.

Mack, John. *Madagascar: Island of the Ancestors.* British Museums Publications, 1986.

MacPherson, Fergus. *Kenneth Kaunda of Zambia: The Times and the Man.* New York/UK: Oxford University Press, 1974.

Maier, Karl. *Into the House of the Ancestors.* Chichester, W. Sussex, U.K.: John Wiley, 1998.

Major Twentieth-Century Writers. Detroit: Gale, 1991.

Makeba, Miriam, and James Hall. *Makeba: My Story.* New York: New American Library, 1987.

Makers of Modern Africa: Profiles in History. 3rd. ed. Africa Books, 1996.

Mandela, Nelson. *Long Walk to Freedom.* Boston: Little, Brown, 1994.

Mandela, Winnie. *Part of My Soul Went with Him.* Edited by Anne Benjamin. New York: Norton, 1985.

Marquard, Leo. *The Peoples and Policies of South Africa.* 4th ed. New York/UK: Oxford University Press, 1969.

Maylam, Paul. *A History of the African People of South Africa: From the Early Iron Age to the 1970s.* New York: St. Martin's, 1986.

Mboya, Tom. *Freedom and After.* Boston: Little, Brown, 1963.

McLynn, Frank. *Hearts of Darkness: The European Explorations of Africa.* Pimlico, 1992.

Meintjes, Johannes. *President Paul Kruger.* Cassell, 1974.

Meltzer, Milton. *Winnie Mandela: The Soul of South Africa.* New York: Viking Kestrel, 1986.

Meredith, Martin. *First Dance of Freedom.* New York: Harper, 1984.

Meredith, Martin. *The Past Is Another Country: Rhodesia UDI to Zimbabwe.* London: Pan Books, 1980.

Modern Twentieth-Century Writers. Detroit: Gale, 1991.

Mondlane, Eduardo. *The Struggle for Mozambique.* Zed Press, 1969.

Moore, Gerald. *Wole Soyinka.* New York: Africana Publishing, 1971.

Moorehead, Alan. *The White Nile.* New York: Harper, 1971.

Morell, Virginia. *Ancestral Passions: The Leakey Family and the Quest for Humankind's Beginnings.* New York: Simon & Schuster, 1995.

Morris, Donald R. *The Washing of the Spears: The Rise and Fall of the Great Zulu Nation.* Abacus, 1992.

Mosely, Nicholas. *African Switchback.* Travel Book Club, 1958

Mosley, Leonard. *Haile Selassie I: The Conquering Lion.* Englewood Cliffs, NJ: Prentice Hall, 1965.

Mostert, Noël. *Frontiers: The Epic of South Africa's Creation and the Tragedy of the Xhosa People.* North Pomfret, VT: J. Cape, 1992.

Mudenge, S. I. G. *A Political History of Munhumutapa: c. 1400-1902.* Zimbabwe Publishing House, 1988.

Murray-Brown, Jeremy. *Kenyatta.* Allen & Unwin, 1979.

Murphy, E. Jefferson. *History of African Civilization.* New York: Dell, 1972.

Murphy, E. Jefferson. *The Bantu Civilization of Southern Africa.* New York: Thomas Crowell, 1974.

Niane, D.T. *General History of Africa.* Volume 4. UNESCO, 1984.

Niane, D.T. *Sundiata: An Epic in African History.* New York: Longman, 1965.

Nichols, Lee, ed. *Conversations with African Writers.* Washington, DC: Voice of America, 1981.

Nkomo, Joshua. *Nkomo: The Story of My Life.* New York: Methuen, 1984.

Nkrumah, Kwame. *Autobiography.* Sunbury-on-Thames, Middx., U.K.: Thomas Nelson, 1957.

Nyagumbo, Maurice. *With the People.* Akron, OH: Graham Publishing, 1980.

Nyerere, Julius K. *Freedom and Development.* New York/UK: Oxford University Press, 1974.

Obeng, Ernest E. *Ancient Ashanti Chieftaincy.* Ghana Publishing Corporation, 1988.

Odinga, Oginga. *Not Yet Uhuru: An Autobiography.* Heineman, 1967.

Oliver, Roland. *The African Experience.* Pimlico, 1994.

Oliver, Roland, and Atmore, Anthony. *Africa since 1800.* 2nd ed. New York/UK: Cambridge University Press, 1972.

Oloka-Onyango, J. "Uganda's 'Benevolent' Dictatorship." In *Current History,* May 1997.

Omara-Otunnu, Amii. *Politics and the Military in Uganda: 1890-1985.* New York: St. Martin's, 1987.

Omari, T. Peter. *Kwame Nkrumah: An Anatomy of African Dictatorship.* Accra, 1970.

O'Meara, Dan. *Forty Lost Years: The Apartheid State and the Politics of the National Party, 1948-1994.* Athens: Ohio University Press, 1996.

Ousby, Ian. *The Cambridge Guide to Literature in English.* New York/UK: Cambridge University Press, 1993.

Pakenham, Thomas. *The Boer War.* Macdonald, 1982.

Pakenham, Thomas. *The Scramble for Africa: 1876-1912.* Jonathan Ball Publishers, 1991.

Parker, Kenneth, ed. *The South African Novel in English.* 1978.

Paton, Alan. *Towards the Mountain: An Autobiography.* David Philip, 1980.

Paton, Anne. *Some Sort of a Job: My Life with Alan Paton.* New York: Viking, 1992.

Peck, Richard. "Nadine Gordimer: A Bibliography of Primary and Secondary Sources 1938-1992." In *Research in African Literatures,* March 1, 1995.

Pedler, F.J. *West Africa.* New York: Methuen, 1951.

Perham, Margery, and J. Simmons. *African Discovery: An Anthology of Exploration.* The Travel Book Club, 1943.

Petersen, Kirsten Holst, and Anna Rutherford, eds. *Chinua Achebe: A Celebration.* North Pomfret, VT: Heinemann, 1991.

Phillips, Claude S. *The African Political Dictionary.* Santa Barbara, CA: ABC-CLIO, 1984.

Pieterse, Cosmo, and Dennis Dueren, eds. *African Writers Talking: A Collection of Radio Interviews.* New York: Africana Publishing, 1972.

Pratt, Cranford. *The Critical Phase in Tanzania, 1945-1968: Nyerere and the Emergence of a Socialist Strategy.* New York/UK: Cambridge University Press, 1976.

Putz, J. H. von Egidy, and P. Caplan. *Namibia Handbook and Who's Who.* Magus, 1989.

Rake, Alan. *Who's Who in Africa: Leaders for the 1990s.* Metuchen, NJ: Scarecrow Press, 1992.

Rattray, R. S. *Ashanti.* New York/UK: Oxford University Press, 1923.

Ray, Benjamin C. *African Religions: Symbol, Ritual, and Community.* Englewood Cliffs, NJ: Prentice Hall, 1976.

Reshetnyak, Nikolai. *Patrice Lumumba.* Novosti Press, 1990.

Ritter, E. A. *Shaka Zulu.* New York: Longman, 1955.

Roberts, Andrew. "The Lumpa Church of Alice Lenshina." In *Protest and Power in Black Africa.* Edited by Robert Rotberg and Ali Mazrui. New York/UK: Oxford University Press, 1970.

Roscoe, Adrian A. *Mother Is Gold: A Study in West African Literature.* New York/UK: Cambridge University Press, 1971.

Sampson, Anthony. *Black and Gold.* North Pomfret, VT: Hodder & Stoughton, 1987

Sampson, Anthony. *The Treason Cage: The Opposition on Trial in South Africa.* 1958.

Sarpong, Peter. *The Sacred Stools of the Akan.* Ghana Publishing Corporation, 1971.

Sarte, Jean Paul. *Lumumba Speaks.* Boston: Little, Brown, 1972.

Scientists: The Lives and Works of 150 Scientists. Detroit: U*X*L, 1996.

Senghor, Léopold Sédar. *Selected Poems.* Translated by John Reed and Clive Wake. New York: Atheneum, 1969.

Shepperson, George, and Thomas Price. *Independent African.* 1958.

Shibeika, Mekki. *The Independent Sudan,* 1959. and P. M. Holt.

Shillington, Kevin. *Ghana and the Rawlings Factor.* New York: Macmillan, 1992.

Short, Philip. *Banda.* London: Routledge & Kegan Paul, 1974.

Slater, Montague. *The Trial of Jomo Kenyatta.* North Pomfret, VT: Secker & Warburg, 1955.

Smith, David, and Colin Simpson. *Mugabe.* Salisbury: Pioneer Head, 1981

Smith, George Ivan. *Ghosts of Kampala: The Rise and Fall of Idi Amin.* New York: St. Martin's, 1980.

Smith, William Edgett. *Nyerere of Tanzania.* London: Victor Gollancz, 1973.

Soggot, David. *Namibia: The Violent Heritage.* Rex Collings, 1986.

Soyinka, Wole. *The Man Died: Prison Notes of Wole Soyinka.* New York: Harper, 1972.

Soyinka, Wole. *Myth, Literature, and the African World*. New York/UK: Cambridge University Press, 1976.

Soyinka, Wole. *Ake: The Years of Childhood*. New York: Random House, 1981.

Sparks, Allister. *The Mind of South Africa*. London: Heinemann, 1990.

Sparks, Allister. *Tomorrow Is Another Country*. Struik, 1994.

Spencer, John H. *Ethiopia at Bay: A Personal Account of the Haile Selassie Years*. Algonac, MI: Reference Publications, 1984.

Spleth, Janice. *Léopold Sédar Senghor*. New York: Twayne, 1985.

Stockwell, John. *In Search of Enemies: A CIA Story*. New York: Norton, 1978.

The Struggle for Africa. Edited by Mai Palmberg. Zed Press, 1983.

Stuart, James, and D. McK. Malcom, eds.*The Diary of Henry Francis Fynn*. Shuter & Shooter, 1986.

Sweetman, David. *Women Leaders in African History*. Portsmouth, NH: Heinemann Educational, 1984.

Taylor, Stephen. *Shaka's Children: A History of the Zulu People*. New York: HarperCollins, 1994.

Theobald, A.B. *The Mahdiya: A History of the Anglo-Egyptian Sudan, 1881-1899*. 1951.

Thompson, Leonard. *History of South Africa*. New Haven, CT: Yale University Press, 1990.

Trimingham, J. Spencer. *A History of Islam in West Africa*. New York/UK: Oxford University Press, 1974.

Tufuo, J. W., and C. E. Donkor. *Ashantis of Ghana: People with a Soul*. Anowou Educational Publications, 1989.

Tutu, Desmond. *An African Prayer Book*. North Pomfret, VT: Hodder & Stoughton, 1995.

Tutu, Desmond. *Hope and Suffering: Sermons and Speeches*. Skotaville Publishers, 1983.

Tutu, Desmond. *The Rainbow People of God: South Africa's Victory over Apartheid*. New York: Bantam Books, 1995.

Vail, John J. *Nelson and Winnie Mandela*. New York: Chelsea House, 1989.

Vaillant, Janet. *Black, French and African*. Cambridge, MA: Harvard University Press, 1990.

Verrier, Anthony. *The Road to Zimbabwe: 1890-1980*. London: Jonathan Cape, 1986.

Von Rensberg, A. P. J. *Contemporary Leaders of Africa*. Haum, 1975.

Wallace, Aubrey. *Eco-Heroes: Twelve Tales of Environmental Victory*. San Francisco: Mercury House, 1993, pp. 1-21.

Warren, Dennis M. *The Akan of Ghana*. Rev. ed. Pointer Limited, 1986.

Weh, Tuan. *The Love of Liberty: The Rule of President William V. S. Tubman in Liberia, 1944-1971*. New York: C. Hurst/Universe Books, 1976.

Wepman, Dennis. *Jomo Kenyatta.* Broomall, PA: Chelsea House, 1989.

Who's Who 1997: An Annual Biographical Dictionary. A & C Black, 1997.

Wilentz, Gay. *Binding Cultures: Black Women Writers in Africa and the Diaspora.* Bloomington: Indiana University Press, 1992.

Wills, A. J. *An Introduction to the History of Central Africa: Zambia, Malawi, and Zimbabwe.* New York/UK: Oxford University Press, 1985.

Wilson, Derek. *A History of South and Central Africa.* New York/UK: Cambridge University Press, 1975.

Wilson, Monica, and Leonard Thompson, eds. *The Oxford History of South Africa.* Volume 2. New York/UK: Oxford University Press, 1975.

Windrich, Elaine. *Britain and the Politics of Rhodesian Independence.* Africana Publishing, 1978.

Wingate, F.R. *Mahdism and the Egyptian Sudan.* Originally published in 1891. 2nd ed. London: Frank Cass and Co., 1968

Woods, Donald. *Biko.* London: Paddington Press, 1978.

Young, Kenneth. *Rhodesia and Independence.* Eyre & Spottiswoode, 1967.

Zolberg, Aristide R. *One-Party Government in the Ivory Coast.* Rev. ed. Princeton, NJ: Princeton University Press, 1969.

Periodicals

Africa Confidential. June 1, 1990; December 6, 1991.

Africa Report, May-June 1981; January/February 1988; July/August 1991; November/December 1993.

Berkeley, Bill. "Paying for Past Crimes: Uganda's Murderous Lessons." In *The Alicia Patterson Foundation Reporter.* Volume 16, number 3, 1994.

Callaloo, winter 1990, pp. 87-101.

"Can He Save the Elephants?" In *New York Times Magazine,* January 7, 1990.

Chicago Tribune, March 20, 1988.

The Economist, August 30, 1997; November 29, 1997, p. 104.

Gilbey, Emma. "The Lady: The Life and Times of Winnie." *New York Times Magazine,* May 14, 1995, pp. 24-29.

Goshko, John M. "Soft-spoken Man Who Gets Things Done." In *Mail and Guardian,* December 20-23, 1996.

"The Green Belt Movement." In *Geographical Magazine,* April 1990, p. 51.

Hultman, Tami. "Portrait of a Grass-Roots Activist." In *Utne Reader,* November-December 1992, pp. 86-87.

"An Interview with Kenya's Zookeeper." In *Audubon,* September 1990.

Los Angeles Times, July 31, 1984; December 7, 1986.

Maathai, W. "Foresters without Diplomas." In *Ms.,* March-April 1991, p. 74.

McNeil, Donald G. Jr. "Coup Charges Dropped, and Zambia's Ex-Leader is Freed," *New York Times,* June 2, 1998.

McNeil, Donald G. Jr. "Its Past on Its Sleeve, Tribe Seeks Bonn's Apology," *New York Times,* May 31, 1998.

Mehegan, David, "Nadine Gordimer's Next Chapter," *Boston Globe,* November 29, 1994, p. 69.

"The Most Dangerous Game." In *New York Times Magazine,* January 7, 1996.

Ms., July 1975; January 1987; September 1987.

The Nation (Nairobi), October 26, 1997; December 22-28, 1997.

New Republic, April 27, 1974.

Newsweek, May 8, 1972; September 4,1978.

New York Times, July 24, 1977; May 27, 1981; July 9, 1984; January 14, 1986; November 7, 1986; April 22, 1987; December 28, 1987; March 8, 1988; March 13, 1988; June 11, 1988.

Time, May 8, 1972.

Paris Review, summer 1983.

"Protectors of Forests Take Home the Prizes." In *Wall Street Journal,* May 10, 1991, p. B1.

Rolling Stone. October 20, 1994, pp. 55-56.

Saidi, Bill. "How the World Is Always Forgiving KK." *Zimbabwe Independent,* January 16, 1998.

The Standard (Nairobi). January 5, 1993.

Sunday Times (Nairobi). December 27, 1992.

Time, September 4, 1978; February 10, 1986; November 23, 1987; November 6, 1989; September 1, 1997.

Washington Post, March 3, 1992.

World Press Review, June 1986.

Other

Breaking the Silence (video documentary), 1988.

Garner, Dwight, "The Salon Interview: Nadine Gordimer," March 1998: www.salonmagazine.com/books/int/1998/03/cov_si_90int.html

Gersony, Robert. *Summary of Mozambican Refugee Accounts of Principally Conflict-Related Experience in Mozambique.* Washington, DC: U.S. State Department, 1988.

Guardian News Service report by Robin Denselow dated August 5, 1997.

King's College Newsletter, December 1984.

Maathai, W. "The Green Belt Movement: Sharing the Approach and the Experience." International Environmental Liaison Center, 1988.

Nwangwu, Chido. "USAfrica: The Newspaper." USAfrica ONLINE. www.usafricaonline.com, August 4, 1997.

"Revolutionary Worker Online." www.msc.net.rwor, #920, August 17, 1997.

UXL Biographies CD. Detroit: Gale, 1995.

WUSB 90.1 FM (Stony Brook, NY) radio broadcast featuring Lister Hewan-Lowe, June 21, 1986.

Index

Italic type indicates volume numbers.
Boldface type indicates entries and their page numbers.
(Iill.) indicates illustrations.

Wangari Maathai

El Saheli *2:* 393
Elizabeth II (queen of England) *1:* 44
England *1:* 19, 53, 68, 110, 141-143;
  2: 204, 295, 316, 326, 334, 372;
  3: 467, 486, 549, 563, 584
Epps, Maeve *2:* 236
**Equiano, Olaudah (Gustavus
  Vassa the African) *1:* 119-124,**
  119 (ill.)
Eritrea *1:* 143, 145, 146, 148; *2:* 337
Erosion *2:* 272
Ethiopia *1:* 138-148; *2:* 220, 330,
  332 (map)
Ezana (emperor) *2:* 222

F

Farewell, Francis *3:* 517-518,
  518 (ill.)
Federal Theological Seminary *3:* 585
Federation of Rhodesia and
  Nyasaland *1:* 53, 166, 170;
  2: 384; *3:* 522, 523-525
Federation of Workers' Unions of
  Guinea *3:* 555
Firestone, Harvey Samuel *3:* 574
Firestone Rubber Company *3:* 574
Forbes, Frederick*1:* 134
Fordham University *1:* 170
Fort Hare College *1:* 188, 190
Fort Hare University *2:* 380
Fourah Bay College *1:* 98
France *1:* 122, 133, 137, 143, 157,
  160; *2:* 207, 257, 335, 347;
  3: 483, 487, 550, 558, 560
Franco, Francisco *1:* 144
Francois, Curt von *2:* 295
FRELIMO (the Front for the
  Liberation of Mozambique)
  1: 90 (ill.), 91; *2:* 363, 364 (ill.),
  365, 398
French West Africa *1:* 161
Frere, Bartle *1:* 76, 77
Front for National Salvation
  (FRONASA) *2:* 398
Frumentius *2:* 222
Fulani-Hausa *1:* 4, 35, 40, 41, 45,
  104, 105, 107, 109; *3:* 542
Fynn, Henry *3:* 517-518

G

Gabon *1:* 13
Gama, Vasco da *2:* 224
Gandhi, Mohandas *1:* 169
Garang, John *2:* 402
Garfield, James A. *1:* 37
Garvey, Marcus *1:* 36, 71, 73
Gelele *1:* 134, 136
General Motors *2:* 345
George V *3:* 533
George VI *3:* 533
Germany *1:* 68, 84, 137, 142, 143,
  188; *2:* 207, 250-251, 294-303,
  397; *3:* 449, 474, 550
Ghana *1:* 28, 29, 35, 36, 38, 46, 52,
  72, 145, 161; *2:* 217, 257-258,
  381; *3:* 426-436, 428 (map),
  478, 480, 482, 498, 542, 554,
  556, 598
Gichuru, James *2:* 327
Girls' Vocational and Industrial
  Training School *1:* 72
Giyorgis, Haylu Walda *2:* 333
Gobir Kingdom *1:* 105
Goering, Heinrich *2:* 295
Goering, Hermann *2:* 295
Gold Coast. *See Ghana*
Gold and gold mines *1:* 52, 127;
  2: 207, 248, 250-251, 295,
  390-391, 394; *3:* 479, 483,
  499, 523, 531, 562
Goldberg, Denis *2:* 317
Goldie, George *1:* 103
Gordimer, Nadine *1:* 125-131,
  125 (ill.), 130 (ill.)
Gordon, Charles George *2:* 286, 289,
  291, 292 (ill.)
Gowon, Yakubu *2:* 217
Great Britain *1:* 4, 19, 50, 68, 110,
  120; *2:* 204, 295, 316, 326, 334,
  372; *3:* 487, 499, 521, 550, 564
Green Belt Movement *2:* 271,
  273, 275
Guezo *1:* 132-137
Guinea *2:* 390; *3:* 554-561, 557 (map)
Guinea-Bissau *3:* 558
Gulf War *1:* 30
Gustavus Vassa the African (Olaudah
  Equiano) *1:* 119

N

National Congolese Movement
3: 564
National Congress of British West
Africa *1:* 70
National Democratic Congress
3: 503
National Democratic Party (NDP)
2: 382
National Party, South Africa *1:* 59,
113-117, 127, 128; *3:* 471
National Resistance Army *2:* 399
National Union of South African
Students *1:* 60
NATO (the North Atlantic Treaty
Organization) *3:* 558
Ndebele *2:* 203, 246-253, 371, 386;
3: 420, 423, 528
Ndlovukazi (Labotsibeni Mdluli)
3: 532
Ndongo *3:* 459
Netherlands *2:* 210
Ngala, Ronald *1:* 184; *2:* 327
Ngqumbhazi *1:* 75
Ngwane V *3:* 531
Nicol, G. C. *1:* 98
Niger River *1:* 35, 99; *2:* 390, 393
Nigeria *1:* 4, 34, 37, 95, 100 (map),
104, 119, 161; *2:* 212; *3:* 433,
466, 492, 536
Nigerian People's Party *1:* 42
Nigerian Trade Union Congress
1: 39
Nile River *1:* 22, 179; *2:* 286, 289,
290, 391; *3:* 405, 407, 508, 551
Njonjo, Charles *2:* 351, 352
Nkomo, Joshua *1:* 172; *2:* 382;
3: **418-426,** 418 (ill.), 524
Nkrumah, Kwame *1:* 34, 35, 46,
47, 52, 145, 164, 180, 182;
2: 257, 258, 326; *3:* **427-436,**
427 (ill.), 434 (ill.), 499, 509,
555, 557, 565
Nobel Peace Prize *1:* 112; *2:* 263,
268, 310; *3:* 581
Nobel Prize, literature *1:* 131; *3:* 536
Northern People's Congress
1: 40, 41
Northern Rhodesia. *See also Zambia*
1: 53; *2:* 238, 377; *3:* 523
Northwestern University *2:* 362

Ntare School *2:* 398
Nujoma, Sam *3:* **437-442,** 441 (ill.)
Nwapa, Flora *3:* **443-447,** 442 (ill.)
Nyamwezi *2:* 374; *3:* 547, 549
Nyandoro, George *3:* 524
Nyangwe *3:* 548
Nyasaland. *See also Malawi 1:* 50,
53, 80, 166, 167; *2:* 240;
3: 523-524
Nyasaland African Congress *1:* 53
Nyerere, Julius *1:* 26, 27;
2: 235 (ill.), 364, 383, 399;
3: **448-458,** 448 (ill.), 455 (ill.)
Nzinga a Nkuwu *1:* 9
Nzinga, Anna *3:* **459-465,** 459 (ill.)

O

OAU. *See Organization of African
Unity*
Obasanjo, Olusegun *2;* 217;
3: 495, 497
Oberlin College *2:* 362
Obote, Milton *1:* 20, 21, 25;
2: 396, 399
Odede, Paula *2:* 327
Odinga, Oginga *2:* 327, 351
Ogun River *3:* 538
Ojukwu, Odumegwu *1:* 48
Okello, Tito *2:* 400
Okigbo, Christopher *1:* 5
Okito, Joseph *2:* 262
Okoya, Pierino *1:* 21
Okri, Ben *3:* **466-470,** 466 (ill.)
Olduvai Gorge, Tanzania *2:* 225-227,
230, 231
Olusanya, Gabriel *1:* 40
Omaheke Desert *2:* 301
Opangu, Pauline *2:* 256
Orange River *2:* 205, 370
Organization of African Unity
(OAU) *1:* 46, 138, 146, 148,
163; *3:* 526, 560
Ottoman Empire *1:* 108
Oxford University *1:* 190; *2:* 326

University of Edinburgh *1:* 52
University of Essex *3:* 468
University of Ibadan *3:* 494, 540
University of Ife *3:* 540, 542
University of Indiana *1:* 52
University of Lisbon *2:* 362
University of London *3:* 584
University of Nairobi *2:* 272
University of Natal *1:* 60
University of Pittsburgh *2:* 272
University of Witwatersrand *1:* 128;
  2: 361
Upper Volta (now Burkino Faso)
  3: 560
Urhobo College *3:* 467

V

Vaal River *2:* 205, 207
Verwoerd, Hendrik *3:* 475, 526,
  589-597, 589 (ill.), 596 (ill.)
Victoria (queen of England) *1:* 78,
  99; *2:* 205, 333; *3:* 480
Von Trotha, Lothar *2:* 300-302
Von Francois, Curt *2:* 295, 297
Vorster, Johannes Balthazar *3:* 526

W

Washington, Booker T. *1:* 81
Watch Tower Movement *1:* 83
Waterberg *2:* 300-301
Wayzaro Manan Asfaw *1:* 141
Wayzaro Yeshimbet *1:* 141
Wayzaro Ejegayahu *2:* 334
Welensky, Roy *3:* 523
West African Slave Squadron *1:* 96
West Germany *3:* 495, 560
White Fathers *2:* 240
Wilberforce Institute *1:* 52
Williams, Ruth *1:* 190
Wilson, Allan *2:* 252
Wincham Hall College *2:* 214; *3:* 494
Witbooi, Hendrik *2:* 297, 300-301
Witwatersrand, South Africa *2:* 207
Wolfe, James *1:* 122
Wolseley, Garnet *2:* 292; *3:* 479, 482
Woodbrooke College *1:* 180
Woods, Donald *1:* 65

World War I *1:* 71, 842: 239
World War II *1:* 128, 169; *2:* 262,
  359, 397; *3:* 474, 494, 521

Y

Yaa Asantewa *3:* 598-602
Yancy, Allen *3:* 576
Yaw Atwereboana *3:* 482
Yeshimbet, Wayzaro *1:* 141
Yohannes IV *2:* 334-336
Yoruba *1:* 4, 35, 40, 45, 46, 49,
  67, 95, 96, 99, 102, 136;
  2: 213-214; *3:* 469, 494,
  538-539, 541, 542
Young Women's Christian Associa-
  tion (YWCA) *1:* 70
Yunfa (Hausa king) *1:* 107

Z

Zaire. *See also Democratic Republic
  of the Congo 1:* 146, 196;
  2: 244, 255, 346, 374; *3:* 562
Zambezi River *2:* 252
Zambia *1:* 26, 53, 166, 168 (map);
  2: 238, 244, 377, 381;
  3: 523, 562
Zambia African National Congress
  1: 170; *2:* 243
Zan Seyum *2:* 220
Zanzibar *2:* 375; *3:* 546, 548,
  550, 553
Zawditu *1:* 142
Zimbabwe *1:* 53, 73, 91, 147, 166,
  167, 187; *2:* 208, 240, 246, 248,
  250, 379, 381 (map); *3:* 517,
  521, 523
Zimbabwe African National Union
  (ZANU) *2:* 383-387; *3:* 527
Zimbabwe African People's Union
  (ZAPU) *2:* 382-383, 386-387;
  3: 527
Zimbabwe Rhodesia *2:* 385
Zinjanthropus 2: 230-231
Zulu *1:* 73, 74, 76, 78; *2:* 247-248
Zululand *73-79; 2: 265; 3: 512-520*
Zwangendabe *3:* 517
Zwide *2:* 248; *3:* 516-517, 520

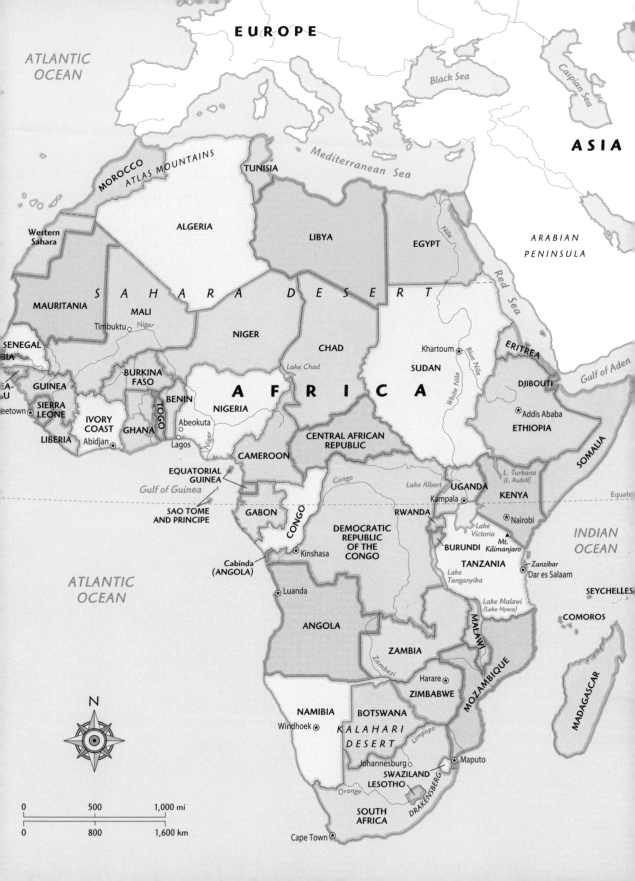